The art and s
large, angr

WHO are These People and WHY are They YELLING at me?

DAVID R. HARDY, R.P.P.
Edited by Marc Huminilowycz

 FriesenPress

Suite 300 - 990 Fort St
Victoria, BC, V8V 3K2
Canada

www.friesenpress.com

Copyright © 2019 by Hardy Stevenson and Associates Limited
First Edition — 2019

Edited by: Marc Huminilowycz

All rights reserved.

No part of this publication may be reproduced in any form, or by any means, electronic or mechanical, including photocopying, recording, or any information browsing, storage, or retrieval system, without permission in writing from FriesenPress.

ISBN
978-1-5255-5625-8 (Hardcover)
978-1-5255-5626-5 (Paperback)
978-1-5255-5627-2 (eBook)

1. BUS052000/BUSINESS & ECONOMICS/PUBLIC RELATIONS

Distributed to the trade by The Ingram Book Company

Contents

Acknowledgements vii
Dedication ix
Foreword xi
Opening xvii
Introduction xix
    Who Does This? xxii
    Deep Experience xxv
Chapter 1: The Making of an Extreme Facilitator 1
Chapter 2: A Gathering Storm: Knowing When a Large,
Angry Public Meeting is Imminent 9
    Unresolved Issues of Health Risk 11
    Perceived Uneven or Unacceptable
    Distribution of Risks or Costs 13
    Rights are Perceived to be Violated 19
    Values are Perceived to be Out of Alignment 19
Chapter 3: Enter the Extreme Facilitator 21
    Delivering Best Outcomes 23
    Basic Facilitation Skills and Qualities 25
    Third-Party Neutral Presence 28
    Understanding Groups 33
    Designing a Group Process 35
    The Process Expert 36
    The Right Stuff Skills 38
        Grounding 39
        Ability to Deal with Strong Emotions and Conflict 44
        Being Nimble When Dealing with Complications 51
        Understanding the Subject Matter 52
        Managing the Evolving Dynamics 54
        Cool Heads: Establishing and Maintaining Tone 56
        All Ears: Being a Strong Listener 58
        Reading and Conveying Verbal and Body Language ... 61
        I'm Listening 63
        Reading the Audience 66

    The Right Moves. 67
    Conductor Gestures. 68
    Team Body Language 68

Chapter 4: Avoiding the Slippery Slope. 73
    Hierarchy of Public Emotion. 77
    Seven Principles for Building
    Trust and Credibility 81
    Investing in the Bank of
    Trust and Credibility 86
    Doing Your Homework 92
    Being Prepared to Discuss
    Ethics and Morality. 94
    Using Common Sense 99
    Preparing for the Unreachable
    Bar of Consensus. 103
    Practicing Horizontal and
    Vertical Consultation 106
    Personifying. 109

Chapter 5: Great Design: Implementing a Sound Community
Engagement Process. 113
    Transparency. 120
    Traceability. 121
    Legitimacy 124
    Accountability. 125
    Inclusiveness 127
    Timeliness 129
    Power Balance 130

Chapter 6: The Dynamics of Large, Angry Public Meetings 133
    The Forming Stage 135
    The Norming Stage. 137
    The Storming Stage. 139
    The Performing Stage 140
    The Reforming Stage 141
    The Closure Stage 142

Chapter 7: Setting the Stage: Preparing for the Meeting 145
    Spider Facilitation 146
    World Café 151
    Roundtables 153
  Choreographing Successful Outcomes 154
  Writing the Script 157
  The Facilitator's Agenda 162
  The Stage 168
  The Architecture of Democracy 169
    Classroom and Auditorium Style Stage 170
    Semi-Circle or Thrust Stage 172
    Circle or Theatre in the Round 173
    Horseshoe or U-Shaped 174
    Roundtable 176
  The Parts of a Stage 176
    Front of the House 176
    Centre Stage 178
    Backstage 178
  Audio-Visual Equipment 179
    Wrangling Microphones 181
    Knowing What's Happening Next Door 182
  The Rehearsal 184
  The Chalk Talk 185

Chapter 8: Safety and Security 193
    The Active Assailant 198
    Security Guards 200
    Police Presence and Plain Clothes Police 201
    Bodyguards 204
    Fire Safety and Emergency Response 208
    Security Checklist 209

Chapter 9: Meeting Day 211
  Introductory Remarks 212
  The Ground Rules 214
  Getting People to Agree on Ground Rules 223
    Enforcing Ground Rules 224

Agenda Progression..224
Managing the Question and Comment Period................................226
    The Listener in Chief..228
    Hogging Air Time..230
    Managing the Response...230
    Managing Storming...233
People and Situational Complications....................................234
    Indignant and Outraged..235
    Children..237
    Local and Internet Experts..238
    Politicians...246
    Anarchists..247
    Intoxication..248
    People Demanding to Hold a Vote...................................251
    Grandstanders...253
    Prolonged Applause..255
    Chanting..256
    Citizen Journalists and the Media.................................257
    Throwing People Out...263

Chapter 10: Final Thoughts...267
References...271
Index..273
Figures..283
Appendices...284
    APPENDIX 1. Social Impact Analysis and Stakeholder Sensitivity Analysis..284
        Sample Stakeholder Sensitivity Analysis......................284
        Sample Social Impact Analysis................................289
    APPENDIX 2. Sample Comment & Disposition Table....................293
    APPENDIX 3. Sample Facilitator's Agenda...........................294
    APPENDIX 4. Chalk Talk Outline....................................301

Acknowledgements

I'm very pleased to acknowledge to the input of clients, staff, facilitators, colleagues and friends who provided comments on the draft text. Dr. Abbie Edelson provided the inspiration for the title and helped with very early drafts of the text. Bob Fleeton and Mitch Zamojc helped with several of the technical details and clarifying the setting for the Region of Peel, 'Clear Scents' program. Jon Spalding and Bruce Gillespie assisted with clarifying how the Spider Facilitation process rolled out for the province wide public consultation program for the 2010 Vancouver Olympic and Paralympic Bid process. Dr. Suzanne Ghais, provided excellent comments and directed me toward the research and analysis of Susskind and Field.

Former staff member, Andrzej Schreyer provided early research on the facilitation literature.

As the prime editor I wish to thank Marc Huminilowycz for helping me organize the thinking and encouraging me to do the work necessary to pull together the research and insight.

Dedication

This book is dedicated to my immediate family members as they've had to endure my many evenings away from home as I worked with members of the public: Frances, Judy, Michelle, Christy, Leah and Asher.

Foreword

Public trust in government is declining. In the United States (from where I write), the problem is acute. By one study, "[o]only 17% of Americans today say they can trust the government in Washington to do what is right," down from over 70% in the 1960s.[1] A Gallup poll similarly found Americans' trust in government had reached "record lows."[2] Beyond the U.S., the majority of OECD countries, including Canada, saw decreases in trust in national government between 2007 and 2012,[3] although Canada enjoyed an upward trend subsequently, to reach above 60% in 2017, significantly outperforming the OECD average.[4] Public trust in business is not faring much better, with only 52% of respondents in one 28-country survey trusting businesses to do the right thing.[5]

Interestingly, however, the trends differ for local governments. Gallup found that trust in local government in the U.S. increased gradually from 63% in 1973

---

[1] Pew Research Center: U.S. Politics & Policy, "Public Trust in Government: 1958–2019," April 11, 2019 https://www.people-press.org/2019/04/11/public-trust-in-government-1958-2019/ (accessed May 24, 2019)

[2] Megan Brenan, "Americans' Trust in Government to Handle Problems at New Low," *Gallup Brain*, January 31, 2019, https://institution.gallup.com/poll/246371/americans-trust-government-handle-problems-new-low.aspx (accessed May 24, 2019)

[3] OECD, "Confidence in national government in 2012 and its change since 2007: Arranged in descending order according to percentage point change between 2007 and 2012," December 10, 2013, in *Government at a Glance 2013*, OECD Publishing, Paris, https://doi.org/10.1787/gov_glance-2013-graph1-en (accessed May 24, 2019)

[4] Keith Neuman, "Canadians' Confidence in National Institutions Steady," *Policy Options*, Institute for Research on Public Policy, Montreal, https://policyoptions.irpp.org/magazines/august-2018/canadians-confidence-in-national-institutions-steady/ (accessed May 24, 2019)

[5] Matthew Harrington, "Survey: People's Trust Has Declined in Business, Media, Government, and NGOs," *Harvard Business Review*, January 16, 2017, https://hbr.org/2017/01/survey-peoples-trust-has-declined-in-business-media-government-and-ngos (accessed May 24, 2019)

to 72% in 2018.[6] In Canada, similarly, trust in local government in 2017 was higher for local government (54%) than for the federal government (43%).[7] Perhaps the difference comes from a greater ability to witness firsthand and understand what local government does,[8] the lower levels of negative campaigning and partisan attacks, or the possibility of face-to-face contact.

These data point to challenges and opportunities for those who call public meetings and the facilitators who help them. Much of the public will react with reflexive skepticism, or even hostility, to an initiative such as a road expansion, a new dense residential development, or even a seemingly benign initiative such as one near my home to convert an erstwhile nuclear weapons plant into a wildlife refuge. That's the challenge. The opportunity hides beneath the data on local government: where there is opportunity for face-to-face contact or meaningful exchange between officials and the public, there is some hope that there will actually be mutual learning, recognition, and accommodation. There is hope that governments will respond to public needs for health, safety, and environmental protection and public demands for transparency and fairness while pursuing growth and development. There is also hope that sensible projects—which may, to be sure, have disproportionate impacts on those who live or work nearest to them—will not be derailed by a community's ill-informed fears or grossly exaggerated grievances.

To realize this opportunity and to overcome the challenges, however, takes an open-minded attitude and considerable skill. Plenty of public officials present their project to the public, eager to explain the benefits, the studies they've conducted, and the mitigation measures already envisioned, fully expecting citizens

---

6 Justin McCarthy, "Americans Still More Trusting of Local than State Government," Gallup, October 8, 2018 https://news.gallup.com/poll/243563/americans-trusting-local-state-government.aspx (accessed May 24, 2019)

7 Ipsos, "Canadians Say They Trust, Get Better Value from Their Municipal Governments than the Feds of Provinces," July 2, 2012, https://www.ipsos.com/en-ca/canadians-say-they-trust-get-better-value-their-municipal-governments-feds-or-provinces (accessed May 24, 2019)

8 Julia Manchester, "Pollsters Say Americans Have More Trust in Local Government than in Federal Government," The Hill, October 18, 2018, https://thehill.com/hilltv/what-americas-thinking/412117-pollsters-say-americans-have-more-trust-in-local-government (accessed May 24, 2019)

Who are these people and why are they yelling at me? | xiii

to warmly embrace the resulting plans. Instead, the officials may encounter hostile interrogation, a room full of protest signs, or worse. A bureaucrat who has been intimately involved in developing these plans is probably the worst situated to listen to the public's concerns calmly, nondefensively, and empathetically. Moreover, someone whose expertise is, say, designing bridges is far from automatically qualified to design a public engagement process. Enter the facilitator, and enter Dave Hardy's book.

In these pages, Hardy describes how he discovered he had "become a noun" when someone referred to a particularly contentious public forum as "a Dave meeting", meaning Dave should have been there to manage it. He'd developed a reputation as fearless and masterful with the most cantankerous crowds. I was honored and humbled to learn that, in developing his skills to manage large, angry groups in public venues, Hardy relied heavily on my 2005 publication *Extreme Facilitation: Guiding Groups through Controversy and Complexity*. That book drew on my years of experience as a facilitator in a variety of settings, both internal to organizations and external—that is, stakeholder negotiations and public consultations on issues of public concern. I'd had the good or ill fortune of facing tough challenges in the groups I'd facilitated—elevated emotions, technically complex subjects, bureaucratic mazes, and intense conflict and controversy—and I set out to share what I'd learned for the benefit of other facilitators.

In the years since my book's release, the field of facilitation has flourished, and with its maturation comes specialization. Dave Hardy has deftly combined his expertise in planning with his earlier experience in community organizing and protest to develop a specialization in facilitating public meetings. In public meetings, government or company officials present plans to the public and obtain their feedback, in order (ideally) to help shape the project and ultimately arrive at an improved plan that serves the original public purpose while better addressing the public's needs and concerns. While I have facilitated a handful of public meetings (among many other types of meetings and group processes), Hardy has facilitated over a thousand of them. In offering facilitators a volume devoted to this specialty, he has indeed, as he says, picked up where I left off.

Another thing that has changed in the years since writing my book has been my own substantive focus. While I am still an active facilitator, and still working in organizational as well as public settings, I have also developed expertise in the prevention and resolution of armed conflict, and I have begun to apply my skills in peace processes. (Maybe I'm a junkie for the "extreme"?!) I've come to better understand the role of good governance in the prevention of violent conflict. In short, it is not differences that causes war—there will always be ethnic and racial divides, religious differences, ideological clashes, and economic disparities—but rather the ability of governance institutions to channel and manage those inevitable differences.

Good governance means that when citizens feel aggrieved, they have someplace to turn—the courts, the police, the legislature, regulatory agencies, the electoral process—and while they might not get their way, they will see that there is some more-or-less fair process in which their voice counts, even if only by aggregation with many others. Presidential and parliamentary democracies are effective in this way—they have plenty of flaws, but at least when there is a groundswell of support for some desired change, it does tend to happen eventually. (I believe other forms of good governance are conceivable, building on traditional practices, such as the Arab world's *shura*, or consultation, and *sulha*, or dispute resolution.) Public involvement processes—including public meetings—take democracy to the next level, such that citizens can make their views known on not just who should represent them in office, and not just in a cursory way (such as a letter to a legislator), but directly and in depth on an issue of particular concern. By contributing to good governance, public participation contributes to peace.

As Hardy writes, "People need to know that, after the meeting, they have been successful, and negotiation needs to occur. Alternatively, they haven't been successful, and the next step is the ballot box. It is certainly not armed insurrection or civil disobedience". This last point may have been tongue-in-cheek, but to me it is deadly serious. Public participation makes governance more effective, and effective governance is critical to preventing violent conflict. It is when citizens believe their voices are consistently ignored that they might conclude that working within the system is futile and they will get better results by forming an armed militia or planting a bomb. There are many factors that contribute to armed conflict, and the U.S. is hardly on the brink of civil war (Canada even less so), but we have in fact begun to see an uptick in small-scale political violence.[9] The need for officials to show communities they are listening is urgent.

But don't let me over-romanticize. The work of facilitators is pragmatic and immediate. We run meetings! The skills to do so well—especially in more extreme cases—take practice and sensitivity, but they can be learned.

Dave Hardy has made an excellent contribution to helping you, the reader, do just that. He draws on the work of many well-established facilitation authors such as Doyle & Straus, Bens, Susskind & Field, and Schwarz, as well as his own ingenuity and extensive experience. The result is a practical, readable, and often humorous guide for facilitating large, heated public meetings. Enjoy!

May 2019
Suzanne Ghais, Ph.D.
Principal, Ghais Mediation & Facilitation, LLC

---

[9] Zaid Jilani and Jeremy Adam Smith, "What's Driving Political Violence in America?" *Greater Good Magazine,* November 7, 2018, https://greatergood.berkeley.edu/article/item/whats_driving_political_violence_in_america (accessed May 24, 2019)

Opening

Public meetings about government or corporate infrastructure, utility expansion or other projects, policies or plans which may have an impact on communities are a regular occurrence in western society. Indeed, they are part of the demographic process.

As a professional facilitator, about ninety-five per cent of the author's work involves services that help clients to achieve the best possible outcomes from public meetings. The facilitation of large angry public meetings, where emotions run high, make up roughly ten per cent of his assignments. Professionals who work at this extreme end of a facilitator's role may be referred to by clients as "hired guns".

There are only a handful of trained "extreme facilitators" in Canada. They are called upon to turn around situations that have spun out of control, where political representatives have not been able to make tough decisions or when public and corporate clients have completely overlooked the community impacts of a decision, conducted shoddy public consultation processes or communicated poorly to citizens.

As an extreme facilitator, the author describes how he has achieved ideal outcomes out of what could have been the ranting of a mob. He shares some of the most bizarre events leading up to and occurring during large, angry public meetings that he has encountered in his career, such as civil disobedience, death threats, children used as pawns, and citizens participating in outrageous behaviour.

In addition to lessons learned from facilitating hundreds of angry public meetings, the author provides personal reflections on why he or anyone in their right mind would want to stand in front of a potential riot, utilizing training, strategy, communications and strength of personality to steer the outcome in a positive direction. The author ends with insights on how to avoid angry public meetings in the first place and the art and science of how to manage these meetings if inevitable.

Introduction

It was expected to be a civil, medium-sized public meeting about a road project, but it ended up drawing 1,200 angry citizens. For about ten years, my company held the record for facilitating the largest and angriest public meeting ever held in Toronto, Ontario.

For the life of me, I still can't figure out whether I should wear the record attendance as a badge of courage or a nose wart. It certainly helped establish the reputation of my company at the time as the firm that knew how to plan for and manage large and rancorous meetings.

We were retained about two months before the record-breaking event by a client who knew that a meeting was being demanded by local residents but had no idea that the public was extremely upset about what was essentially a road-widening project. In fact, the politics then were so hot that a coalition of local community groups in Toronto's west end had almost managed to bring down the provincial government over the issue.

Our client, proposing to widen a road for high occupancy vehicle lanes, was in denial about the potential for the meeting to be large and angry until the last moment, believing that we were overblowing what was going to happen. But the new widened lanes were to be built along the same route as a previously proposed expressway that had been successfully opposed by residents a half a generation earlier. So, the public was seeing the project as an "'expressway – version two".

On the day of the public meeting, about an hour before the start time, the client and project team realized that they were being held up travelling to the pre-briefing because police were redirecting traffic near the venue. This was the result of a rock concert-sized traffic jam created by the number of people driving to attend the meeting and finding that they had no place to park.

Our client showed me over two hundred and fifty hand-written (not form-written) letters of protest, a significant number not to be ignored. Large global corporations will consider changing a global brand if they receive several letters of protest. In the hierarchy of community dissent, hand written letters rank very high as an indicator of community opposition.

In preparation, we put the art and science of managing large public meetings to work. First, we set up an internal planning and communications process for the client. Whether the client would admit it or not, we knew that they were in for a hot night and we needed to be prepared. We started focusing on the logistics: Is the venue big enough? Can we get a sound system that works well? What about fire exits, and what happens if someone pulls an alarm?

We then moved on to what I call "meeting choreography", the minute-by-minute planning of the meeting: How do we want the meeting to play out? Who speaks and when? How do we deal with questions? How do my clients show they are listening? How do we address the demand by opposed citizens groups to speak and have equal time on the agenda? How do we address the requests to be heard from local politicians? What are we and aren't we able to control when it comes to the media?

At the end of the pre-meeting planning process, which was initially developed several weeks earlier, we at least had the basis of a plan for the evening. I knew that it would also be important to meet with the residents in advance. Thankfully, my clients agreed to allow us to convene and attend what is known as a "kitchen table" meeting; an opportunity for a small group of residents and clients to sit down and discuss issues frankly with the neutral facilitator face to face. These meetings can be critical to a successful outcome of a large angry meeting.

The other challenge was introducing me to the larger community as a professional facilitator. People are typically very suspicious of a facilitator; what they are, who are they and what they do? They may ask themselves, "Do facilitators advocate the interest of the other side? Do they control the meeting so rigidly that we can't get their message across?"

The answer to both questions is "no". While we are paid by the client and understand what the client wants to get out of the meeting, we let the residents know that our role is to be neutral. We don't live in the area. We may not be working with the client after the meeting, so we have no reason to be biased. In addition, we have no position with respect to the ultimate decision about the project. I'm honest with people, letting them know that we will be paid for our work, and that the client will be footing the bill.

During the kitchen table meeting, we learned that one of the non-negotiable items demanded by residents was for our client to share the meeting airtime. Reluctantly, our client agreed. Our choreography then involved coaching our client on their role and their messages within a shared agenda, in order to at least provide information that might help both sides understand each other.

Typically, our clients are more interested in telling rather than listening. Specifically, they feel that their only role is to tell the public what the project, policy or program is about, trying to get people to listen to and accept their views. If the public is not listening, then they feel they need to speak louder or explain more clearly. More often than not, clients want our help in getting the public to accept their position. That is not our job.

In addition, people attending large public meetings will not be patient enough to listen to a forty-minute long PowerPoint presentation on issues with which they completely disagree. For this large meeting, we needed to change the expectations of the client in terms of how things would be run, negotiating with them to present a truncated version of their PowerPoint after the expert appointed by the public had their turn to speak.

We knew that security would be important. Members of the public are generally respectful, but the dynamics change during large, angry meetings. These types of meetings sometimes attract people who have axes to grind or may not appreciate the boundary of what constitutes acceptable public behaviour. The subject of safely interacting with a range of people at meetings will be discussed in later sections of the book.

We worked with the police who in this instance, were requested to have uniformed officers in attendance. The police needed to know what I'm doing and what boundaries I'm setting. It's good to have someone with formal authority available at meetings to throw people out if need be, keeping in mind that yelling or having strong views doesn't constitute a reason to do so.

As the facilitator, I can use a strong voice and use any tacit authority that I might earn from the public to keep interactions civil. I can't touch anyone, and any person acting out can ignore me if they wish. If you have no formal authority, threatening to throw someone out of a meeting and then doing so comes with a risk. For this reason, I usually have one eye on the person being thrown out and the other on the exit door. (I joke with my clients that I'll be the first to run out the back door if my authority isn't working.)

By the way, the name of my company is Hardy Stevenson and Associates Limited. As a collection of about eight public consultation specialists, social scientists, policy researchers, land use planners, engineers, geoscientists and communicators, we are all a bit adventurous and will take on assignments that even lawyers won't touch.

Who Does This?

On the morning after another large angry meeting involving about seven hundred suburban Toronto residents who were upset over a proposed off-shore wind turbine project on Lake Ontario, one of my former staff who attended the meeting told me that the exasperated meeting facilitator was heard to say, "This should have been a Dave meeting!"

On that day, I came to the realization that I had become a noun. Why? Because I'm one of a few professional facilitators in Canada who's trained and has enough experience to facilitate meetings that have the potential to take a turn for the worst. In fact, throughout most of my career, I've been called upon to take on these assignments by companies and governments who had somehow managed to infuriate so many people that they could no longer handle the outrage themselves. So, they phone me or one of a handful of my colleagues.

The scenarios vary: an announcement to locate a landfill site beside an idyllic, back to the earth rural community; informing homeowners that they will have to move because the Ministry of Transportation needs their home to widen a road; announcing that a homeless shelter or drug injection site will be located in the community; locating a cellular telecommunications tower in the community; initiating dialogue between a public agency responsible for blood transfusions which, due to a bureaucratic oversight, managed to spread Hepatitis C and, in a few cases kill the relatives and friends of people who they now realize they have to talk to.

My colleagues and I get the call: "We need a facilitator and your name has been suggested." As extreme facilitators, we've probably seen it all during angry public meetings: people dying; domestic disturbances; physical violence and death threats; radical groups trying to "game" the meeting; the media manipulating members of the public and trampling over clients to stage a story; and even children being used as pawns.

We have also had large meetings turn into constructive and conciliatory sessions where all sides learned something and went away thinking about how to reposition their views to accommodate the other side. Even if they don't agree with my clients at the end of the evening, that's the outcome I'm normally seeking.

I have learned and applied techniques that have helped to avoid large, angry meetings. And I have learned how to successfully manage these meetings when they occur. I don't always get it right, and I've seen them spin out of control. The flawed meetings gave me a chance to reflect, ponder what happened and determine how I could do a better job the next time.

Having worked as a community organizer in my youth, I must admit that I also learned how to organize and deliver angry meetings. So, I have seen many sides. The work that I do when I run these meetings is technically called "facilitation". I refer to the large angry public meeting assignments as "extreme facilitation". There's an art and science to managing these meetings, and that is what I want to share with you.

The title of my book, "Who are these people and why are they yelling at me?" was based on an idea that came from Dr. Abbie Edelson, a community organizer, colleague and friend. Pointing out to me that this is exactly the question many of my clients ask before they engage the services of an extreme facilitator, Abbie's observation was the inspiration for the title.

A good facilitator usually knows as much about his client's subject matter as does the client and, after facilitating 1,500 meetings, you learn a lot about a wide range of subjects. Learning about the subject matter allows you to fully understand the conversation and share prompt questions that allow the group to explore the issues and reach consensus.

After years of standing in front of angry crowds, the irony of various situations becomes apparent. Many years ago, I facilitated numerous meetings involving people wanting to stop coal-fired electricity generation and nuclear energy. The wind and alternative energy advocates, mostly made up of vocal anti-nuclear, anti-coal global warming activists, were the angry people that I had to deal with. With missionary zeal, they shouted out from every hilltop that the world was crying out for wind power as the solution to the world's energy problems. "The public is on our side," they proclaimed. "God is with us!"

In 2008, the Province of Ontario passed the Green Energy Act (Green Energy Act S.O. 2009, S 12 as updated). The solar and wind power lobby had achieved its goals. For the first time, funds were available for wind, solar and other alternative energy projects. For my colleagues and me, this meant a new group of clients who might need our services.

We pointed out to the pro-wind activists and now potential clients (with little success) that they might run into the same public opposition as proponents of nuclear, coal and other fossil-fueled generation sources. We suggested that they would need to initiate excellent public consultation and engagement the same as any other energy project proponents. And, that they might need a facilitator for their meetings.

Time after time, I saw these naïve green entrepreneurs march into rural communities waving high the banner of wind energy, convinced that the public would throw rose petals at their feet. Unfortunately for them, there was huge community opposition. Thus, raising the question, "who are these people and why are they yelling at me?"

They fully believed that all of society would embrace wind turbines; they were the new messiahs who had cast out evil nuclear and coal, were now spreading the message, "I am here with your wind turbines!" - only to be stopped dead in their tracks by angry rural residents wishing to run them out of town.

My company is one of only a few firms in Canada that provides professional services (urban planning, socio-economic development, engineering and geoscience) to environmental and citizen groups as well as "bread and butter" work with corporate, agency and government clients. We are happy to work for citizens' groups from time to time.

Who are these people and why are they yelling at me? | xxv

As professional urban and environmental planners, public consultation experts and communicators, engineers and geoscientists, we are also asked to be experts hired by a client or community to give evidence at a hearing or tribunal. Or, we are hired to peer review a technical report or give technical advice. We work with many corporations, agencies and government departments. Compared to these clients, it is quite a juxtaposition to work with citizens leading the cause and "fighting the good fight".

Leaders of citizens' groups opposing projects often find themselves involved in the most intense public profile and political activity of their lives. Normally, they are well-organized to challenge city hall or take on a corporation. At times, they will dally with notions of civil disobedience, typically taking the form of removing information posters or perhaps standing in the way of an official trying to get to a podium.

Deep Experience

The citizens we work with often don't know that, as extreme facilitators, our experience and understanding of civil disobedience runs deep. We've been schooled in Saul Alinsky's "Rules for Radicals". Not that I've ever participated in such activities but, over the years, I learned how to wet a scarf to minimize the effects of tear gas and the correct way to throw a Molotov cocktail. One of my colleagues built a youthful reputation by holding a boycott and student protest. Another colleague started her career leading a large, successful environmental organization.

Corporate or government leaders who typically hire us may find themselves embroiled in the biggest issue they have ever faced. Achieving peace with a community or an interest group, or having a project cancelled, costing millions of dollars, can make or break their careers.

Those hiring us for the first time may not know that, as extreme facilitators, we work on these high-controversy, high-profile projects every week. We have helped clients successfully carry out highly demanding and complex approvals. And, we've worked with communities at a grassroots level when the solution requires changes to government and corporate plans and policies, to the chagrin of bureaucrats and corporate officials convinced that their policies and projects should remain set in stone.

Large angry meetings are often the peak event in the evolution of a community fighting city hall or rallying for corporate change. They bring together political representatives, the media, government and corporate decision makers, residents and businesses. Our role as facilitators is not to stand in the way of change. By the time the meeting happens, the residents have usually made their point. Either the change they are seeking is underway, or they've hit a brick wall that's not going to crack.

At this stage in the process, our job is to begin patching up the rips and tears in the fabric of democracy. People need to know that, after the meeting, they have been successful, and negotiation needs to occur. Alternatively, they haven't been successful, and the next step is the ballot box. It is certainly not armed insurrection or civil disobedience.

Even when emotions are running high and the cause is right and just, there are lines that cannot be crossed in civil society. (I say to citizen groups that I work with, "Your rights to protest and civil disobedience stop at the end of my nose".) At the peak of intensity in an angry meeting, my job as facilitator is to use my experience, solid preparation, carefully-placed attitude, a practiced calm demeanour, an internal sense of humour and a very thick skin to direct all sides to a constructive outcome.

For community leaders, these meetings involve placing their issues at the forefront. They are rallying large numbers of people and businesses, organizing the media, running a large communications campaign and staging the politics toward the outcome they are seeking. They have typically managed to pull together hundreds of residents, mobilize print, radio and television, reign in political representatives and identify true corporate and government decision makers in order to hold their feet to the fire.

I have often met in advance with local community leaders organizing or planning to attend big angry meetings. It is always my preference to do so. More frequently than I'd care to admit, I've found community leaders who are a bit intimidated by the public anger they've unleashed. On occasion, they have privately asked me for help in keeping their fellow residents under control. After the meeting, I often have these same members of the public comment that, even though there were several hundred people in the room and emotions were high, the meeting ended up being calm and constructive. And, they got what they wanted.

What these clients don't realize is that a meeting like this will likely be the most intimidating situation they have ever experienced in their careers. On the day they are hired, few corporate managers, project engineers or project developers envision a time when they would have to defend their actions in front of a large group of angry residents. I've never seen that requirement in a job description.

A lot of my pre-meeting coaching is focused on helping clients to not take public anger personally. It's their job. The day after the meeting, they will normally have the respect of their employers and colleagues. Sometimes the respect comes because their colleagues were glad that my client had to "do" the meeting and not them, and most often because my client got through the meeting with no more than minor flesh wounds. My clients are usually on the receiving end. They are the spokespeople standing in front of the room. By the time the meeting finishes, they get what they want out of the meeting: to get it over with.

What either side typically doesn't grasp is that, what happens once in a lifetime or once in a career for them, is a full career for me. There isn't much that extreme facilitators haven't seen or experienced.

To my knowledge, this is a body of skills, science and art that has rarely been documented. It is my hope that, by opening the door a small crack to the skills and techniques extreme facilitators bring to these meetings, we can help to teach people what to expect, so that all sides can have positive outcomes.

All of the anecdotes in this book are true. I have changed the names and circumstances of situations and people in order to protect the reputations of great clients, staff, colleagues and passionate residents whom I have in some small way helped to get through some of the most difficult situations they've faced.

Chapter 1:
The Making of an Extreme Facilitator

When I was a teen in high school, I had a friend, Harvey. Harvey was a socially awkward type who was quite nerdy. He went around telling people that he was either going to be a nuclear physicist or a rocket scientist. In grade nine, letting this out to other high school students was like walking around with a target on your back. As a result, plenty of kids picked on and bullied him.

My problem was that I had a bit of an "equalizer" complex and got upset when I saw my friends being picked on. One day, when two players on the school football team were bullying Harvey, I told them to stop. The conversation when something like, "And who's going to make us stop?" I responded that Harvey and I will. They replied, "Then why don't the two of you meet us on the school lawn after school?" I agreed.

Unfortunately, as it turns out, the timing was not good for Harvey as he had a violin lesson after school and he decided to cut afternoon classes early that day so he wouldn't be late. So, it was just me and the two football players on the front lawn. I weighed about one hundred and thirty-five pounds at the time. They were considerably bigger.

I knew that the day would not finish well, so I figured the best I could do was get in the first punch. When they started by pushing me around a bit, I let a punch fly that caught the bigger guy right in the face. Now I was dealing with two really pissed off football players, and the kicks and punches from both of them flew in my direction.

If you have ever been punched hard, you know that you feel the pain before the punch actually arrives. I suppose it's the adrenalin. After a while, I ended up in a crouched position, figuring that the best they could do is kick in or facture my ribs, which they tried to do with gusto. I was also hoping that an adult in the school, someone walking by or someone driving buy might tell them to stop. I was lucky that my ribs were only bruised and not broken.

To my dismay, the bullies weren't tiring of kicking me as quickly as I hoped they would be. I suppose the biggest mistake I made was getting up. The bigger of the two was wearing tough leather cowboy type boots and took advantage of my head being down. His kick caught me in the mouth and knocked me backward off my feet. (I kind of wonder if he was a field goal punter, because it was very good kick.)

When you are being beaten up you can hear bones fracturing and breaking. The cracking sound I heard was my lower teeth being loosened by the kick, which had also driven my lower teeth right through my bottom lip. (I have the facial scars today, and sometimes joke with my friends that kicking someone in the toe of their boot with my face is my signature punch.) By that point, I was covered in blood, but I still got in the last punch. I think the only reason they stopped beating me is because their clothes were also becoming covered in blood – mine.

Walking home that evening, I remember the blood coming out of my nose, occasionally forming bubbles as I exhaled. The knuckles on my right hand were bleeding, so I guess one or two of my punches landed. I remember walking into home room class the next morning. When my teacher arrived, she looked at me and started screaming. The swelling, bruises and cuts had magnified overnight. My face looked like chopped liver.

Soon, the whole school knew that I had stood up to two football players. No one touched me for the next five years. The football players had the rest of their lives to live as bullies, and I lived my life knowing that I could and did stand up to them. Today, I believe that purposely fighting anybody else is stupid. I'm not sure what happened to Harvey. We didn't talk much after that. Perhaps he became a professional violinist.

What does this experience mean for extreme facilitation? I know that there are consequences to what I say. And, I know what it feels like if someone sincerely wants to challenge me. And, I know how far my informal authority as facilitator can go and the potential consequence of exceeding that limit. The lesson I also

Who are these people and why are they yelling at me?

learned is that, while people often complain loudly and want change, they don't always show up when the change they desire requires heavy lifting or needs to be paid for. Sometimes the battles that community leaders take on are just not worth fighting.

Everybody needs inspiration in their lives. I was influenced by three notable people. One of them was Saul Alinsky[10], a union and community organizer in Chicago during the 1950s and '60s. Alinsky developed innovative civil disobedience techniques that were very effective in motivating meat packing barons to provide their employees with proper pay and working conditions. The techniques were creative, lawful and very intimidating.

Saul Alinsky also used a wide range of community organizing techniques. For example, he had dozens of union members buy tickets and attend a Chicago Opera Company performance that was also attended by their corporate bosses, the meat packing barons. They were coached on how to make their working conditions known to well-dressed patrons during intermission.

Alinsky fed each meat packer a large plate of beans before the performance so as to make their presence known. Once opera company patrons got wind of who was protesting, they realized that the meat packers would continue communicating in an odorous manner and create a very uncomfortable operatic experience.

This odious display of public flatulence achieved the effect of embarrassing the meat packing barons, causing them to explain to their corporate colleagues and fellow opera patrons what the union protest was about. The meat packers got their union contract. Alinsky also had union members picket outside the country club of business owners. Bringing the issue home to the families and communities of corporation executives had a very powerful and positive effect.

The closest I got to meeting Saul Alinsky was on a university sponsored trip to Chicago in the mid-1970s, where I met another community organizer named Jessie Jackson. Reverend Jackson was leading a grassroots organization named People United to Save Humanity (PUSH), the focus of which was providing

---

10 Alinsky, Saul, Rules for Radicals: A Pragmatic Primer for Realistic Radicals, Vintage Books, Random House, New York, March 1972

4 | David R. Hardy, R.P.P.

civic services to people in the Oak Park and South Side sections of Chicago. My PUSH experience eventually led me to follow activities centered around the Riverside Church in New York, at the time a hotbed of community and tenant organizing in New York proper and the Boroughs.

My second influencer was Don Keating[11], a community organizer in Toronto during the 1960s and '70s, and my professor at the Ontario Institute for Studies in Education (OISE). Don was very effective in initiating grass roots organizations among poor, working class and disenfranchised people in Toronto, particularly those being bulldozed from their homes for the sake of urban renewal.

Don Keating's focus was on the St. Jamestown and Riverdale areas of Toronto, where developers assembling land and building apartment buildings caused people to be evicted from their homes. Leading sit-ins and demonstrations at City Hall, Don's core strength was his ability to use grassroots door-knocking as a way to mobilize residents and develop a strong political organization.

The third person who influenced me was Norm Brudy[12], with whom I worked as a community organizer for Toronto's Federation of Metro Tenants. When I met him, Norm was an ardent Communist. I was certainly not.

While I didn't agree with his Norm's politics, I saw him use incredible communications and oratory skills to instill a sense of shared anger and empowerment among people who, an hour before, didn't know each other. Oppressed people sometimes need to have someone to hold up a mirror to help them see their plight. Through his oratory, Norm was able to ask critical questions: "Is this the way you are living now?"; "Is this the way you want to live?"; "Do you want to do something about it?"

My challenge as a young community organizer at the time was to cool off Norm's oratory before he could also offer his opinions about nationalizing Canadian housing, mines and the auto sector. If the meeting reached that point, people were turned off and things would quickly deteriorate. Norm

---

11 Keating, Don, The Power to Make it Happen: Mass Based-Community Organizing, What it is and How it Works" 1975

12 https://en.wikipedia.org/wiki/Norman_Brudy

never knew when to stop. He could not understand why everybody didn't want to be communists.

Regretfully, my association with Norm resulted in my being visited by the RCMP, who wanted to know what my politics were all about. I wanted people's lives to improve in a practical and real manner. Where I differed from Norm was that I didn't believe in pushing others to accept a different ideology in the process.

Through my early personal experiences, I learned the techniques of confrontation politics. On the path I travelled during my youth, also I learned what the extreme side of politics was about. Following the May 4th shootings of students at Kent State, Ohio, I participated in the infamous May 9, 1970 anti-Vietnam War protest and police riot in front of the U.S. Embassy in Toronto.

May 9th protest organizers coached participants on how to bring down police horses with ball bearings, use fire crackers to simulate gunfire (forcing security officials to think twice about advancing on protesters), and the intimidatory presence of protest signs stapled to baseball bats.

For the record, I never threw any ball bearings, lit any fire crackers or swung any bats. Nor did I break any windows. But I watched others behave badly. Following the demonstration, I received another call from the police, who knew that I was taking photos and wanted them for themselves. As a kid from the suburbs who respected the police, I promptly surrendered most of my photos. I never did get them back.

They say that if you don't have passion in youth, you don't have a heart. And, if you don't turn conservative in your old age, you don't have a brain. Today, as a proud Rotarian, my activism is filtered through a wonderful global organization dedicated to poverty alleviation, polio eradication and world peace. I get quite upset when I hear confused purposes and witness the disobedience of some of today's youth demonstrators. I don't like what I see. If you are going to protest, at least get the facts right.

I learned a lot about civil disobedience techniques as a grass roots community organizer. During grad school, I was very involved in fighting for tenants' rights. One issue that I was passionate about was the growing number of children living in apartment buildings who were falling to their deaths due to the failure of the Ontario Building Code to require builders to install child-proof windows.

When the former City of North York failed to implement a model window lock by-law, my fellow students and a tenants' group in which I was involved[13] organized a sit-in at the Council chambers. Researching and writing the draft by-law at the Faculty of Environmental Studies at Toronto's York University, we and about a dozen other protesters chanted and refused to move until the City passed our proposed legislation.

Within two hours, our by-law was fine-tuned and passed, and no one was arrested. Because we had prepared the draft before we held our demonstration, the politicians knew exactly what they needed to do in order to get us and the media to leave. Happily, that by-law is still on the books today.

Back in the early 1970s, there was no rent control legislation or security of tenure in the Province of Ontario, so my colleagues and I organized twenty-five tenant associations across Toronto and the province. This organization technique involved responding to a request to meet with someone in an apartment building, then planning a whole-building meeting in a nearby school or community centre.

A fellow community organizer[14] and I would print the invitations, then find a way to enter an apartment building. Since there was a high likelihood of being thrown out by a building superintendent or being detained and charged with trespassing, it was our practice to always have two or more of us start on different floors, knocking on doors in a leapfrog fashion. That way, the "super" believed that he/she had caught and ejected the organizer, and that the organization effort was over. In fact, another organizer would finish the job.

As the community organizer, it was my job to lead the off-site tenant meeting and facilitate a conversation until I could identify one tenant in the audience with the leadership skills needed to take charge. I would first ask the participants to share what it was like to live in the apartment building. Often, they would describe huge rent increases, infestations or minimal repairs.

---

13 North York Tenants Council
14 Eric Novick

Who are these people and why are they yelling at me? | 7

I would ask everyone to introduce themselves, describe what they did for a living and any skills that might be helpful in discussing the issues with the landlord. Interestingly, this meeting was often the first time that tenants living in the building for many years had ever talked to each other.

The objective of the tenant meeting was to, over the course of an evening, have a small group of tenants identify a leader, form an executive committee and agree to take the next steps on a "pro tem" (for the time being) basis. Other organizers and I would be asked to return and convene the first meeting of a new tenant association, then approach the landlord to seek improvements in building conditions or reductions in unreasonable rent increases. I call this technique "Lone Ranger" community organizing: move in; get them organized; show them how to take action; ride off into the sunset and on to the next group of tenants.

As an odd part of this work, I learned to never entertain a public question about cats and dogs as pets - in apartment buildings or anywhere else. It's strange, but people attending tenant meetings will often spilt along species lines and fight with one another about cats running loose and dogs defecating in public spaces - rather than focusing on rising rent levels and poor living conditions. I had several community meetings completely disintegrate for this reason. All I could do was put my hands over my face and shake my head.

I also learned how to stack meetings and use the media to get our message out. Just before rent control and security of tenure legislation was brought into Ontario in 1974, our tenant coalition made a major announcement and managed to get the Minister of Housing to show up to explain the province's response. With the Minister coming, we also attracted the interest of most of Toronto's radio and TV media. The media always follow senior politicians.

The problem we had is that we couldn't get many of our own members out to the event. Having the Minister attend with few tenants in the audience would weaken the story, so we managed to convince the Toronto District School Board to let us hold the meeting in a public-school classroom. In that small space, the meeting appeared to be packed with members of the public, creating the impression that there was huge public attendance and support. As there was no facilitator or anyone to screen questions, the Minister was on the defensive throughout the entire evening – the media story we wanted and got.

Many years later, my colleagues and I were involved in supporting a local environmental group called Save the Rouge in their fight over the Oak Ridges Moraine. Taking street theatre to a new level, dressed in squirrel and deer costumes, they marched outside of a government meeting with protest signs. Those were the media shots.

Eventually, I had the opportunity to serve on the executive of the Federation of Metro Tenants in Toronto. But, with a young family under way and another career path available, I had to step aside. Instead, another community organizer, Jack Layton, stepped up and became the next leader of the Federation.

Over the years, the table turned. Perhaps it was because I was getting older and needed to support a family, but I realized that the techniques I had learned as a community organizer could help me build a career. And so, after twelve years working for an electric utility, I entered my mature career as a professional facilitator – a role that involved helping public sector and corporate clients to avoid becoming embroiled in rancorous public debates, get through angry public meetings and occasionally coach citizen's groups on how to raise hell.

Chapter 2:
A Gathering Storm: Knowing When a Large, Angry Public Meeting is Imminent

There are causes and signs of a consultation process going off the rails. Thus, it is essential that public consultation and communications programs be integrally linked to a well-informed strategic analysis.

It is important to understand the process of public dialogue and public/client interaction. For a new highway project, we were doing the analysis, but the client was not listening. Strategic analysis of public consultation programs allows you to assess whether your method of engaging the public has fundamental structural issues or is on track. For most community engagement programs, I recommend a mid-point evaluation step that asks: "Is the engagement process rolling out as planned? Are mid-course corrections required? What's the temperature of the public?"

Knowing the signs that the public is angry and that an emotional response is brewing is essential. These are some of the indicators I use to determine if an angry meeting is imminent:

- Local resident groups are coalescing with other groups around an issue.
- The public is raising money to oppose a project, policy or program. Funds are being used for anti-project websites. Lawyers and consultants are being hired by the public.
- There is active lobbying of senior political representatives by people who generally don't talk to these officials.
- A vacuum exists, where there are no government or corporate policies to provide a context for the discussion.

- Hand-written letters are submitted in opposition.
- Media coverage is becoming more frequent, in-depth and intense.
- Issues of health and safety, risks and rights are being raised but not addressed in the minds of the public.
- The public is confused about the need or rationale for a decision.
- The proponent cannot answer fundamental questions about why the policy, project or program is needed.
- During earlier internal team meetings, the purpose of the meeting is fuzzy or seems untruthful. An internal lack of logic and absence of rational thinking is apparent to everyone except the person leading the project, program or policy.

Cellular communications companies trying to site cell phone towers, and government agencies attempting to route electrical transmission lines are both particularly susceptible to rancorous public opposition due to a perception of health effects associated with electromagnetic fields (EMF).

For example, the issue of health effects was front and centre during a Saturday morning public meeting in Muskoka, Ontario in a community centre auditorium. Our client, a Canadian mobile phone company wanted to locate a cellular tower in this affluent region of "cottage country" in order to improve mobile phone service for residents.

Mobile phone companies siting cellular towers tend to have more than their fair share of big angry public meetings. One reason is that the cellular phone companies are faced with communicating the risks and perceptions of harm due to electromagnetic effects in a public meeting format. Although everyone has a mobile phone, no one wants a cell phone tower. Many of the participants in this case were wealthy cottagers who wanted the company to know that they have the resources to block the cell tower.

The meeting I was facilitating started angry. There was no, lets get to know each other phase. One of the residents, who had a serious heart condition, desperately needed improved cell phone communication to place a 911 call in an emergency. My staff and I facilitated the meeting by arranging to have health and safety issues addressed openly and frankly. Given that the cell tower

Who are these people and why are they yelling at me? | 11

would provide positive health outcomes for at least one resident, we arranged to have people opposing the cell tower for health reasons to talk to the individual needing the cell tower for health reasons.

Effectively, we helped to steer the discussion to the need for cell phones in health emergencies and the need for cell towers in the area to service emergency calls. Our client, a representative from Rogers Mobility, was an excellent communicator who brought the sincerity and credibility needed to build trust and provide the necessary assurances. After the initial anger, the meeting went smoothly.

Overall people don't like change. Doyle and Straus bluntly comment, "People don't want change unless they have to."[15] They note that many people feel there is already too much change going on and until members of the public recognize and agree that they have a serious problem or see payoffs for changing they aren't going to change. In the next section, I look a little deeper into why there is concern about change resulting in public anger.

There are four main causes I look for when assessing whether or not an angry public meeting is likely: 1) unresolved issues of health risk; 2) perceived unequal distribution of risks or costs; 3) rights are perceived to be violated; and, 4) values are perceived to be out of alignment.

Unresolved Issues of Health Risk

Although there are exceptions, there are many layers of science-based rules and regulations supported by government review that keep the public healthy. That said, health risk and particularly, perceptions of health risk, are among the strongest reasons for people to act angrily and show up at meetings.

Many issues of perceived health risk are resolved or incited by whether or not science communication has been effective. For example, many lay people question climate science while climate scientists almost universally agree that climate change is a real and serious issue. Opposition to climate science has as much to do with how effectively the social sciences are used to support communication of the science as it does with the raw politics that characterize both sides of the issue. Similarly, some people believe that there is scientific evidence

---

15 Doyle and Straus, How to Make Meetings Work, Berkley Books, New York, 1976, p. 19

linking vaccinations to autism, while the scientific community has concluded that there is no such link. Part of the challenge in both instances lies in the effective communication of science, facts and values.

Many of the meetings I've facilitated involving health risk involved electromagnetic fields of electricity transmission lines and cellular towers. Humans have been exposed to electromagnetic effects for over one hundred years. Indeed, at one point in the last century, exposure to electromagnetic and electrostatic effects was believed to be healthy and curative. Utility workers around the world have been exposed to these effects throughout their careers. There have been well over one hundred and fifty thousand studies of the possible effects of EMF on human health which, in total, indicate that there may or may not be an association with certain health effects, particularly cancer.

In the scientific research on EMF and human health, an association between EMF exposure and cancer does not necessarily mean that electromagnetic effects cause the disease. Yet at most public meetings that I have facilitated on behalf of mobile phone companies trying to get the approval of a site for a cellular tower, a sizable number of people will claim that there is a cancer effect. There is usually a member of the public at the meeting who has searched the internet and found the one study indicating a causal effect between EMF and cancer. Instead of the scientific experts, the information shared by that person is believed.

These are some techniques I recommend to the client to advance science and health communication and avoid, or at least temper, public anger focused on perceived health risks related to a project:

- Invite a respected medical doctor or scientist familiar with the research as a speaker.
- Acknowledge the health concern and convene one on one discussions with members of the public before or after the meeting to discuss health effects in depth.
- Set up a health committee, workshop or colloquium of experts and members of the public to review the scientific data and draw conclusions.

- Partner with staff at a university or hospital so that the public sees a third party – with no interest in the decision - commenting objectively.

The Region of Waterloo in the Province of Ontario has completed excellent scientific risk communications programs. One particularly good program is focused on the science around biosolids. Biosolids are the residual products of sewage treatment plants. It can be used as fertilizer, as a fuel source or disposed. Biosolids also may be odorous and they are perceived to have health risks due to perceptions of endocrine disruptors in the material. One of the Region's large biosolids master plans ran into stiff public opposition.

Following this opposition, and to address the issue of biosolids and human health, they retained as a spokesperson Bob McDonald, respected host of the CBC Radio show Quirks and Quarks and a science reporter for the Canadian Broadcasting Corporation.

Through a You Tube video, Bob MacDonald shares a folksy discussion of the programs and science in a way that is both easy to understand and credible. The You Tube video is clear, easy to understand and to the point:
https://www.youtube.com/watch?v=F6eD83Zuptk

It's excellent health risk and science communication.

Perceived Uneven or Unacceptable Distribution of Risks or Costs

From time to time projects or programs that are discussed at public meetings do have a tangible effect for local communities and the natural environment. For most projects or programs seeking approval, studies can determine in advance who lives close to the project, who might have more frequent interaction with the change, and if there are any socio-economic and socio-cultural indicators of who receives or perceives higher risk. Typically, if there is an uneven distribution of risks or costs, the fairness of the risks or costs is brought before an administrative tribunal and a decision is made as to whether the risks and costs are acceptable. Mitigation actions can change to reduce social or environmental risk. There are also social mechanisms for ensuring the distribution of risk is acceptable. For example, proponent programs that allow for avoidance, management or compensation of risks or costs.

Anger can be anticipated when higher risks are going to be imposed by an outsider on some members of the public and not others, and when some members of the public are required to experience a risk for the larger society to benefit. For example, people don't choose to have a highway located beside their homes or communities. However, it is an agency and ultimately a government that chooses the location. Local residents are therefore required to accept the risk imposed from outside. They experience disbenefits and risks so that the larger society can benefit.

In addition, locating a highway beside an existing community means people living closest to the highway will potentially experience health risks from noise, dust, odour and emissions. In comparison, people travelling along the highway will benefit through reduced travel costs and more effective delivery of goods and they don't experience the disbenefits. Once again, risks are unevenly experienced by individual residents and the local community so that the larger society will benefit.

A third issue is the differences between probabilistic risks and perceived risks. There is a large body of literature including early research by Sandman,[16] and Slovic, Lichtenstein and Fischoff[17] that explain the differences between measurable, probabilistic risk versus perceived risk. Probabilistic risks are those mathematical risks calculated to occur based on scientific study. Experts calculate, what is the mathematical probability of the risk occurring at any particular time and what are the consequences if the risk occurs. Relative risks can be ranked and rated on this basis. For example, there is a higher probability of death from falling off a ladder than an airplane crash.

Perceived risks are those the public experiences psychologically even if the math and science say there is a low likelihood of the risk occurring. Essentially, if the consequences of harm are very high, but the probability is very low, the public will act on its perceptions of harm because of the consequences over perceptions

---

16 Sandman http://www.psandman.com/media/RespondingtoCommunityOutrage.pdf

17 Slovic, P., Fischoff, B., & Lichtenstein, S. (1985) Characterizing Perceived Risk, in R. W. Kates, C. Hohenemser, & J. X. Kasperson (Eds.), Perilous progress: Managing the hazards of technology (pp. 91 – 125) Boulder, CO. Westview Press

Who are these people and why are they yelling at me? | 15

of harm based on low probability. The weight placed on consequences becomes the root of the angry response.

When designing public communications and engagement programs, and assessing whether an angry meeting is likely, I look for project characteristics that usually lead to at least some people concluding that the risk is unacceptable. Characteristics of these projects include association with hazardous materials, chemicals, endocrine disruptors, electromagnetic effects, radiation, germs, atmospheric pollutants, etc.

One approach for elevating the discussion of risk to a point where all sides can at least engage in dialogue is to ask, "What risk are you willing to accept?" Most activities in life involve some sort of risk. There are consequences associated with living in a world with very few risks compared to a world with risks that most people would see to be acceptable.

It is rare for project approvals, associated communications and public engagement programs to start at this level. And, that's a problem. Notable is the leading edge work of Canada's Nuclear Waste Management Organization, which began the process of siting of a high-level nuclear waste repository with several years of Canada-wide conversations about the most fundamental questions: What questions should we be asking? What should a siting process look like? In my view, this organization has some of the best community engagement and communications programs in the world.

An important discipline helping to shine a light on how people view risk is anthropology.

I am a big fan of the work of Michael Thompson[18], particularly based on his research on energy tribes at the International Institute of Applied Systems Analysis in Austria. Michael explores the theory that the values of communities in relation to risk can be understood tribally. From this perspective, communities in North America and Europe are as tribal as those of the Brazilian jungles. Each community I work in can therefore be viewed as tribes which

---

18 http://www.iiasa.ac.at/staff/staff.php?type=auto&visibility=visible&search=true&login=thompson

have developed an informal consensus on what is right and wrong thinking about the subject my client is discussing.

Modern individuals identify with certain tribes, which may have an opinion about a project being proposed, the science, what constitutes facts and who has 'right' thinking about a particular subject. Simply put, across North America there are tribes of people for whom high risks are acceptable and tribes who believe high risks are totally unacceptable. For the same change, such as the siting of a new cellular tower, people view risks along tribal lines in the same community. Some people will be totally opposed or totally supportive of the science, because that is the norm of the tribe.

Following a career as a Himalayan mountaineer, Michael observed[19] the Sherpas, who frequently risked their lives carrying supplies up Mount Everest for wealthy dentists from New Jersey while, in the Sherpas' village, there were ironically people who were exceptionally risk adverse. From an anthropological perspective, your view of risk comes down to the mores, values and belief system of your tribe.

In Canada, we have tribes of people who embrace technical facts, probabilistic risk assessment and science as a core part of their belief system - 'the science and facts show there is nothing to be concerned about.'

We also have tribes of people for whom a fundamental belief and acceptance of science as a basis of decision-making is inconsistent with their beliefs. People who use facts and science to justify their opinion are, in their opinion, heretics - 'we don't need facts because as a matter of faith we are right'. Or more commonly, we don't need their facts because our facts are right. Having faith means holding a set of beliefs, i.e. nuclear energy is wrong, pipelines are wrong, country wisdom is right. Or, nuclear energy and pipelines are right and the risks are acceptable and the math and science shows it. Country wisdom is wrong because it is not based on scientific fact.

---

19 Micheal Thompson, "Political Culture: An Introduction", 1980. "An Outline of the Cultural Theory of Risk", 1980, "The Social Landscape of Poverty", 1980, "Beyond Self-Interest, A Cultural Analysis of the Risk Debate", 1981, International Institute for Applied Systems Analysis A-2361, Laxenburg, Austria.

Who are these people and why are they yelling at me? | 17

The thinking goes deep and I'll often encourage my colleagues to be equally deep in their probing of where consensus between two tribes might lie.

As the respected academic Dr. George Pickering observed[20], the values fight between various tribes goes far back in time, particularly on the debates over matters of science and technology. One social tribe is fundamentally Aristotelian, with faith in science grounded in the philosophy of Athens. Logic, scientific technique and observations are at the core of wise and right thinking. It is the basis of their morality. These are more often my clients, regulators, academics and political representatives.

But I can assure you that it would be very rare for a large mass of Aristotelian's to show up angry at a public meeting, outside of academia or professional societies.

The other tribe views science and technology with their faith grounded in beliefs originating in Calvary. These are often activists, community leaders, some academics and faith leaders who show up to meetings to protest a cellular tower or pipeline.

For example, both groups will see the science related to a proposed cellular tower differently based on their specific perspective. And, in their group, the prevailing perspective on how science and facts should be viewed is held by all members of the group and it is seen to be right thinking. If you hold an alternative view about science and facts you are not part of the group.

To me, the issue is not whether the tribe of science should prevail over the tribe of faith. Nor is it a matter of "science" versus faith. It is an issue of faith versus faith. In other words, faith in science vs. faith in faith. The best example I've seen is in the scientific study of dark energy. Scientists lament the Heisenberg principle that is apparently interfering with the ability to measure through astrophysics that dark energy is real. You can't see it and when you try to measure it goes away or the cosmological constant changes. Yet, to scientists working on dark energy, it is real. The same scientists who advocate for their colleagues to have faith that dark energy exists (even though we can't measure it) will also

---

20 "Moral and Ethical Issues relating to Nuclear Energy Generation: Proceedings of a Seminar", Canadian Nuclear Association, Toronto, Ontario, 1981, ISBN 0-919307-15-9, p. 7 "Integrating Ethical and Technical Considerations in the Energy Debate, George Pickering.

advocate against people who have religious faith, because God can't be shown to scientifically exist.

While it's not my purpose here to get into the science or faith, it is my purpose to suggest that many of the issues that are at the core of angry public meetings run deep.

George Pickering provides good insight about the depth of division sometimes at the core of these meetings. He points out that the division between science and faith we see being acted out today goes as far back as the Reformation, when Galileo drove a wedge into "natural science", which at the time combined science and religion. According to George Pickering, it was a divorce that didn't take.

I see this division fought out at many angry meetings involving science and risk. For this reason, an understanding of tribal characteristics and the moral and ethical underpinnings of technological change is important to predicting when an angry meeting will occur and understanding what is happening when these meetings are underway.

Allegiance to the person's tribe determines whether or not they share the values of the proponent and other people at the meeting. Ignoring the tribal characteristics of participants means that you are only talking to one segment of the people at the meeting. Making wrong assumptions about the tribe you are talking to will inevitably contribute to public anger.

How does an extreme facilitator prepare to communicate from this perspective? It is important to craft communications that acknowledge and speak to the following tribes:

- Risk takers and those who are risk adverse.
- People for whom economics and property values are important.
- People who see health risks being associated with every change and those who have less concern about health risk.
- People who trust scientific data and accept facts, and those who don't.
- People who will never trust scientific facts over trusting the values of their community members.

Above all, members of the public need to know that all perspectives at a public meeting are important and will be listened to, no matter what their tribe.

Rights are Perceived to be Violated

When people in a meeting perceive that their rights are being violated, they feel that they are not being treated fairly. And, the likelihood of the meeting becoming angry intensifies. For example, a local municipal council may be opposed to a change, but a higher level of government may support and approve the change. In this case, members of the public voted in the municipal councillors and their Councillors are supporting the position of the residents. But, they feel their local vote is not being acknowledged because senior level politicians voted in by others are making the decision instead.

To address rights issues, it is important to clearly present: the decision-making process; opportunities available to members of the public to influence the decision; and the role of the political representative or project proponent in making the ultimate decisions. Rights occur at many levels but the complexity of who has rights and whose rights should prevail is rarely discussed.

Values are Perceived to be Out of Alignment

If only I had a dollar for every time I've heard members of the public saying that they are opposed to a project because it is out of alignment with their values!

I have heard residents of small communities in the Ottawa Valley claim to be more eco-superior than anywhere else. I've seen members of an upscale left-leaning urban community advocate for social justice until an agency wanted to locate a homeless shelter in their community. 'We will still fight for social justice but, the shelter is inconsistent for the values of this community.'

During one urban transportation project meeting, local urban residents didn't want suburban residents driving through their community to get to work because it would alter their wonderful community; no matter the socio-economic costs to the suburban residents and their families.

On another occasion, I was retained to facilitate an angry meeting in York Region because local residents were upset about the proposed colour of the paint on the garage doors of an addition to a regional waste water treatment plant. They were demanding that the colour had to be right for the community. And, that was the reason why a 20-million-dollar project was being held up. My advice to the client was simple: tell them that's going to be the chosen colour and that the decision is made, move the agenda along and close off the meeting. I'll facilitate the discussion. They did, and that was the last the client heard about the colour of the garage doors from the community.

In contrast, I was once asked to work with members of a Mennonite community on the matter of improving the economic health of the broader community. Before I met with about 20 elder members of the community, I wrongly assumed that they would be opposed to the programs because they were inconsistent with their values. Instead they were very supportive.

People in every community in which I've worked hold the opinion that their community is uniquely special - better than any other community and therefore deserving of special attention. This means they believe they should not have to endure a risk or cost associated with a project because it is inconsistent with the values intrinsic to the community.

In reality, every community is special to its residents, because each resident has made a choice to live there. Choosing to live there is consistent with their values. They believe that they would not have made a bad choice. If a project is inconsistent with their values, they show up in masse to public meetings to plead for the uniqueness of the community and the inconsistency with their community values.

Sometimes, I am asked what I observe when I look out onto a crowded hall full of hundreds of people. What I see is a wide variety of values - rarely a single set of values, as members of the community suggest.

In sum, while I will discuss later other signs that indicate when a large angry public meeting is imminent, these are some of the fundamental signs I look for.

Chapter 3:
Enter the Extreme Facilitator

In Ontario, there are a handful of extreme facilitators who are well trained in group dynamics, communications skills, listening, logistics and event organization. All of us have been involved in advocacy movements of one sort or another, and are used to being on both sides of an issue.

I cringe when I see someone with no facilitation training in front of a large group of concerned residents. It happens. Too often, an untrained facilitator will make statements implying judgements that the community doesn't agree with instead of being neutral and independent. Or, they may view their job as maintaining order, which causes tempers to rise in a group that will perceive the meeting to be stacked against them.

The public will normally eat up public relations professionals who run meetings, as their focus is on communicating a message and getting people to listen to their client. Hearing the repetition of the client's point of view is the last thing the angriest members of the public want.

Susskind and Field have a rather negative view of the way public relations sometimes occurs vs how it is supposed to occur in the context of public anger. "While public-relations textbooks may highlight the need for quality information, effective communication, and mutually beneficial relationships, public relations as practiced often employs techniques such as stonewalling, whitewashing, as well as blocking and blaming....They commit to nothing and admit to nothing."[21] I don't agree as the public relations professionals I've worked with are ethical and have integrity. Telling the truth is important to them.

---

21 Susskind, Lawrence and Patrick Field, "Dealing with an Angry Public: The Mutual Gains Approach to Resolving Disputes", The Free Press, New York, 1996. p 9

Sometimes, an organization will ask a respected ex-politician to facilitate the meeting. This person will not be aware that their job is about serving the group, not preserving their personal credibility or maintaining control. The problem with politicians as facilitators is that they usually don't know how, or are technically unable to stay neutral.

At other times, the facilitator is the client who has decided to take on this role. The point is that facilitation is not about the client's opinion[22]. It is about the group. And 'clients as facilitators' are usually challenged when they find themselves in the weeds. How can they be seen as an honest, trustful and an open broker if it is obvious to the public that the chief listener has a stake in the outcome of the issue being discussed?

While most of our clients chair public meetings from time to time, Doyle and Straus[23] present four potential issues that arise when the proponent of a project, program or policy 'facilitates' the meeting: 1) the client has a personal investment in the subject matter; 2) they can't hide their bias for a particular outcome; 3) they want to talk more than everyone else; and, 4) they are taking on too many roles at one time.

They state, "it is almost impossible to run a fair, nonmanipulative meeting when you have a personal investment in the subject matter. There is no way you can objectively lead a group that is considering whether or not to discontinue a project of your own." Furthermore, they can't run the meeting without the public observing their bias. And, if they are controlling who speaks and how the meeting is proceeding, they are effectively controlling the outcome of the meeting. The public will typically feel they are being used and object strongly.

The last issue is, the client finds themselves doing too many roles at once: controlling how the meeting proceeds, dealing with conflict, presenting or talking more than anyone else and then making a final decision. Facilitator's who play multiple roles cause confusion and irritation.[24]

---

22 Ghais, S, 'Extreme Facilitation: Guiding Groups Through Controversy and Complexity', Jossey-Bass, San Francisco, CA, 2005, p. 14

23 Michael Doyle and David Strauss, op cit, pgs. 32, 33

24 Michael Doyle and David Strauss, op cit, p. 29

Yet, project proponents who manage public meetings without a facilitator is the norm. And, they will manage to get through the process, but with additional battle scars.

Suzanne Ghais, author of "Extreme Facilitation: Guiding Groups Through Controversy and Complexity" shares the frustration that most extreme facilitators feel about the perception of the public and clients of what they do. Ghais states, "The average person probably thinks of a facilitator as someone who does more or less the same thing each time, assembling an agenda from a list of topics provided by the group or its leader, standing in front of the group and calling on raised hands, signalling times to change to the next agenda item, and perhaps curbing members who dominate or encouraging the quieter ones."[25]

While extreme facilitators do perform these tasks, the core of our profession involves being clear on the goals of the group, exercising judgement on how the group is proceeding and making the right interventions at the right time. Extreme facilitation requires additional skills.

Delivering Best Outcomes

Tough public policy decisions need to be made in every sector: health, housing, telecommunications, energy, transportation and public safety. These decisions may create a high emotional response among members of the public. And, the facilitator has a key role to play in delivering best outcomes.

There are fundamental reasons why issues blow up and lead to large, angry public meetings. That's when a client, be it a company, government department, non-government organization or institution, may decide to hire a professional facilitator. This person will usually begin to work with a client to see if a large, angry public meeting can be avoided. Preparation and planning skills are essential. As observed by Ghais, the majority of the work of the facilitator occurs before the meeting.

Needless to say, an extreme facilitator must possess fundamental facilitation skills, including the basics: setting a cordial and collaborative tone; focusing the discussion; summarizing the main points; and managing closure. I define facilitation as encompassing a range of roles: moderator, chairperson, group

---

25 Ghais, S. op cit; p. 29

psychologist, public consultation specialist, chief listener, communicator and manager of the conversation.

Facilitation is classically defined by Killermann and Bolger as follows: "…a style of engaging others toward a goal. We generally assume that the goal is learning, which we define learning in the broadest of ways: learning content knowledge, learning about oneself and others or unlearning…. Creating and holding that space for everyone to bring their voice to the table."[26]

Certainly, when large public groups come together, learning about a project or policy is an important goal and something that I will always promote. Doyle and Strauss describe a facilitator as a person who focuses on the process of meetings as distinct from the person who makes the substantive decisions.

Roger Schwarz adds: "…a group facilitator is a person who (1) is not a member of the group, (2) is content neutral, (3) has no content decision making authority or input, (4) is acceptable to all members of the group, and (5) diagnoses and intervenes in a group, to (6) helps it improve the processes by which it identifies and solves problems and makes decisions in order to increase the group's effectiveness."[27]

Ghais provides a further insight into the definition of public facilitation: "Facilitation can be so much more than just keeping a group on its meeting agenda, keeping order and taking notes. It can be an intervention that transforms how group members interact with each other and view the issues. It can help large publics work through a complex array of issues efficiently. It can often enable resolution of the most divisive organizational or public-policy conflicts. It can provide a way for strong emotions to be channelled into productive decision making or improved relationships."[28]

---

26 Sam Killermann and Meg Bolger, "Unlocking the Magic of Facilitation" Impetus Books, Austin Texas, January, 2016 pps. 2, 66.

27 Schwarz, 3rd Edition, p. 14

28 Ghais, S. op cit p. 3, 4

Who are these people and why are they yelling at me? | 25

Basic Facilitation Skills and Qualities

An extreme facilitator needs to have an excellent understanding of the theory of facilitation and be able to put the theory into practice when the circumstances are challenging. A great deal of theoretical material is available on meeting management and facilitation skills. The earlier and majority of the literature focuses on meeting management and interpersonal relations required for making meetings productive. Doyle and Straus, "How to Make Meetings Work"[29], is an often-cited resource. Associated resource works such as "Emotional Intelligence"[30] is also recommended reading. The later work addresses the psychological underpinnings necessary for understanding the human side of the transaction of information and the skills required to build relationships between parties.

The literature also addresses the theme of building consent at an individual and group level. "Getting to Yes"[31] and its successor volumes is a valuable resource because of its focus on the techniques of bringing people to a point of agreement. Moving to group and nation agreement, "Managing Public Disputes"[32] by Carpenter and Kennedy and "The Third Side: Why We Fight and How We Can Stop" by William Ury are good foundational works, although the latter is geared to reinforcing positive behaviours of those who choose not to fight. For the management of large, angry public meetings, people involved are often well beyond hearing the good advice that Ury shares.

Sam Kaner, "Facilitator's Guide to Participatory Decision Making"[33] is an excellent resource for bringing groups together to facilitate open discussion, building sustainable agreements and reaching closure. In terms of group process, I've found an early paper by Joseph Luft[34] to be particularly useful in diving deep

---

29 Doyle and Strauss, op cit

30 Goleman, D 'Emotional Intelligence', Bantam Books, New York, 2005

31 William Ury and Roger Fischer, 'Getting to Yes', ISBN 0-395-63124-6, Houghton Mifflin, New York, 1981

32 Carpenter, Susan and W. J. D. Kennedy, 'Managing Public Disputes', Jossey-Bass, San Francisco, 2001

33 Kaner, Sam with Lenny Lind, Catherine Toldi, Sarah Fisk and Duane Berger, Facilitator's Guide to Participatory Decision Making, Third Edition, Jossey-Bass, San Francisco, 2014

34 Joseph Luft, Group Process, National Press Books, University of Michigan, 1963

into understanding the group processes I've observed during many of my meetings. In particular, the notion of 'group mindset' that sometimes occurs and needs to be understood.

There are three theorists and practitioners who I quote generously here, as they discuss facilitation skills specifically important to extreme facilitators. I have often referred to their wisdom and experience to enhance my thinking and because they present good practice. Each author helps to answer the question, "Why is this aspect of the practice of extreme facilitation important?"

Among the works presenting practical skills, my staff and I found "Facilitation Skills for Team Leaders"[35] by Donald Hackett and Charles Martin an easy, helpful read. It is a good primer that we refer to when we are in the design stage of a facilitation assignment. Roger Schwarz, "The Skilled Facilitator: A Comprehensive Resource for Consultants, Facilitators, Coaches and Trainers"[36] provides a deep foundation of the practice of facilitation. I refer to Schwarz frequently in this section, quoting both Edition Two and Three.

Schwarz's work is used as a standard reference for facilitation training. The facilitation objectives advocated by Schwarz are designed to help groups achieve stronger performance and productive working relationships, and promote individual wellbeing. These objectives are ideal for the committees I work with. But, even coming close to achieving individual well being during a large angry public meeting typically falls in the category of "being on my heavenly wish list."

Schwarz's work is an excellent source for understanding facilitator roles, such as why a facilitator needs to intervene and when? It highlights important facilitator roles such as diagnosing and intervening when certain issues arise. Further, the work assists in understanding the emotional aspects of group process. Schwarz's third edition addresses technology and virtual meetings. While important, technology issues related to large, angry public meetings have more to do with social media and how it can influence meeting outcomes; a topic to be discussed in a later chapter.

---

[35] Hackett and Martin, Facilitation Skills for Team Leaders, CRISP Publications, Inc. Menlo Park, California, 1993 Library of Congress Catalog Card Number 92-082933

[36] Roger Schwarz, The Skilled Facilitator: A Comprehensive Resource for Consultants, Facilitators, Coaches and Trainers, 2nd Edition (2002) and 3rd Edition (2017), Jossey-Bass, San Francisco.

The facilitation theory that I have found most helpful is one associated with group conflict and emotions. For most of the meetings I facilitate, the conflict is most often between the public and my clients, who are usually proponents of a particular policy or project. However, it is often the case that conflict is occurring among members of the public at the same time. Everyone is emotional, including the facilitator.

Ingrid Bens has written extensively on group conflict and emotional response in relation to group process. I have extensively quoted her work, "Advanced Facilitation Strategies: Tools and Techniques to Master Difficult Situations"[37] and a handy pocket book created as a reference for addressing conflict situations called "Conflict at a Glance"[38]. (The list of thirty conflict scenarios and facilitator responses is quite helpful.)

"The Magic of Facilitation"[39] by Kellerman and Bolger is a parallel work which is more focused on helping individual participants in a group and supporting group process. The section on "yes/ and" language is helpful. I have used this language in large groups with great success.

Most facilitation theorists refer to the profession as a technique designed to avoid anger or manage short moments of anger among specific individuals. The work by Suzanne Ghais that I refer to most in the following pages helps to understand and address people who are already angry and groups already experiencing emotion in the midst of conflict. Books and courses that address facilitation skills also support team leadership, empowerment, and the arbitration and facilitation of issues.

In some cases, facilitators and formal team leaders assume the role of providing structure and focus for a team. In this way, conventional skills provide an important foundation for the more extreme form of facilitation. The challenge is that most of the literature is generally focused on helping the professional facilitator working in an agency, corporate or government setting. Or, their intent is to provide skills

---

37 Bens, Ingrid, "Advanced Facilitation Strategies: Tools and Techniques to Master Difficult Situations", Jossey-Bass, San Francisco, 2005

38 Bens it al, "Conflict at a Glance", GOAL/QPC, Salem, New Hampshire, 2013

39 Kellerman and Bolger, op cit.

for facilitators working with people in small groups. I have facilitated hundreds of internal committees, Stakeholder Advisory Committees, Citizen's Advisory Groups and small groups where the more traditional facilitation skills apply.

Large, angry public meetings are different, however. It will be a rare day when a company employee or stakeholder will be angry enough during a meeting you are facilitating to pull a fire alarm. "Extreme Facilitation: Guiding Groups Through Controversy and Complexity" by Suzanne Ghais comes closest to explaining the situations discussed in this book, nicely covering off what it takes to be an extreme facilitator, how to help unwieldly groups achieve consensus and the process of preparing to facilitate these groups.

What I find ironical, however, is Ghais' observation that the "Extreme Facilitator … picks up where other books on the topic leave off". She states, "public meetings (ones open to the general public rather than only the invited stakeholders or members of intact groups) are the most volatile forums for facilitators."[40], Ghais provides some advice on physical threats and the potential for violence. In part, this is where Ghais closes the topic of extreme facilitation and where my advice begins.

Third-Party Neutral Presence

Most theorists agree on the need for a facilitator to be independent and neutral, although there are variations on the definition of what neutrality means. Very few facilitators believe that there can be "pure" neutrality in their profession. Killermann and Boyle discuss facilitation against the backdrop of social justice, where the subject matter is anything but neutral. In this case, being clear on your own views while looking for clarity on the views of others is important as you encourage their expression without judgement.

Schwarz picks up on the concept, pointing out that a facilitator can be "content neutral", but not "process neutral'". Being content neutral means that you have no preferences regarding the solutions identified by the group. Process neutral is a misnomer because "you know what kind of behaviour and processes lead

---

40 Ghais, S op cit, p. 277

Who are these people and why are they yelling at me? | 29

to effective problem solving and other group outcomes"[41], but your biases come through because you "signal your belief of what makes for effective process."[42]

However, at some meetings, having a group reach a decision can be just the opposite of what the public wants. In this case, the determination to stick with a process that will arrive at a decision does not demonstrate facilitator neutrality.

Schwarz and others point out that a facilitator may be called upon to perform other roles that are less than neutral. Indeed, I have been asked to do so on many occasions. Hired as an "expert consultant", I have facilitated processes geared towards discussing specific topics, where I'm not neutral about wanting the group to learn specific information and have that discussion. Sometimes I am asked to facilitate as a "group leader", which involves using my technical skills and providing advice on how to move the yard sticks forward for the client. I have also facilitated as a "coach", which may involve working off-site to help a client navigate through a specific situation. And so, my actions may involve coaching or being the leader.[43] But these roles characterize normal and not extreme facilitation.

Ingrid Bens points out that it's a mistake to assume that being neutral on the content of the agenda means staying neutral on the process. In fact, she states that the opposite is true: "…the facilitator should be directive on process issues. Besides selecting the approaches, facilitators also need to point out process problems and to redirect dysfunctional behaviour. In other words, effective facilitators know how to be appropriately assertive on the process without compromising their neutrality about the content…" For particularly troublesome processes, Bens adds, "Nowhere is it written that facilitators are expected to suffer abuse at the hands of ill-behaved groups, no matter what their rank or perception of self importance."[44]

While I tend to address the skills of the facilitator in more depth when discussing the unique skills of extreme facilitation, what is common to both is

---

41 Schwarz, R. 3rd edition, p. 17
42 Schwarz, R. 3rd edition p. 18
43 Schwarz, R. 3rd edition, p. 19, 20
44 Bens, I. Advanced Facilitation Strategies, p. 82

the challenge of presenting yourself as neutral to a large public audience or an angry group. Facilitators always have to do a bit of a dance at the beginning of a public meeting in order to establish their neutral presence. The issue is that we are asked to be neutral, but we are also being paid by the client.

Killermann and Bolger describe the neutrality conundrum nicely: "Part of what is so appealing about 'neutral' is the thought of some absolute truth, an unquestionable right or wrong.... [Neutrality] would nice, and so would Santa Claus. Being a facilitator is not about being neutral, but instead about being honest and open with your group about your goals together and recognizing the implicit bias in those goals. Just because neutrality isn't possible, it doesn't mean you can't achieve some of the goals that neutrality espouses. "[45]

To get the neutrality question out of the way during a large, angry public meeting, I will usually start by saying, "I'm being paid by my client to be here. That said, my job is not to take a position, but to allow you (the people in attendance) to say what you need to say, and allow the client to say what they need to say." I will discuss later the technique of speaking using neutral language during the meeting, but the need to remain a neutral presence extends throughout the meeting and after.

As a facilitator, you are managing the process but can't help listen to the rationality of the arguments on all sides. We hear and perceive the actions and beliefs of others in relation to what might be our own actions and beliefs. Referring to the study of 'naïve realism', Susskind and Field observe that when others disagree with our point of view on the matters being discussed, there is a tendency to assume one of three things: 1) the person wasn't exposed to or had limited access to information that we have (we know what they don't know); 2) the person is biased due to mistaken beliefs, ideology or self interest (they are misinterpreting the facts because of their beliefs); 3) the person is simply too irrational to arrive at my conclusion given the evidence at hand.[46] They state the danger of seeing others as irrational are substantial.

Thus, it's imperative that the extreme facilitator learn to set their beliefs and opinions aside for the sake of achieving neutrality.

---

45 Killermann and Bolger, op cit; p. 6, 26
46 Susskind and Field, op cit; p. 19

Achieving neutrality can be achieved by: 1) listening without bias to real issues that the public is raising, which need to be resolved or at least voiced in the meeting; 2) adjusting the process somewhat, if required, to ensure that both sides can make the points that they feel are important; and, 3) unhinging their role as facilitator from their relationship with the client and project team during the meeting. To assure the public I'm listening to all points of view I might ask, "So what I heard you say is …?" By saying that, someone with a unique point of view has been assured that at least one person has heard them even if the larger group wants nothing to do with the comment.

Because most of angry public meetings are politically charged, there are many perspectives that need to be heard. Adding to the advice given by Killermann and Bolger, it is important to point out the political charged atmosphere during the facilitator's opening remarks and ensure that people with different opinions are welcome to share their views. If there is an elephant in the room, its up to the facilitator to point it out.

On this point, Killermann and Bolger state: "If something is politically charged, address the political charge. Most social justice topics are couched in a lot of different belief systems: political, religious, personal and beyond. Recognizing that there are multiple perspectives from which to view any one issue allows others to be more comfortable adding their views to the conversation." [47] I will often say, "I know many of you have opinions on the matters being discussed tonight and that's why you are here." And, "I want to hear all opinions."

I make much of my living facilitating. When I do so, I'm not there to solve specific issues or deliver client outcomes. I might have a personal interest in how a decision gets made, but not a professional interest. For example, I was asked to facilitate a small meeting of scientists fighting over how to measure an environmental contaminant. The result of their discussion would find its way into national mining regulations and have a large economic impact. I wanted the dialogue to arrive at a result that they could all agree on, but I simply wasn't there to take a side.

---

47 Killermann and Bolger, op cit; p. 29

Listening to the core issues being discussed at meetings, I have facilitated a few where the client is totally off the mark. The client's staff, the consultants hired by the client, and the residents know the issues. When there is a wisdom in the room coming through, I will spend a lot of time allowing the issue to be heard through public comments, even though I know that it is uncomfortable for the client.

At times, consultants and staff will spend a lot of time agreeing with the public. Consensus is being reached, but the client is squirming while the residents and others can see change occurring. What I'm hoping for is that, by the end of the meeting, my client will see the change as a learning moment. My goal is to have them hear these views in a respectful and constructive manner.

At other times, the public is way off the mark. I've facilitated meetings where the public was opposing a person of a different background living in their community. And, where there was simply no merit to their point of view based on the evidence. Key facts held by the public may be untrue and assumptions may not be supported. In this situation, I will give my client a lot more time and latitude to explain why. While it might seem risky to give preference and time to the client where there may be two hundred and fifty members of the public and only five members of the client team, I generally have faith that the wisdom in the room will lead to at least some people placing value on having additional information pointing out that their facts are not accurate.

When I adjust the process, it is usually because someone, either the client or a member of the public, has provided a perspective that needs to be addressed. In the most uncomfortable case, facts are wrong or relevant information has been overlooked. For this reason, the extreme facilitator needs to have a good understanding of the subject mater, which will be discussed later.

In terms of separating myself as neutral, the last thing I want to do after a particularly good meeting is go to the client for a high five. Neutrality needs to be maintained during and after the meeting. Staff and I will usually pack up and say good night to the client and the residents at the same time.

Who are these people and why are they yelling at me? | 33

Understanding Groups

The ability to understand groups and organizational behaviour is a fundamental skill that facilitators need to possess. University sociology faculties include courses on organizational behaviour and organizational development. (Group dynamics are discussed in Chapter 6.) Most of the theorists referenced in this book discuss group process and confirm the need to understand groups at this level.

On this topic, Schwarz points out that a group is a social system with its own dynamics. The facilitator enters this system when taking on the assignment of helping the group.[48] He states, "The challenge is to enter the system – complete with its functional and dysfunctional dynamics – and help the group become effective without becoming influenced by the system to act ineffectively yourself."[49]

Luft[50] provides an early but important description of what is happening in groups when they come together in a meeting format. He examines the concept of 'group mind'. When groups of individuals come together, they create an atmosphere. Groups have personalities, they present an emotional tone, they may be more or less cohesive and there may or may not be pressure to conform. When people come to large angry public meetings, they don't know who the other people are. But group process leads to them examining their own behaviour in relation to that of others.[51] People have a natural tendency to want to belong, to be accepted by peers, to be understood, to express themselves and for self esteem and status.[52]

Effective communications with the public are essential at every interaction. Without strong communications, rumours and misinformation breeds. That's why my firm also tries to work with clients early and define their Community Engagement and Communication Plans.

---

48 Schwarz R., 2nd edition p. 13
49 Schwarz, R. op cit p. 13
50 Luft, J. op cit, p. 17
51 Luft, J. op cit, p. 8
52 Luft, J. p. 51

Luft states, "Rumours tend to develop when there is a strong need to know what is going on but, for various reasons, information and communication are limited. Rumours reflect the anxiety and the hopes of individuals as they attempt to piece together what is known from the little that is unknown."[53] In contrast, public meetings tend to be information rich and the member of the public will want to make sense of what is being said. They are trying to understand and learn about the group mind.

Doyle and Strauss observe that people in groups have much more difficulty in solving problems than they would as individuals for the following reasons: 1) multiple ideas come their way from other individuals who see the problem differently; 2) each person attending the meeting can be focused on a different part of the problem at a different time; 3) the group is searching for a single focus and this may be difficult.[54]

As individuals, most members of the public do a reasonable job of assessing the information and drawing conclusions about what their opinion should be. But in a large angry meeting, they are hearing multiple and conflicting opinions from others attending. They observe that group problem solving is a messy business. This makes it all the more important for the facilitator to help them navigate the sensory and knowledge tapestry rolling out during the meeting and to assist them to draw their own conclusions.

To understand group process, I typically observe where the group is at, how the group is evolving, and the changing roles of individuals within the group as the dynamics unfold as I'm facilitating. The need for Stakeholder Sensitivity Analysis and Social/ Cultural/ Economic Impact Analyses studies, to be discussed in a later chapter, also helps to diagnose where the group is starting from and what is likely going on in the group.

Every group has leaders and followers: people who bring the group together and others who threaten the vitality of the group. I watch to see whether an individual might be helping the group to reach consensus or whether the group is doing so on its own. Understanding the group helps my judgement on when to intervene.

---

53 Luft, J. p. 26

54 Doyle and Straus, op cit. p 22

Who are these people and why are they yelling at me? | 35

We have all been part of groups that either work well or don't. (The latter scenario can be painful.) When groups work well, we often grow personally as a result of the people we've met and the ideas we've shared. It is important for the facilitator to see and understand that group processes are under way that will influence whether or not facilitation efforts will be successful.

Designing a Group Process

Effective group processes don't necessarily happen without some attention to how the group is designed to function. At a minimum, someone needs to put an agenda together, chair the meeting, track time and take notes.

When a facilitator is involved, the group and group process is specifically designed with attention to detail. A critical skill of the facilitator is the design of a process that will ultimately be effective, where the group understands and internalizes what they are there to do and individual members know the role they should be playing. Group process design allows for resetting the vision and mission of the group, if required, and establishing methods for managing disagreement.

Other facilitation design skills cited by Hackett and Martin[55] include: planning team meetings; knowing how to ask questions; knowing how to use a flip chart; remaining neutral on content issues; encouraging open communication; tolerating conflict and smoothing the waters. They state, "Because the facilitator is visibly positioned in the group, this person has the ability to bias the team either intentionally or unintentionally. Thus, the role of the facilitator is to manage the meeting structure while remaining neutral regarding the meeting content. The meeting content is the responsibility of the team."[56]

For most meetings that I facilitate, the team is the client, their staff and consultants but, when I am retained to conduct extreme facilitation, there is only one group, comprised of the client and the public.

Haskett and Martin go on to say that, when you deal with the meeting structure, you are dealing with the "how" questions: 1) how the meeting issues and

---

55 Hackett and Martin, op cit.
56 Hackett and Martin, ibid, p. 14

subjects are dealt with; 2) how the meeting proceeds in terms of the agenda and team tools; 3) how the discussion will take place; and, 4) how the physical environment of the meeting will be arranged. Content is about the "what" questions: the meeting subject, the issues, the recommendations, the supporting data, and which subject matter is to be dealt with in what particular sequence.[57]

While my focus is on the "how" questions when I'm on my feet in front of an audience, I usually have an opportunity to also direct the "what" questions, which are discussed ahead of time with the client in preparatory meetings. This extreme facilitator skill, used long before the meeting, involves circling the "what" questions and responses for the client before they are in public. I may ask my client, "Do you really want to say that?" "What do you want to get across to the public?"

While facilitation is about process, not content, there are important exceptions for the extreme facilitator. Although the design of the facilitator agenda is discussed in later chapters, it is important to note that 'agenda design' is one of the fundamental design skills that every facilitator needs to have.

The Process Expert

When an untrained meeting chair or facilitator asks questions of the public, they are usually along the lines of, "Do you have any questions or comments? Does anyone have anything to say?" Of course, they do. That's why there are two hundred people sitting in front of you!

Formulating and asking good prompt questions is where facilitators make their money. In small group facilitation, questions are designed to move the group toward a goal. The group often has to make a decision. For larger, public meetings the decision is usually multi-faceted. As research, data and analysis have been shared with the public, there are many probing questions that can be formulated.

Doing my very best to avoid questions that don't lead to a "yes" or "no" response, I try to formulate questions that prompt people to think deeper about their response. Perhaps there's a common problem that both the members of the

---

57 Hackett and Martin, ibid, p. 14

audience and the client need to solve. Questions beginning with "should" are ideal for many situations. "Might, would and could" questions are also effective, depending on the circumstances. In fact, my default is to always frame a prompt question with 'would, should, could' as a start point, unless there is a reason not to. It is these questions that open doors to a deeper conversation.

A question might be, "The client has had to evaluate whether or nor this is the right choice. Would you have made the same choice? Were the matters that were studied by the client the same matters that you would have studied? If you had the same data as the client and same set of options, could you have come to the same conclusion?" By asking questions in this manner, I am acknowledging the intelligence of the audience and asking them to think instead of giving me their "gut" reactions.

Killermann and Bolger present six types of prompt questions that they use in every facilitation activity. While these are foundational questions for most facilitators, they are also helpful for extreme facilitation:

1. **Challenging questions** are used to suggest an alternative idea or different way of thinking about something that grants agency to the person who had the idea you are challenging. Are the alternatives being proposed by the client acceptable for some people and not others? How best do we find alternatives we can all agree upon?

2. **Clarifying questions** involve rephrasing another person's point or question, helping to ensure that what was communicated was heard. "What did you mean when you said …?" Also helpful are questions that both clarify and explore greater depth, i.e. "describe, tell, explain"

3. **Gauging questions** help to get a sense of where a member of the audience or the group is at mentally, emotionally or physically. The response can help to identify what the next step of the meeting should be. "How are you feeling about what you've heard or about what other participants are saying? Are we ready to discuss the next stage?" Open-ended questions are used, such as, "How do the rest of you feel?

4. **Leading questions** are used when an answer may be apparent and, when posed, help participants to get to the answer on their own. "From what

we said to each other, should I understand that there is general acceptance of this way forward?"

5. **Probing questions** open up the discussion or help to follow up a broader question. They help to highlight, expose or better understand where comments are coming from. "Can you speak more to that idea? Tell me why you think your idea is important?"

6. **Reflective questions** help participants to think about themselves, what they've learned and how they are engaged, with the hope of bringing better understanding to the greater group or as an opportunity for learning. "What was it like to experience that change? For example, describe to me how you experienced these outcomes for another project."[58]

It is important to have a solid understanding of the facilitator's role in terms of content versus process. In extreme facilitation, the facilitator is the process team member, not the content team expert. An answer requiring content knowledge is always directed by me to the technical team member.

Because I'm working closely with a note taker, I usually take a moment to tie the comment to the process, so that, in the middle of a lengthy exchange, I will say to my note-taker, "Did you hear that comment and record it in your notes?"

I know that the note-taker has heard it already, as they are usually well aware of the subject matter. However, publicly asking if we understood and recorded the comment helps the public to see that we are taking their comments seriously. It helps to build trust and allows the group to move on. It also gives the technical team time to sort out who will confirm a response and who will deliver the response. I provide additional comments on the note taker and note taking process in later chapters.

The Right Stuff Skills

What special skills are required for extreme facilitation? What are the differences between the basic skills of the professional facilitator and skills of an extreme facilitator?

---

58 Killerman and Bolger, op cit, pps. 68, 69

In my experience, there are eight skills that are required to successfully facilitate a large angry public meeting, which either add to or strengthen the foundational skills of professional facilitation. The extreme facilitator needs to be: 1) more strongly grounded; 2) comfortable dealing with strong emotions and conflict; 3) nimble and able to deal with complications; 4) competent in their understanding of the subject matter; 5) able to manage meeting dynamics; 6) able to establish and maintain tone; 7) a strong listener; and, 8) able to read and convey language (body and verbal) at a more demanding level. Let me elaborate.

Grounding

Why is 'grounding' an essential requirement for extreme facilitation? All theorists and practitioners stress the need for the facilitator to not only understand the emotions of the groups, but to also be in charge of their own emotions. It is especially important for the extreme facilitator to have emotional grounding.

Schwarz, for example, states that as a facilitator, "your emotions and how you deal with them profoundly determine your effectiveness."[59] All facilitators experience emotions. In this profession, you need to perform in a skilled way in front of a potentially hostile audience. If you don't have butterflies in your stomach, you aren't showing respect for the task at hand or the people with whom you will be working.

Schwarz adds that it's not so much about of having these feelings as it is about being aware of these feelings in ourselves and others. Moreover, you need to be able to manage your feelings as part of your own emotional intelligence.[60] You need to know who you are, what you stand for and why you have chosen your career.

Donald Hackett and Charles Martin[61] cite critical grounding-type characteristics that a facilitator must have, including "patience, a tolerance for ambiguity, and the need to have a sense of timing that aids in knowing when to push for more ideas, more information and more participation, and equally important

---

59 Schwarz, R. 2nd Edition, op cit, p. 14
60 Schwarz, R., 2nd edition, p. 15
61 Hackett and Martin, op cit.

when not to push. Finally, they should have the ability to organize, handle details and bring events to a closure."[62]

A few years ago, I was hired to facilitate a cell phone tower siting meeting that promised to be particularly nasty. The issue had already been covered by local print, radio and television media. Politicians were threatening to change legislation in a manner that was unfavourable to the client, while the local residents were already well-organized to oppose the cellular provider.

I got the meeting going and shared the ground rules, one of which included showing respect for all views. When speaking to the public about ground rules I always provide a dual perspective on what "respect for all views" means. The public should be respectful of the views of the presenters and the presenters will show respect for the views of the public.

As usual, the meeting got off to a rocky start, with loud outbursts and interruption of the presenters. I intervened on several occasions and, after about ten minutes, the mood quieted down. Several community leaders had done their homework and were starting to ask good questions about electromagnetic field effects on health. They and the client were having constructive dialogue, which is something I aim for.

At one point, the client thought that a question would be better responded to by a government official with expertise in electromagnetic field health effects which, in the telecom industry relating to cell towers, range from "no effects" to "unknown but unlikely". Given that virtually everyone on the planet has been holding some sort of radio frequency devices to their ears for fifty years, it is an answer that I'm personally happy to hear.

The government official responding to the health concern was not kind with the person asking the question. They not only began their response dismissively by stating that the question was, in not so many words, stupid, but also following up with a statement to the effect that anyone thinking of such an effect must be an idiot.

---

62 Hackett and Martin, ibid, p. 8

In a split second, I had two hundred and twenty-five people looking at me to see what I was going to do. I had established the ground rule of showing respect, and that rule had clearly been broken. People in the audience expected me to walk the talk.

Meanwhile, I knew that my client was depending on this particular government official for their approval of the project, and that calling the official out for disrespectful behaviour was going to result in repercussions for them.

Given that situation, my implicit commitment was to the group (the client and the public as the group), and involved asking the government official to apologize in public. It was the right call. That's what I did, and that's what he did. The repercussions ended up being minor, as the client, whose personal grounding also involved telling the truth and being respectful, also saw and understood what was going on.

Suzanne Ghais defines extreme facilitation as being about "…how to facilitate in the most challenging situations – ones that are controversial, complex, large-scale, emotional, or otherwise exceptionally difficult".[63] According to Ghais, an extreme facilitator is an architect of a custom process - someone who has a deep understanding of the group, knows a wide scale of possible facilitation techniques, has a strong personal presence (the right stuff) and is able to draw on all of the group's capabilities: physical, intellectual, emotional, intuitive, creative and even spiritual.[64]

Personal presence is the most important part of grounding, especially during the most difficult public meetings. Ghais elaborates, saying that an extreme facilitator's personal qualities should include: being authentic; having a presence and confidence; being trustworthy and being seen to be trustworthy; knowing their own values and being able to act on them consistently; being centered and focused, and able to find calm; being able to show caring and respect.[65]

"Finally," Ghais says, "the extreme facilitator must be able to confidently handle the challenges we most fear, such as individuals who dominate the discussion,

---

63 Ghais, S., op cit; p. 2
64 Ghais, S., op cit; p. 4, 5
65 Ghais, S., op cit pps 14 to 27

efforts to undermine the facilitator's authority or the process, hidden agendas, cultural clashes, angry outbursts, altercations between participants, and physical aggression."[66]

Extreme facilitation requires the facilitator to transcend narrow, immediate and self interests. Facilitators are there to serve the group, even if serving the group results in negative personal consequences. On many occasions in the midst of an angry meeting, I have been strongly tested. Some members of the public may want me to make a process change that, under the circumstance, I need to resist. In one specific instance, the process change in question would have been deleterious to the group as the individual, at the time, had the motive of disrupting the group to achieve a political outcome.

I know I need to think calmly and rationally about what to do about disorderly and disrespectful conduct. And, I may be subject to a personal attack by someone who sees that I'm not about to let a presenter be tarred and feathered. Or a process to be disrupted.

Indeed, protecting individuals and fostering comments from quieter participants is an important part of the role of the facilitator. I've often seen individuals with good ideas and an important contribution to make back off if they know the group or a vocal individual will jump on them.

Doyle and Straus refer to this phenomenon as 'group rape syndrome'. They state, "two problems limit participation: 1) difficulty in getting a chance to speak and 2) fear of personal attack (the group-rape syndrome) …. By consent of the group, a facilitator is empowered to act as gallant police officer. A good facilitator promises to make sure that every member of the group has an equal opportunity to be heard and is protected from personal attack. This includes group members who are absent from the meeting."[67] I make sure that the group knows I will protect people with all opinions when setting ground rules and hold the comment of louder vocal people to make space for quieter individuals. I let people know that partially formulated ideas are welcome as quantity is just as important as quality.

---

66 Ghais, S. op cit; p. 7, 8
67 Doyle and Straus, op cit. p.99

On those occasions, I will reach deeply into the personal characteristics that ground me. Firstly, I'm in the middle of this conflict because I have the training and experience to be there, and my client and the public want me to be there doing my job. They have given me the power to lead.

Secondly, people acting out are emotional but, under normal circumstances, they are normally friendly people with nice families. Their comments and behaviours may be out of character in this circumstance.

Thirdly, I have a personal standard that I won't compromise. I know who I am. I know my values, my strengths and weaknesses. My standard is rooted in family, friends, and faith. It is my deep grounding that allows me to weather some of the toughest situations.

Grounding is important and is the core of having the right stuff skills. Ghais describes grounding as the basic presence that we bring into the room where we are facilitating, stating, "Presence is largely based on personality, which is formed early in life…. In extreme facilitation, you will need every resource you have – and the easiest way to maximize your resources is to build on your strengths."[68]

One of the most important strengths of a facilitator, and an aspect of grounding, is the trait of being trustworthy. Ghais states, "A facilitator who does not earn the trust of the group will fail. Participants in a facilitated process often feel vulnerable or skeptical. They look for ways to test us. If they don't trust that our process is fair, honest and reasonably safe, they will rebel or withdraw, and the process will lose credibility or even fall apart."[69]

Schwarz adds to the discussion of grounding stating, "Facilitation involves developing a relationship with a group – a psychological contract in which the group gives you permission to help them because they consider you an expert and trustworthy facilitator…without the foundation, you lose the essential connection with the group that makes your facilitation possible and powerful."[70]

---

68 Ghais, S. p. 19, 21
69 Ghais, S. p. 21
70 Schwarz, R. 2nd edition, p. 12

In summary, the depth of grounding required is the primary characteristic that is different between competent facilitation and extreme facilitation.

Ability to Deal with Strong Emotions and Conflict

Being able to deal with strong emotions and conflict is a pre-requisite of extreme facilitation, and every book on the subject deals with how to address emotion.

To set 'emotion' in context, it's important to understand that in the meetings I facilitate, emotions are tied together with reason. Susskind and Field observe, "It would be a frightening world if people used only reason or only emotion. In reality, it is far more likely that both "sides" will use both reason and emotion. After all the public has both hearts and minds, and those who wish to advance their cause most always appeal to both. It is best to acknowledge strong emotion and at the same time, appeal to reasoned arguments."[71]

The facilitation training that I received was faith-based. It was led by a group called the LOGOs Institute (no longer in existence), associated with the Anglican Church of Canada.

The "Fifth Discipline: The Art and Practice of the Learning Organization"[72] by Peter Senge and other authors was the text that we used at LOGOs, along with other support material - mainly paperclipped photocopies of pages from a variety of books and manuals. Our training involved a weekend retreat followed by several classroom sessions over the next three months. We then formed teams and did our field work.

A handful of other novices and I were trained on how to serve faith groups facing challenges such as a clergy person in trouble or a parish in conflict over a significant issue. Occasionally, we would help parishes develop a strategic plan. We would learn in the classroom setting, then co-facilitate in parishes, repeating the process until we felt confident enough to lead a group on our own.

---

71 Susskind and Field, p. 184

72 Senge, Peter, Art Kleiner, Charlotte Roberts, Richard B. Ross and Bryan J. Smith, "The Fifth Discipline Fieldbook: Strategies and Tools for Building a Learning Organization", Doubleday; New York, 1994

Who are these people and why are they yelling at me? | 45

Because faith was at the core of our work, we were trained to also lead people through personal reflection and discernment, asking "What is your faith telling you about the choices that the congregation needs to make?" Our trainers took great care to help us facilitate this part of the process with sensitivity and care because its was very emotional for participants.

Being involved in the group was a significant and emotional moment for these participants because their comments spoke from the core spiritual beliefs that they held dear. Furthermore, someone was truly listening to them at a deep and emotional level and, at times, reaching them spiritually. These sessions were designed with an understanding of the emotional terrain that we would travel. We made sure that group dialogue also allowed time for emotional release, singing popular hymns and taking food breaks along the way.

The most important part of each session was the closure period, as the group, having usually accomplished a lot, was collectively proud of what they had achieved. They had solved a problem or charted a new direction and the whole community was emotionally invested in the result. Along with the emotional pride was a reluctance to let go. As the facilitator, I needed to be sensitive to where people were emotionally at every step in the process, right up to the end.

In large, angry public meetings, it is easy to know the emotions of the most vocal people. It would be difficult not to. What is more challenging is knowing the emotions of those who are less vocal. This is something that an extreme facilitator needs to watch for.

The emotional charge happens in public meetings as well. About twenty years ago I co-facilitated a session with my former business partner, Mark Stevenson. We were helping the staff of a provincial ministry to decide on a long-term plan. The process was designed to be creative, with the goal of developing concrete recommendations for organizational change. Because the changes could unfortunately result in some people being relocated or losing their jobs, participants discussed agenda items with personal concern about what they could mean to them and their families.

In the afternoon plenary session, we heard from a young woman who began accusing her bosses of being insensitive and stating that the whole process was a sham. If she had stopped there, we could have explored her concerns and found out what could be done to have the process shift in the direction that she desired. But she didn't. In the midst of about ninety work colleagues, the young woman ranted about various conspiracy theories, the medications that she was on (and the medications that the pharmacy refused to give her), her father, and his treatment of her. At times, she was crying. At other times, she was yelling loudly.

Mark and I looked at each other. None of the government staff was stepping up to help, and both of us realized that we couldn't allow the woman to continue to eviscerate herself in front of her fellow employees. At this point, she was either having a nervous breakdown or perhaps having a bad reaction to the medications that she talked about.

We decided that Mark would go over and talk to the woman and ask her whether it would be better if she could share her thoughts with us one on one in a quiet place in the hall outside of the meeting room. Mark is a very friendly person who naturally speaks calmly and respectfully. We decided that I would continue to facilitate the group alone. Mark spent the next few hours with her, listening until she regained her composure. At the end of the day, she had regained enough self-esteem to smile and apologize to people. We could only deal with emotions at this level because we were co-facilitating. I couldn't do it if I was the only facilitator. More importantly, we understood in advance that the session would be emotional and we were prepared.

Too often, I've seen undertrained facilitators stop the meeting when people have emotions in order to help to address their emotions. While dealing with emotions is a core requirement, stopping meetings is not the extreme facilitator's role. Schwarz provides an excellent reminder of how far a facilitator should go in terms of people's emotions, saying "…group facilitation is not group therapy. The purpose of dealing with emotions that arise in facilitation is to help the group become more effective at its work, not to change people's personalities or to focus on emotions for their own sake."[73]

---

73 Schwarz, R. 2nd edition p 247

Who are these people and why are they yelling at me? | 47

While these are perhaps unique examples of the emotions and conflict that can be expected, Ingrid Bens[74] has done a fine job of highlighting thirty conflict scenarios that a facilitator can expect. For each, she summarizes: the challenge; facilitator pitfalls; an analysis of what's going on, and; intervention strategy. Of these scenarios, five conflicts that I see most frequently are summarized as follows:

Figure 1 Facilitator Challenges		
CONFLICT	**EXPLANATION**	**HOW TO DEAL WITH IT**
The Personal Attack	An attack on the facilitator, client or experts hired by the client to speak. At times, it will involve personal attacks on other members of the public.	• Stay calm • Ask them to repeat their comment so as to have them own it. • Push back somewhat by asking, "What's your concern?" • Point out why you've been asked to facilitate and that you are there to serve the group. • If it's an attack on the client or experts, ensure that people are informed of the person's qualifications, if that's the issue. • If it's an attack on another person, ask them to restate their comment in a manner that shows respect for others. • Thank the person for the comment and continue facilitating.

---

74 Bens, I. Advanced Facilitation Strategies, op cit

Lack of Authority	People challenge the facilitator by starting to ask questions before the meeting has begun and disrespecting ground rules. At times, they will ask why a facilitator is needed and challenge your authority. For example, a prominent individual in the community at one of my meetings stated at the beginning of the meeting, "I don't want to be facilitated".	Most people attending the meeting will want information before providing comments. And, they will see the facilitator who's helping to organize dialogue to allow an exchange to happen. Responses include: • Restate what I'm there to do. • Point out that I've made a commitment to the people attending that we will hear their views and trust me to stay with that commitment. • Ask them to check with me at mid meeting and point out if I'm not allowing issues to be raised – and I'll make a course correction. • Keep going.
Agenda Overload	Agendas that are overloaded and front-ended. Also, agendas that don't allow the public enough time to participate and share their comments.	• Split up the presentation. • Shorten the presentation. • Inform the participants that the presentation will be long and ask for their permission to show the complete presentation. • Make sure the agenda stays on time and on track.
The Over-Participant	The "air hog" is discussed later, but this conflict issue involves people who need to speak at length over everyone else. They have no sense that there are other people who want to speak or might have something important to say.	• Set a time limit for comments at the beginning of the meeting. • Point out that the agenda is tight and lots of people want to speak. • Point out that their time is up or ask them to summarize so that others can speak.

Who are these people and why are they yelling at me? | 49

The Positional Debaters	This conflict occurs when people are arguing passionately that someone else is wrong – usually my client. They have arrived at a solution and won't listen to any other point of view.	• Active listening and paraphrasing. • Point out there may be strong alternative points of view and that it's OK to hear them. • Hear from other members of the public. • Give the client time to fully respond.

Schwarz observes that conflict also may also have positive features as it shines a light on an issue that the client or facilitator needs to address. He states, "A principle of the Skilled Facilitator approach is to move toward the conflict. By publicly identifying the conflict in the group and engaging people in a conversation about it, you can help the group explore how people contribute to the conflict, how they are feeling about it, and how to manage it."[75]

While all of these conflict issues occur during angry meetings, working with clients who want to stack the agenda with a long presentation is a recurring challenge for me. As many of my clients are engineers, planners and other professionals, a great deal of my work is done in the context of an Environmental Assessment Study - a process that is prescriptive, sometimes requiring only two public information centres as part of a very long and complex study. Combined with poor requirements for public dialogue, some clients believe that the public will come on side if you simply give them enough information. "How can they ignore the facts?" they ask.

One of the most challenging facilitation assignments that I accepted had to do with bringing a new light rapid transit rail line on a separate right of way to an established community with an existing, older-style transit line at street level.[76]

---

75 Schwarz, R., 2nd edition, p. 254

76 This light rail line is a different line than the one referred to for the HOV meeting.

On the face of it, modern public transit on a separated right of way should be seen as a good thing for any community. But not this community.

I was the first facilitator in the project, meaning that I was the first one who had to deal with a client with strong views about how to present information, and even stronger views about how I should do my job. As it turned out, I was let go and other facilitators were hired in my place. I said a prayer for them.

I knew that the first meeting I facilitated would be tough. Among the local residents were professional organizers and agitators who were part of Toronto's "alt left" scene. One of them was a good friend of mine, so I knew what to expect. I'm exaggerating a bit here, but tempers were so high that the image of a crowd of people with pitch forks, burning torches and a noose would be a good depiction of the people attending the meeting. Three hundred people attended - as many as the venue could legally hold.

To start the meeting, my client insisted on presenting a five-minute film arguing why light rail transit was right for the community. About three minutes of the film involved a camera shot of a car making a left hand turn on the street-level rails, blocking a crowded trolley with eighty people on board from moving forward.

Perhaps if the people on the trolley were also at the meeting, things would have been calmer, but all hell broke loose. People got the point after the first fifteen seconds. Not wanting to be forced to watch the rest of the film clip by the client and wanting to state their views, the audience completely ignored the agenda and chanted to stop the film. About a dozen people intimidated every other presenter.

I explained to my client then, as I do to every client, that tensions and emotions rise in the audience when you try to pack an agenda. In this case, the people in the meeting were being inconvenienced in the same way as the people on the trolley.

Thinking through the presentation and how the audience will respond is essential. Doyle and Straus point out that the client needs to ask, why am I doing this presentation? What do I want to get out of it? And how will the public respond? What's the desirable interchange between the client and the audience? Most presentations flop because too much information is spilled out. They state the purpose of most presentations should be to inject new information to assist

Who are these people and why are they yelling at me? | 51

group problem solving. The client can start by keeping it simple and return to additional Power Point slides that provide more detail during the question and answer period.

They state, "Poor presentations waste participants' time even after they are delivered because the relevant information is not in a form that can help the group in its deliberation and so people spend a lot more time wheel spinning, trying to reorganize and digest it before they can make a decision."[77]

Being Nimble When Dealing with Complications

Complications are discussed at length in the Chapter 9: Meeting Day. Being nimble in the context of facilitator skills, involves the extreme facilitator needing to accept that complications will arise. When you are on your feet, it's your job to deal with complications on the spot. Much of this comes down to planning for the worst and hoping for the best outcomes before the meeting is under way. The rest comes down to the trained facilitator knowing alternative meeting structures that can be implemented if the current structure isn't working. It also involves knowing what public engagement techniques are available and not being afraid to make a change mid-stream.

While the facilitation skills and techniques discussed here do not apply to engaging Indigenous people, which requires a deeper level of knowledge and understanding, I have been asked on several occasions to facilitate a meeting where a high percentage of Indigenous people were present. One meeting involved a review of forest management policy options in Northern Ontario. I needed to be very nimble in order to deal with a complication that arose.

My client wanted me to manage the meeting as if everyone attending was of European ancestry. I knew that this was going to be a problem since a lot of First Nations communities had been invited, and participating in a meeting was not in keeping with their cultural engagement practices. I didn't get too far past the ground rules before an aboriginal elder spoke up and said that my rules did not work for his people. I responded with great respect by asking, "What would work

---

77 Doyle and Straus, op cit, p. 256

for you?" He replied that the process needed to be separate, with parallel professional staff working with his people in a manner that was appropriate to them.

My response to the elder was that, if I could find a separate suitable meeting room and borrow one or two of the agency staff to work with them throughout the day, would that work? If so, a process of dialogue that is acceptable to them could be used. I added that we could all come together again over lunch and debrief together again at the end of the day. The elder agreed with the revised "dual meeting" structure, which ended up working very well for all parties. After facilitating a respectful sharing of comments, I was thanked at the end of the day by the elder for allowing an alternative way of having dialogue.

Understanding the Subject Matter

Facilitators who manage potential high-emotion issues are usually very well-educated and are typically trained in several disciplines. Having an excellent knowledge of group psychology, philosophy and sociology is important. Related disciplines could include urban planning, medical professional, emergency response, communications and others. Even though you may be well informed, facilitators should always direct the content questions to the client.

Doyle and Straus state that the 'content' is the 'what' problem, topic or subject matter. The 'process' is the 'how' approach, method or procedure. Getting it wrong means the meeting isn't going to work. To clarify, they refer to ice. "The 'process' of melting is not the state of the ice or state of the water; it is what happens in between. In problem-solving, the process is how an individual or group solves the problem. The problem and solution are whatever is acted upon; it is the content."[78]

The better extreme facilitators know a great deal about subject matter content that draws public rage. Taking the time to read the background technical reports, learn the facts, understand the range of opinions and become familiar with the details of the issue is important. Extreme facilitators are almost always significantly more informed about the issues on the agenda than members of the public. In fact, those facilitators who have researched and facilitated particular issues for many years may even be as informed as their clients. However,

---

78 Doyle and Straus, op cit p. 25

they know enough to never tip their hand during the meeting. Their focus is on process, not substance.

There are three reasons why understanding the subject matter is important. Firstly, it helps you to recognize the content of the questions being asked. Sometimes, questions are carelessly formulated, or a member of the public doesn't know the technical terms needed to describe their concern. My client wants to know as accurately as possible what's being asked, as do members of the public. I will usually know what the member of the public is getting at because I've done my homework and approached the subject matter with a critical eye.

In an instance like this, I will intervene to suggest some rephrasing, such as "So, you are asking whether there has been a peer review for Section 4, the ecological protection part of the study?", to which the person might reply, "Yes, that's what I said. Did anyone else look at nature?" I had read the study in advance and knew that this is what the individual was referring to. My client will then know the exact section of the study that was a concern and respond accurately.

The second reason for understanding the subject matter is so that the facilitator can determine whether or not questions being asked by the public are germane. While I welcome all questions when facilitating, there are times when a query refers to a completely different study, a study or policy that had been decided on many years earlier, or a study that is outside of what the client can deal with, since it not their responsibility. I won't block the question, but I will provide a suggestive response that might bring the discussion back on topic.

I might say, "It sounds like you are referring to a matter that is the responsibility of a different agency. No one here tonight can provide a response, I'm not sure if I can find anyone from the project team who can help." To this statement, the client will usually respond with body language that says, "No one can answer", so l will close the question in a respectful way saying, "Let's note your question and perhaps we can find someone to respond after the meeting'"

The third reason is to help the group sort out the smorgasbord of information flowing during the most intense parts of the meeting. Conceptually, I'm helping the public to place the information in the right boxes so that they can keep pace and understand the information transaction. I don't want anyone to say, 'I don't understand what's going on' or 'what went on'.

In larger, more dynamic meetings, questions may stimulate a range of completely different questions over a fifteen-minute period, so my clients need to be on their toes. My assistance will come from knowing what each questioner is getting at (often well before the person finishes their question), and pointing to a gatekeeper from the project team.

A meeting gatekeeper is someone who, during the rehearsal part of the meeting, has agreed to direct questions to the right technical expert for a public response. This person or I will alert a technical specialist that they are on deck and should be ready to respond. In this instance, the facilitator knows the subject matter as well as the expert familiar with the subject matter who, via body language from me, knows that they should be ready to provide a response to the question.

Managing the Evolving Dynamics

This role of the extreme facilitator involves intervening in group processes to help manage meeting dynamics toward a positive outcome. Suzanne Ghais points out the following actions that can be taken to manage dynamics:

1. **Paraphrasing or Summarizing:** I use this mainly when responding to an individual. (It's somewhat risky to do so for a group.) Paraphrasing assures the person that I've heard them. With groups, it is unlikely that you've been able to accurately capture all views, which results in many people concluding that you haven't heard them.

2. **Reframing to Interests:** This technique is helpful when members of the audience, the client and the specialists appear to have agreement on the fundamentals, but are at odds over the details. To reframe the dialogue towards interests, I will state, "We all seem to agree on the fundamental principles, so we need to work on how to get there." For example, most people want healthy outcomes but can't agree whether or not a new cell phone tower would achieve this.

3. **Stating Observations:** I use this technique often during an angry public meeting because, as an independent party, it allows me to draw some closure on both the formal or informal parts of the agenda, so that a

Who are these people and why are they yelling at me? | 55

group can move on. Ghais[79] observes that vocalizing observations helps to point out unspoken dynamics, allows self-correction of the group process, and allows people to hear procedural suggestions and help them to be cognizant of their own dynamics. Sometimes, I observe that the group is spending a lot of time on a small issue, while there seem to be larger issues that may have brought them here.

4. **Making Process Changes:** This role involves being aware of where the group is and, if the process is not going well, make a change in how the group proceeds. For smaller groups, I will ask people how it's going and poll them on how to move forward. For larger public groups, I might suggest that a citizens' advisory group be formed after the meeting to give a group representing the community more time to comment in depth.

5. **Capturing Points of Agreement:** This involves the facilitator listening closely to what people seem to be agreeing on and "noticing what's not being debated."[80] I will sometimes use a flip chart to capture comments and themes that people agree on. When I'm making a comment on areas of agreement, flip chart notes serve as a bit of a fall-back shield in case I get it wrong. I discuss in later chapters the important role of note taking and note takers.

Facilitation text books discuss many techniques for managing meeting dynamics. For large, angry public meetings however, the skills required centre on four areas: 1) the ability to read the group (client and public); 2) being able to formulate the right prompt/intervention questions and comments; 3) knowing how to move the group through the meeting structure; and, 4) knowing when to intervene.

Being able to read the group is an essential skill. It is easier for the facilitator to read the group by including the client as a group member. You and the client have done rehearsals and chalk talks, and reading the client really comes down to body language and short bits of communication while the meeting is

---

79 Ghais, S., op cit, p. 140
80 Ghais, S, op cit, p. 144

under way. Large, angry public meetings pose a greater challenge, as you have a minimal idea of who's shown up for the meeting. (The art of reading body language will be discussed in a later chapter.)

People at large public meetings will certainly be on their feet providing comments and asking questions. But the question is really, where are the two hundred people at in terms of their learning and emotions? Are they responding to information? Are they formulating a group opinion? Are they rejecting the comments and ideas being discussed?

Interpreting the dynamic based on subtleties and nuances requires a fine level of skill. Ghais observes that large, angry public meetings pose a special challenge, acknowledging that the conventional wisdom of typical facilitation simply doesn't work. Consensus is often not the best process goal.

When listening to the exchange of information between the public and the client, facilitators will know how long to let the line of questioning go on, how deeply to probe for comments, what comments are inside and outside of bounds and which client representatives should be asked to respond to specific questions. The facilitator should try to keep the meeting on track. Ghais observes that good facilitators intervene when necessary to keep a meeting going, use their judgement to determine when not to intervene, and know which questions to ask. Extreme facilitators deal with all of the complexity associated with these decisions.

Cool Heads: Establishing and Maintaining Tone

Emotions are contagious.[81] My role is to start positive and be encouraging. Having the facilitator set a tone through opening remarks, emotional dispositions, suggestions of ways for people to talk to each other, and posture, helps to guide the meeting along the path of dialogue. The issue arises in establishing and maintaining tone when the atmosphere is strained. Observing and supporting positive group interactions is important.

It is also important to note that the extreme facilitator is not tasked with controlling the group or being a drill sergeant. In a group of several hundred

---

81 Ghais, S op cit p. 25

Who are these people and why are they yelling at me? | 57

people, this type of behaviour won't be tolerated for long. Nor is the facilitator a "Pollyanna", assuring everyone that everything is OK. There is a right and wrong in terms of process, and the public expects you to exercise control in a metered and measured manner. You are there to serve the group, not stand by while the process disintegrates.

Both Bens and Ghais discuss setting and maintaining the tone of a meeting. Bens observes the importance of questioning skills in maintaining the tone of the group. It is questioning that sends the group in the right direction. She presents twelve types of questions, also referring to other literature that highlights many other types and styles[82]. Specifically, there are questions that: help to set and maintain the context; invite positive and constructive dialogue; help to foster a conversation and link different ideas as a good host would do; test ideas and create synergies; probe for reasons of anger, emotion and conflict; and turn anger and conflict into positive and constructive comment.

Bens states, "If the atmosphere becomes strained, advanced facilitators show self-control and are able to refrain from becoming overly emotional. They're able to manage their own emotions, even in difficult situations. They never lose their temper, become embroiled in disputes, or show their displeasure."[83]

Ghais takes the matter a little deeper. Discussing the spiritual aspect of tone-setting, which I've found helpful when facilitating, she says, "What could spirituality possibly do with facilitation?"[84] If you look at the essence of spirituality, separating it from religious institutions or traditions, much of it concerns helping people rise above our biased, selfish and animal natures – to transcend them."[85]

Adding to the common themes that Ghais identifies, I find that the tone I bring to a large angry meeting also helps to set and maintain the tone of the meeting. Ghais starts with love. When I'm in the midst of emotional and angry people, it is my hope that they will see me as a leader with nothing against them - no animosity and no wish to harm - possessing a truthful desire to get to know them

---

82 Bens, I. Advanced Facilitation p. 34
83 Bens, I. Advanced Facilitation, p 13
84 Ghais, S. p 231
85 Ghais, S. p 231 – 252.

when they are more representative of their true selves. It involves appealing to people to be their best selves.

Regarding other values, I have hope that the dialogue will be successful and that I'm doing everything I can to lend hope to the situation. Continuing with Ghais' themes: I express gratitude for every comment and idea that I hear; I genuinely enjoy hearing people's views on a matter; I'm doing my best to speak the truth, at the same time looking for others (both clients and members of the public) to speak their truth; when appropriate, I appeal to our sense of community.

Often my clients are asked to make tough decisions for the greater good of the community. The meeting may be angry because some people don't agree on what defines the common good. This is my opportunity to push back a bit and ask the question of all meeting participants. By setting out the challenge for the group to identify and speak to the common good, the tone of the meeting changes considerably.

All Ears: Being a Strong Listener

Perhaps the most important skill that both a facilitator and an extreme facilitator should possess is being an active listener. Noting that "…great facilitators spend more time listening than talking"[86], Killermann and Bolger recommend a mnemonic for facilitators, clients and technical support staff to use before responding. "WHALE" refers to Wait, Hesitate, Ask (again), Listen, Explain. Being silent and letting yourself pause before answering ensures that you aren't dominating the discussion or, as they say, "vomiting words all over your participants".[87]

Luft provides great insight about the listening process relevant to facilitation and group process. He states, "Listening may be a simple thing, as when we hear someone tell us directions to the post office. It is another matter in a group where people have come together to work on significant issues. Listening is a skill that is imbedded in one's attitude toward the immediate group and bears

---

86 Killermann and Bolger, op cit, p. 32
87 Killermann and Bolger, op cit, p. 32

Who are these people and why are they yelling at me? | 59

significantly on the personal qualities of the individual. Listening takes time and a special effort in attending to the speaker and to the communication process." [88]

He states questions pertinent to effective listening include:

- Do I understand literally what the other person is saying?
- To whom is the comment addressed?
- What is the speaker's frame of reference?
- What feelings is the person conveying?
- Do I understand what the person is trying to get across? [89]

I am always pleased when active listening skills work. As an example, I was asked to travel to a beachfront town to facilitate a meeting where people were vociferously opposing the location of a cellular phone tower[90]. The issue was electromagnetic effects potentially causing health problems. Because it was the middle of the winter and the town was particularly prone to lake effect snow storms, my staff and I were monitoring the latest weather forecasts all the way there.

The beachfront town was quite lovely even in the depths of winter, so I concluded that it must be quite a wonderful place to live in the summer. Situated below a bluff, there was no other location for the cell tower except in the middle of the community.

Local emergency services personnel had reported that there had been a drowning and several serious situations at the beach, and no one was able to use their cell phone to call the police or an ambulance. They had to locate a telephone call box; an increasingly rare thing.

Even though the community was opposed to the cellular tower project, the irony was that almost every resident had a cell phone that relied on radio frequencies to deliver a signal once they were out of town. The cell tower protest

---

88 Luft, J. op cit p. 25

89 Luft, J. op cit p. 25

90 Note: While I keep picking on the cell phone tower industry, its only because the public interactions about the technology are interesting. Similar issues arise in other sectors and with other technology.

was led by a diplomatic and distinguished-looking cottager who had worked as an economist with the World Bank in New York. To local residents, this background qualified the man as a trusted expert on cellular communications. The meeting was smaller than I expected, with only thirty-five people attending, but the participants were very vocal.

This particular community leader talked with presence and authority about the EMF effects of cellular tower radio waves on his body, referencing, at great length, medical articles that he had read to support his case. He declared that he could actually feel the effects of radio waves on his brain in the form of periodic buzzing and ticking. Knowing that the authors of the articles the gentleman was referring to had long ago been discredited, I did my best to show respect for him as a neutral facilitator. "Interesting," I said. "I hadn't heard that before." It is not my job to judge. It is my job to listen.

The meeting ended with all sides disagreeing. Except for a few libelous and slanderous remarks hurled by two members of the public towards the radio frequency scientist retained by the proponent (for which I extracted apologies from the perpetrators), the meeting ended with no one hurt and only a few people learning.

That said, to try to achieve dialogue, I made every effort I could to show that I was actively listening. After the meeting ended, another resident who also talked about being affected by radio waves came up to me and thanked me for my expert facilitation. It is not unusual for residents to come up and talk to me about their issues after the meeting. I usually continue to listen, but I gradually direct them to the client or program proponent.

This resident told me that she too occasionally heard voices or music, attributing the sounds to the effect of radio waves, but she was unsure if the cause was her teeth or some wiring in her brain. She remarked that no one had ever really understood what she was experiencing until she met me and saw how I responded to her comments that evening. Noting how attentive I was when listening to her, the resident hoped that we could continue the discussion of how her and other people heard voices and their ability to tune in radio programs in their heads. She asked for my card and I gave it to her. Continuing to be respectful, I thanked her for the opportunity to get to know her, told her that I hoped she would be able to find a solution, and wished her the best.

Reading and Conveying Verbal and Body Language

Extreme facilitators must be very careful and skilled in the reading of and use of verbal and body language.

I once got caught by my own sloppy language while facilitating a small meeting in the York Region, just north of Toronto. The issue was how to deal with and develop regional and local municipal policy and regulations to prevent surface water from rain, snow and other sources from polluting local streams.

The session was going well and comments were constructive until someone mentioned that ground water from wells was also an important subject. While relevant, the issue of ground water was outside of the subject matter for the evening. Using a flip chart, I stated that I was going to flag the issue for the "parking lot", meaning, "We're not going to discuss this now, but will be discussing it later so we'll 'park it' by writing the comment on the flip chart." Writing "ground water" on the flip chart, I titled it "PARKING LOT".

Soon, a hand went up and a person commented that we had to do something about the pigeons and geese "pooping on parking lots". The next questioner added that we had to do something about oil from cars and salt for de-icing on parking lots. Another felt that a special study of parking lots was probably required.

Realizing what just happened, I needed to explain that, even though it looked like I had changed the subject to include a discussion of "parking lots", the term was one used by facilitators, not an item on the evening's agenda. Looking over at my clients who, at this point, were trying to stifle their laughter, I saw a look on their faces that said it all, "You're not as smart as you think, Mr. Facilitator."

Being aware of verbal and body language is a very important when facilitating a public meeting. Schwarz[91] lists several guidelines for words to use and avoid:

1. Use words and phrases that have one meaning – the meaning you want to convey.

2. Use descriptive words when they can be substituted for evaluative words.

3. Use proper nouns or nouns other than pronouns.

---

91 Schwarz, R., 2nd edition, Exhibit 8.2 Guidelines for Words to Use and Avoid, p 189

4. Use an active voice unless the identity of the actor is not clear.
5. Use words that give equal recognition to all members and tasks.
6. Chose words that distinguish the facilitator role from the group members' roles.
7. Avoid imperatives; focus instead on cause and effect.
8. Avoid humour that puts down or discounts members or that can be misinterpreted.

Verbal and non-verbal language is also used in the norming stage to help establish norms. I discuss the 'norming' and other stages in Chapter 6. When facilitating, my language changes to be (and appear to be) presenting myself as neutral and independent. The conversation I've had with my client before the meeting is characterized by the words "we", "us" and "they". In other words, "We (the client) are going to have a tough meeting and I'm working to ensure that they (the public) are not too hard on us (the project team) at the same time as encouraging public comments."

When I'm on my feet as an independent facilitator, however, the language changes in the use of "you" and "they". "I'm hearing the point you (the public) are making and I'm sure that they (the client) are listening carefully. So what we (the public) are saying is…" It is a conversation from the perspective of the group and not centred on the client.

Because a great deal of communication during large, angry public meetings occurs through body language, I chose to give the subject considerably more attention than other facilitation theorists have done. Being aware of body language is a very important aspect of facilitating any meeting, but it is an essential consideration for larger, angrier situations.

Extreme facilitation involves one person standing in front of several hundred potentially loud, emotional and angry people. Everyone can see everything you are doing, and will be listening to every word. It is very important to be aware of and check your own body language. A lot of eyes are on you, and your credibility is on the line.

Matt Giordano states, "What you say is thirty percent of what people think of you. Seventy percent is your body language: your posture, speech pattern and eye movements.[92] It goes without saying that being able to infer what's being communicated via body language is essential.

There are typically three main parties in a meeting displaying body language: 1) members of the audience; 2) the facilitator; and, 3) the client along with members of the expert team. Being aware of body language involves a facilitator looking for, interpreting and managing non-verbal signals. Amy Cuddy discusses the subject in depth, identifying three interactions associated with body language: what my body language means to you; what your body language means to me; and what my body language means to me[93].

I'm Listening

Elaborating on Cuddy's observations, in my experience there are is a fourth way that body language can be used to influence a positive outcome of a large, angry public meeting. The first priority is to physically show members of the audience that you are listening and responding. This applies to both the extreme facilitator and the proponent/client. The public can see you folding your arms, smiling, frowning, pointing, slapping your head, looking impatient, appearing bored, acting surprised or confused, and more.

Navarro observes that our body language telegraphs our intentions and whether we are comfortable or not, stating that it is, in fact, more truthful than the spoken word[94].

Giordano[95] points out that a closed posture indicates that you are afraid to be around other people, while open posture means confidence.

---

92 Matt Giordano, Three Types of Body Language, Ted Talk, TEDxBucknell, May 3, 2016 UNiversityhttps://www.youtube.com/watch?v=S_xe649Ug3Q

93 Amy Cuddy, October 1 2012, Author of "Presence: Bringing Your Boldest Self to Your Biggest Challenges Paperback – Jan 30 2018' Quoting: Ted Talk - https://www.internet.ca/search?q=ted+talk+body+language+youtube&rlz=1C1GCEA_enCA775CA775&oq=ted+talk+body+language&aqs=chrome.1.69i57j0l5.17320j1j8&sourceid=chrome&ie=UTF-8 by Amy Cuddy (Author)

94 Joe Navarro M.A, The honesty of body language, Posted Aug 21, 2011 https://www.psychologytoday.com/ca/blog/spycatcher/201108/body-language-basicsBody Language Basics

95 Giordano, ibid.

64 | David R. Hardy, R.P.P.

Words and body language need to mesh. According to Giordano, slowing down your speech and enunciating allows for clear communication. Speaking rapidly without clear phrasing shows fear and worry. He suggests looking at the bridge of people's noses or into their eyes when they are speaking. All of these gestures, representing secondary ways of communicating with the audience, are to be understood and discussed with the client prior to the meeting.

Haskett and Martin[96] prepared the following list of body language "no-no's":

1. **Looking at your watch.** The non-verbal message you send when you look at your watch is, "I wish you'd stop talking". Because every facilitator needs to keep time. I usually place a large-face stand-up watch on the floor in front of the first row, or I find a wall clock, so that I don't have to look at my watch.

2. **Gazing out a window or looking at a mobile phone.** Even if it's only for a spilt second, the non-verbal message is, "I'm not listening to what you're saying."

3. **Yawning.** The message is, "I'm bored with what you're saying."

Good body language practices that I typically use include[97]:

1. **Leaning forward and maintaining eye contact.** "I'm interested in what you're saying."

2. **Scratching my chin and nodding.** "I must have said something important."

3. **Taking a note or checking with the note taker.** "I want to remember what you're saying."

4. **Smiling or showing an empathetic facial expression.** "I caught the subtlety in what you said."

Many people are accustomed to going to a meeting where people are stationed at a microphone or behind a head table. My meetings are different. As a facilitator

---

96 Hackett and Martin, op cit, p. 28, 29
97 Hackett and Martin, op cit, p. 28, 29

Who are these people and why are they yelling at me? | 65

I have the opportunity to move around the room and I do so. If necessary, I get into people's personal space or stay distant. I use many hand and body gestures throughout the course of a meeting. My default gesture involves placing my finger to my chin to show a pensive, thoughtful listening pose. It's not insincere. I'm usually very interested in what people are saying. And, because I'm on the hook for approving the notes of the meeting, I need to understand what is being said.

I also try to set a tone by smiling and appearing to be as friendly as possible. (For some particularly painful meetings, I will jot down a "smile" reminder on each page of my facilitator's notes.) Empathy is important, as is sincerity. I've facilitated many meetings where a corporation or a bureaucracy has really messed up, causing many problems for residents. I want to make sure that those residents have been heard and that my body language shows it.

My body language also helps in the transaction of information. I will nod my head up and down as a positive acknowledgement that I am listening to a comment from the public. If someone is waiting to speak, I continually check back with them by making eye contact, pointing or nodding to them to show that I haven't forgotten that they have information to share.

I also use "mirroring", a classic facilitation technique which, for an extreme facilitation, needs to be magnified. When I observe that a member of the public feels they have an important point to make, I will come close to them. If a person raises a comment that is particularly disturbing, I show by frowning that I too am disturbed, making sure that I see their face and they can see mine. At this point, I'm making an extra effort to let them know I'm trying to understand what they have to say. To be clear, my responses are sincere and not contrived. When people are upset, I get it.

Many other facilitators and I recommend the use of the "yes/and" rule. This involves practicing, then using these words when responding to people with whom you may disagree. Our natural response is to say "but" or "no", then provide a response. The word "but" means, I'm not accepting what you have just said to me. The rule is, when you disagree with something said you begin your rebuttal with "yes" and then say "and". You communicate, "I've heard and understood what you said and I wish to add my thoughts."

Killermann and Bolger observe, "By adding to someone's reality rather than negating it, you can often learn much more about a person's perspective, understanding and ideas than any 'no' could ever bring you." [98] Assuming that you are listening, this simple technique helps to assure people that you are doing so.

Reading the Audience

The extreme facilitator needs to be very skilled at reading the body language of people in the audience. Individual members of the public may verbally agree with something being said, but their body language might tell a completely different story. When I notice this, I will second-guess the verbal comments and try to suss out the true views of participants, saying, "Everyone is quiet and there are no hands up, but I sense there's something on your minds. What is it?" Or I'll say that "I seem to be getting mixed signals".

Watching to see how members of the public react to a speaker's or expert's comments during the presentation part of the meeting helps me to anticipate issues that will come up during the open part of the session. It also allows me to plan how much time I should allocate to the public discussion of an issue. This will help me to understand situations when people react strongly to a particular statement, don't seem to believe a particular fact, and like or dislike a particular policy presented to them.

For example, while facilitating a meeting in York Region, in Ontario, I spotted a member of the public sitting almost at the back of the room. There were about one hundred and twenty-five people in attendance. The subject matter had to deal with a water main to be constructed in front of their homes.

As usual, four or five people had done their homework by reading the client's information in advance and asked the first couple of questions. Before I turned to them again for a second round of comments, I scanned the audience and noticed an older gentleman with his arms crossed and a deep furrow on his brow.

I pointed to the gentleman and said, "It looks like you've got something on your mind." He responded, "How did you know?", to which I replied, "I can see it

---

98 Killermann and Bolger, op cit. p 7

Who are these people and why are they yelling at me? | 67

through your body language." Sure enough, his response was, "Well, I do and this is what I'm concerned about."

When I'm facilitating a public meeting, I continually monitor the body language of members of the public. When in the storming stage and energy levels are peaking and people are really upset, you don't need a primer on body language to know what's going on in their minds. You can be certain of the message you are getting when people are standing up in the aisles, shaking fists in the air and waving hands as if to slap down a comment they don't like. I discuss 'meeting stages' in Chapter 6.

It is really the subtler body language that I'm watching for. Does their body language show that they understand a comment? Is it showing that they have something on their minds, or that some matter is unresolved? Is group body language indicating that more than one person agrees or disagrees?

As there will often be twenty hands in the air, I will ask myself, "Does the body language show that they are frustrated because they have to wait to speak, or are they willing to wait? How are they putting up their hands? With energy? Subtly? Are there sizable numbers of people in the audience who look like they actually agree with what is being said?

When I facilitate a meeting, I constantly watch for what is on people's minds based on nonverbal cues: who is frowning, who's still smiling and who's disoriented. I'm watching for people who feel that they need to talk to their neighbour about something that has been said, so that I know there's something else on people's minds that is not being communicated.

I often tell people at the beginning of a meeting that they may be asked questions, so I will start with a question, "I can see that there's something important you want to talk about. Can you share it with everyone?" I'm looking for arms crossed and people taking notes. Are they sitting back in their chairs as if relaxing or are they sitting forward as active listeners? Do they have doubts? Have they heard enough? Are they evaluating what you are saying or are they bored?

The Right Moves

Another use of your body involves thinking about where you are standing during a meeting. As an extreme facilitator, my practice is to move around the room. Moving up and down aisles assures people that you are looking for and have seen the hands of everyone wanting to speak, including those at the back of the room and in the aisles. In response to a comment, I might direct the attention of members of the audience to key displays or exhibits. As I walk up and down aisles, backwards and forwards, and across rows, I'm scanning the audience the whole time, and people will see my eyes.

I want to let members of the public know that the person running the meeting has a physical presence and is not a distant talking voice at the front of the room speaking from a podium. If there is an individual or cluster of people who feel that they can act out, I will stand closer to them while managing the meeting at the same time. Even though nothing is being said, I'm watching for what is really being said.

Conductor Gestures

The fourth use of body language involves using gestures to "conduct" the meeting. In a large, dynamic meeting, many people will want to be engaged at the same time. I've told them that I will call upon them in the order in which they put up their hands but, being the impatient people that we are, they want to know where they are in the queue.

My facilitation involves a fair amount of memorization as to who put their hand up first. Using hand signals to confirm who's next, who's number two, etc., I will point to a person to let them know that I know they want to have a follow-up comment. If I sense impatience, I might take two or three questions at once before allowing the client to respond. Recounting who's on the list several times during the meeting, my gestures communicate, "I'm going to come back to you". "Okay, who's one, two, three, four? You are five, six and seven."

A lot of body language is going on. Members of the public are focused on the speaker, but through my gestures, they're understanding that there is waiting process, that they will be heard and that listening is occurring.

Team Body Language

The project team and its consultants also need to be aware of their own body language. Amy Cuddy observes that our non-verbal communications govern how people think and feel about us. "What," she asks, "is the presence that *we* are bringing to the presentation? Do we want a powerful person or a laid-back and friendly person presenting?[99] What is the non-verbal feedback presented to the audience when the client is presenting and answering questions?

Over the course of my career, I've experienced some meetings where things have gone wrong as a direct result of inappropriate body language of my client and the project team.

For example, my staff and I facilitated a meeting for Provincial Ministry of Transportation staff who were planning the route of a highway. Ministry staff wanted to have a simple Public Information Centre (PIC), a consultation technique where a series of display boards are set up on easels around a room. The idea is that people visit, ask questions, provide comments and go home. Based on my research, I tried to get the Ministry staff to understand that, even though they were planning for a PIC, it was going to be a loud and well-attended angry meeting.

"You are going to have two hundred and fifty people," I advised. "No, we're not," they insisted. "We'll get thirty people at best," To this, I replied, "No. You need to bring lots of staff and consultants to manage the crowd. Please, I want at least a dozen people there from the Ministry, and I'd like to do some staff training before the meeting." The client responded, "Even if we could, we're not sure if we can find people who are doing nothing that night."

My client was in denial, and they were reluctant to prepare. I also heard a few comments floating around questioning if they had hired a facilitator who had a grip on reality.

The venue was an agricultural display and exhibit hall in rural Ontario. The hall was large and could handle about fifty display boards on easels placed in rows around the perimeter walls. Because the meeting was taking place during spring thaw break-up, the gravel parking lot was wet and mushy. From my experience, a tell-tale sign that a large meeting is going to happen is the number of people showing up early, usually at least half an hour before. When we arrived an hour early to unload and set up, there were already people in the parking lot waiting for the door to be unlocked – an ominous sign.

---

99 Cuddy, op cit

Concerned that we wouldn't have enough people on hand for a large crowd, I brought all of my staff, who are all well trained as facilitators and know what they are doing. The client was balking at paying for more than me.

Twenty minutes after the start of the PIC we counted two hundred and seventy-five people, a clear indication that members of the public were expecting a public meeting. The Ministry staff were very inexperienced. Not knowing what to do, they stood in corners talking to each other. They certainly didn't want to talk to the public. At the same time, senior Ministry staff were standing in the centre of the room in circles talking to each other. The non-verbal body language, signalled by Ministry staff with their backs to the public was, "We don't want anybody asking us questions." Meanwhile, the only thing that the public wanted was to talk to them. At that point, the public information centre evolved into a public meeting.

Eventually I looked around and asked, "Where the hell are the Ministry staff?" I could see my staff, but they were the only ones on the floor. Where did all the Ministry staff go? Almost to a person, they were standing behind the display boards, now effectively hiding from the public. Their body language was quite clear: "We don't want to be here." So, I approached them and said, "Folks, you can't stand here. This is your meeting. This is your subject. You can't stand behind the boards and hope nobody's going to speak to you. Get out and talk to the public!"

In essence, a meeting was formed with no agenda, no speakers and no information being shared with the public other than what was on the display boards. Groups of about twelve to fifteen people began to surround single engineers and technical experts, peppering them with angry questions and comments.

The situation got to a point where I could see several engineers going into a psychological shut down mode. When they got up in that morning, none of them anticipated that this is how their day would end. Instead of watching the hockey playoffs that evening, they found themselves standing in the midst of screaming people. At least one of the engineers was acting catatonically, not able to respond to even the simplest question.

Finally, my client acknowledged that it was indeed a meeting and asked me to do what a facilitator does best. Gathering my staff, we held an impromptu meeting to coordinate our approach. I instructed each of my staff to proceed immediately to

Who are these people and why are they yelling at me? | 71

specific locations where, by this time, Ministry staff were about to be drawn and quartered. Their job was to break things up and begin dialogue.

Pushing our way into the middle of each cluster of angry residents, we started asking probing, calming and mirroring questions. Each of my staff also carried a clipboard, so that people could see that we were writing down what they were saying. Knowing how to stop the yelling and start the dialogue, we said things like, "Tell me more about that; What I hear you saying is…; I can see you are really upset about this highway; Tell me how this will affect you; What's the solution you would like to see?"

To give the client and staff the break they desperately needed, we added, "And by the way, the engineer standing beside me is wanted in the other part of the hall so she's going to have to leave you." In this way, we managed to rescue the engineers and Ministry technical experts, although they were the worse for wear. And, we managed to get a lot of good ideas from the public.

During large public meetings, presenters or people answering questions often come across as bureaucratic, stiff and stilted rather than showing humanity and empathy. I do my best to coach them on their body language, reminding them that this is their opportunity to hear from the public and learn from them. Body language should show that they welcome those comments, some of which may also improve the decision that they will be making.

Susskind and Field list the characteristics of a credible spokesperson in a crisis situation. These characteristics are also attributes of a credible spokesperson in a public meeting. The person:

- "is likable, affable, and straightforward;
- has a reputation for honesty, internally within a company or agency as well as externally with others;
- has a reputation for collaboration rather than confrontation;
- is familiar with the technical subject and can explain it in a clear fashion;
- already has experience in public settings."[100]

---

100 Susskind and Field, op cit; p 84

Chapter 4:
Avoiding the Slippery Slope

Unless you are a masochist, you normally wouldn't want to be in the position of being yelled at by hundreds of angry residents. So, before presenting the techniques of extreme facilitation I want to share two important pieces of advice: avoid angry public meetings in the first place; learn to understand if you are headed down the slippery slope towards the inevitable.

One of my clients has a saying: "Governments give permits. People give permission." Isn't that the truth? I have had more than one client raise glasses of Champagne after a difficult public and political approval, only to have political leaders thrown out of office in the next election. They win the battle, but not the war, and end up having to seek public approval all over again.

In my world, engineers, scientists and accountants are often at the head of the pack when it comes to the respected professions. (Accountants? Only in Canada!) When projects, policies, programs and plans need approval, these professions typically define the public approval process, schedule and budget for each project. They are usually aiming for a permit or other type of government approval based on a fixed time and cost.

For more complex or expensive project, program or policy approvals, they hire or include a public consultation specialist on the team. And, less frequently, they will hire a professional facilitator. When public consultation specialists are involved, the public process normally goes a lot smoother. Big angry meetings are avoided, and the public still has input. But there are times - when the issue is too large, decisions are poorly conceived, or the approvals strategy is designed and implemented in a way that upsets people – and large angry public meetings happen as a result.

I have been called in early enough to see future angry public meetings in their infancy. Typically, there is tension within the project team, with various professionals uncertain about the approach to the public before the public is engaged. Often, there is not a lot of listening. There may be time or financial pressures to move a project forward. And, risks are taken when key public interactions are missed. When I see or hear that the planning process has a challenge and indecision, poor decision-making and tension spills out onto the street.

Why does tension based on team conflict or poor leadership evolve into an angry public meeting? In general, its is due to a lack of sensitivity, where project leaders and professionals, lacking emotional intelligence, are unaware of the "people" aspects of project management. It is also due to inexperience or the inability to see the big picture - knowing that it is ultimately the people who give permission. Short-term expedient actions might be the right decision at the time but, in the long term, they result in significantly more time and expense.

When I'm asked to join project team meetings as a facilitator, I watch for 'group think' within the team as a potential reason why the team may not be seeing how the public is responding to their project or plan. In this case, 'group think' is a structural problem within the project team and one of the causes of people becoming angry. Paraphrased here, Doyle and Straus[101], citing the psychologist Irvine L Janis, list eight signs of group think. (See Figure 2 - Eight Signs of Group Think)

Sometimes the circumstances and social environment mean that the project proponent cannot avoid an angry meeting. In a democracy, tough decisions are sometimes necessary which don't sit well with a large number of people, who often don't see the big picture or understand that their withdrawal of permission will result in harm for someone else.

Unfortunately, I have facilitated meetings in a few communities where residents could be classified as self-righteous, ideological fundamentalist, arrogant complainers. As privileged residents, they are used to getting their way and have little concern for the larger public interest in a matter. At times, their concerns are deeply rooted in prejudice against a racial group or financially weak people in our society, even though they espouse compassion for people in poverty and need.

---

101 Doyle and Straus, op cit, ppgs, 168 to 170

	Figure 2 Eight Signs of Group Think
1.	The group believes they can do anything they want because 'we believe in the right things and we are all good people and well meaning and our decision will be right'.
2.	The group is insular and isolated from a range of opinions – they are only receiving information from people whose views are similar to theirs.
3.	The group is homogeneous and they stereotype the opposition.
4.	Mutual trust occurring in the group and their feelings of belonging trump the airing of alternative views and potential alternative decisions.
5.	The group has developed a conformity of beliefs such that people who believe otherwise are seen as disruptive.
6.	Members of the group are too eager to concur. This means that those who are silent are not asked for their views. The group doesn't ask them for their views because they assume they concur with the majority opinion.
7.	Time constraints (or cost or political or other constraints) are pressuring a group into deciding.
8.	A group leader, perhaps the senior client, is making the decisions and there is an unspoken pact to not challenge the leader.

For example, I have facilitated meetings where the community is protesting group homes, low-income housing or new places of worship being proposed by a specific minority, cultural or racial group. In other instances, the community has either got the facts wrong or choose to ignore acceptable public mores.

These are some meetings that I enjoy facilitating. While I don't and can't take a position, I can see representatives of an agency, government department or a private corporation advocating a positive social change. They admirably work past the local public challenges to seek approval for a project that will ultimately benefit the greater good or people who don't have a voice.

In other instances, the community has a perfect right to be angry. I'm indebted to Suzanne Ghais, for pointing out late in the editing stage of this book, the important work of Lawrence Susskind and Patrick Field[102]. As cited earlier, the authors examine effective ways (and many not so effective ways) of interacting with the public based on case studies and a comprehensive analysis of why the public becomes angry. While there is a good deal of overlap with the observations I make, I've taken care to add their insight where it enriches the practice of avoiding angry meetings and managing the public process where these meetings are inevitable. Susskind and Field make the salient observation that the public may be mislead or harmed by business and government leaders. They ask: "Wouldn't you be angry if you had been hurt, mislead, or threatened?"[103]

It is not always the case that an angry public meeting should be avoided at all costs. In fact, there are times when such a meeting is exactly what is needed or wanted. For example: 1) a project team that actually needs media and political attention focused on a problem that is not having political resolution; 2) where matters need to be drawn to a head; 3) where a public group is on the wrong side of an issue, such as opposing homeless shelters, requiring both sides to "have it out"; 4) to shine a light on politicians manipulating the public to win political brownie points.

While it may seem odd, I have had a few clients who actually want to have a large, angry meeting. For one such meeting, my clients insisted on doing exactly the opposite of what I was suggesting during preparation. They were purposely aggressive and disrespectful of public questions all evening, which created a lot of grandstanding and resulted in media attention. Sitting as a panel, a practice which I discourage, they set up the meeting venue to create a show.

At the end of a very long night when I thought I could bring the meeting to an end, my clients insisted on continuing. I later learned the client actually agreed with most members of the public. But they were forced to have the meeting by

---

102 Susskind and Field, ibid.
103 Susskind and Field, ibid; p 1

Who are these people and why are they yelling at me? | 77

senior decision-makers. And, they were counting on public anger and media attention in order to focus internal blame, resulting in political heat being directed back toward senior decision-makers.

In most cases, the art and science of managing potentially large, angry public meetings begins with taking steps to avoid these meetings in the first place. The question is how? When you've had an opportunity to assess why programs and projects have gotten so messed up as much as I have, you are able to diagnose the difference between well-managed public processes and messy, rancorous procedures. It begins with an understanding of 'what is on the mind of the public?'

Hierarchy of Public Emotion

I've been involved with the approval, permitting and construction of hundreds of projects. The short list includes: landfills, aggregate pits, new highways, oil pipelines, water and waste water plants and homeless shelters. Whether the projects are in their approval stage or construction stage, I've learned there is a hierarchy of public awareness levels and emotions to watch for. Knowing where the public is at helps to scope out whether you need a more traditional public consultation and engagement process or whether we are going to be faced with public anger or civil disobedience.

To understand the hierarchy, you need to consider three questions.

First, are members of the public aware of the program, proposal, project? Additional questions include: Who is aware? How are they aware? Are small groups aware or is everyone aware?

I'm always a bit surprised when we announce a potentially contentious project affecting a local community and there's not a peep of concern. But it happens. For example, we once initiated a public consultation project in advance of the Windsor-Detroit Ambassador Bridge Expansion, where changes required a separate parking area for hundreds of trucks. The proposed parking location was on the Canadian side in an urban area because there was no other convenient vacant land. Land had to be expropriated and people would have to be removed from their homes. Whether the public knew the implications or not, I knew this requirement could be highly disruptive. Notices of a Public Information Open House located at a local school went out. Very few people attended. The local community was working class, many residents were tenants and few had ever been involved in civic matters. The lack of attendance was due to an attitude that 'we'll have no say, so why bother'.

As a second example involved a different client proposing a very large 2400-mm (2.4 metres or 8 foot) diameter water pipeline through a community. The Durham West route outside of Toronto went through a well-established neighbourhood. Roads, parks and sidewalks would be disrupted for the duration of construction. In this instance, the water would serve people in York Region to the north of Toronto. York Region is a completely different community so there was no 'public good' benefit for local residents to put up with the disruption. Again, we held a Public Open House and few people attended.

Over the years I've had great clients. In both instances I pointed out that the lack of attendance should not be seen as a sign that they could anticipate smooth approvals and construction. I suggested that it had to be up to the client to 'stir things up'. For a public consultation practitioner, suggesting to a client that you be paid as an *agent provocateur* could only go one of two ways. First, you're fired. Or second, the client hopes you know what you are doing and they take a risk. Fortunately, we had two clients who were gifted strategic thinkers and we got the nod to start going door to door. At the end of the day, members of the public became aware of the project. They also became aware that the proponent cared enough about potential impacts on the local community that they would go to individual homes to engage the community.

The second question is, what are the characteristics of their awareness?

Whatever stage a project is in, we are trying to determine the level of public emotion. For projects in the approval stage we are trying to understand what's going on in the community. Are community responses approaching the threshold where people will become angry? We look at matters such as the history of how the community has responded to other projects or any social justice issues the community may perceive. For projects under construction its more of understanding the emotions leading up to a complaint. I've had colleagues suggest that if you want to evaluate communications and consultation success for a construction project you count complaints. In my opinion, counting complaints is tantamount to measuring failure. Good project managers avoid complaints.

Who are these people and why are they yelling at me? | 79

We use the following public emotions awareness continuum that helps us to measure where the public is. Figure 3 depicts the continuum. Effectively, how people respond to information about change falls somewhere along the continuum. If they are on the 'Thrilled to Curious' part of the continuum the likelihood of an angry public meeting is reduced. If they are on the 'Inconvenienced to Outraged' part of the continuum, the likelihood that there will be an angry meeting will be higher. Where people are on the continuum can be measured through community surveys.

The third question involves understanding how the public is communicating their emotions?

For some projects we will do public polling in the community to measure just how they are responding as a way of getting advance notice. For the expansion of the Lakeview Wastewater Treatment Facility (renamed in 2007 as the G. E. Booth Wastewater Treatment Facility), in the Region of Peel outside of Toronto we completed seven years of community-wide surveys as part of the "Clear Scents" communication and consultation program. The expansion involved a large sewage treatment plant that in the eyes of the community was odorous. The expansion and upgrades would solve most of the odour issues but, we had to get the construction right. We wanted to measure how the construction project was performing through the eyes of the community. While we were monitoring construction effects, e.g. trucks, dust, traffic and noise our main measure was the response to odour.

So, we measured[104] the following indicators of either supportive or complaining behaviours. Figure 4 – Measuring Public Response, shows the community indicators we measured. For example, how significant was the effect the community was experiencing? How often were they experiencing an effect? And, when the data is analysed, what is the public emotion level in the community.

---

104 Findings of the Clear Scents Survey, Region of Peel, Hardy Stevenson and Associates Limited, 2004

Figure 3 Emotional Awareness Continuum					
When hearing about a proposed project are people….?					
Thrilled	Delighted	Supportive	Pleased	Interested	Curious
ACTION: Monitor but no action required.					
Inconvenienced	Bothered	Disgruntled	Annoyed	Aggravated	Outraged
ACTION: Prepare for potential public emotional response.					

1. Are people aware that construction is going on?
2. Are they experiencing odour?
3. If they are aware, what is the characteristic of the awareness?
4. If they have concerns toward having a negative emotional response, how significant is and what is the frequency of the response?

Figure 4 Measuring Public Response		
Measures of Significance		**Measures of Frequency**
Mildly annoyed and do nothing		Rarely notice
Talked to a neighbour		Occasionally
Phoned in a complaint		Sometimes
Written complaint	**Cross Tabulation of Responses**	Often
Phoned a politician		Very Often
Pushed regulators		
Attended a public meeting		
Spoke at a public meeting		
Started an opposition group		

Who are these people and why are they yelling at me? | 81

Seven Principles for Building Trust and Credibility

Susskind and Field define trust from four perspectives:

Economists view. 'A rational individual determines that sufficient benefits will flow from cooperation so that the individual will adopt a cooperative pattern of behavior toward another in exchange for reciprocity.'

Sociologists view. 'Behaviors that allow individuals to interact in a cooperative, reciprocal fashion in order to supply material wants, meet social needs such as companionship and status, and establish an individual identity in a larger society.'

Psychologist view. 'An expectation of benign or favourable intent by another actor based on previous experiences with parents, siblings and peers.'

Common Sense View. 'People with a common-sense notion tied to honest, reciprocity and reputation. Trust involves predictability, consistency and forgiveness. It allows room for mistakes.'[105]

For the Clear Scents process we built trust and credibility by using an additional set of principles that we formulated based on polling completed by Environics Research.[106]

First principle: Focus communications on the similarity of 'our' values [107](project team staff values and the public's values) instead of focusing on educating the public about our actions.

In theory, trust rises when the public knows the project team thinks like they do when team members are making decisions, in this case, about odour control. Trust and confidence decline if the public perceives that values leading to economic, engineering or political solutions to control odour are going to ultimately 'trump' their interests for quality of life. More information is not

---

105 Susskind and Field, op cit pgs. 79, 80
106 https://environicsresearch.com/
107 Susskind and Field op cit pgs. 154,155

necessarily going to deliver the benefit. In the worst instances it may function to create more anxiety.

For the Clear Scents program, the reality was, Peel Region staff the public would be talking to were living in the same communities as the public and cared for their families and neighbours the same way members of the public do. The proponent cared for their quality of life the same way they do.

We felt that only providing the public with more information about the project and odour and what Peel Region staff was going to do to address odour is not likely to deliver the increased confidence we were looking for. We decided to take actions and provide information that also allowed the public to understand the proponent's values and communicate the values of the project team.

For most of the projects I've worked on, groups will bring interests to the conflict. As a facilitator I'm careful to observe where the conflict is occurring: Is its conflicting interests or conflicting values. Susskind and Field note the difference between 'interests' and 'values' within public debate. Citing William Ury[108] they state, 'interests' are needs, desires, concerns and fears – the things one cares about or wants. They underlie people's positions – the tangible items they say they want. Interests explain the positions that people take in any negotiation.

I find that in the public setting, interests being articulated tend to be local and tangible. Whereas, for project team members, values are broad and deep. Project teams may not agree with the public about their interests but fully agree with them on their values. Using the example of childhood vaccinations, we can't agree with your interest in not having your child vaccinated, but we can agree with you on the value of having the best health for our children.

Fundamental value disputes point to differences in moral world view. Citing Christopher Moore, they state, "Values disputes focus on such issues as guilt and innocence, what norms should prevail in a social relationship, what facts should be considered valid, what beliefs are correct, who merits what or what principles should guide decision making."[109] In summary they state, "values involve

---

108 William L. Ury, Jeanne, M. Brett, and Stephen B. Goldberg, Getting Disputes Resolved, Cambridge Mass: Project on Negotiation Books, 1993

109 Christopher Moore, The Mediation Process, San Francisco: Jossey Bass, 1986

strongly held personal beliefs, moral and ethical principles, basic legal rights, and more generally, idealized views of the world. While interests are about what we want, values are about what we care about and what we stand for."[110]

In support of this first principle, "a reference to common values can alter adversarial relations by validating the core identify of others who value those same principles."[111]

Second principle: Focus communication and public engagement efforts on the general public, and those who have complained, not groups organized to oppose.

Before the project team started the communications and public engagement program, the general public in the vicinity of the G. E. Booth Plant were complaining about odour along with members of some ratepayer groups. Many members of the public were not complaining. Both of these groups (those who complained and those who had not) were open-minded and amenable to dialogue. Our research indicated that they were waiting to be asked to provide their opinion and they wanted to assist with finding a solution. These were the groups we focused on as a place to establish dialogue.

At the time the project team did not have strong vocal environmental or third-party stakeholders involved in the issue or expressing opposition. We concluded that it would be difficult and perhaps impossible to expect to engage in meaningful dialogue with these groups as their threshold for entering into meaningful dialogue would be higher than the project teams would ever be. So, the second principle involved 'triaging' who the project team would focus their communications and public engagement efforts on.

Third principle: Focus on building trust and confidence.

Given that the G. E. Booth plant is one of Canada's largest waste water treatment plants, the real or perceived odour problems would not be addressed overnight. The project team needed to focus its efforts on trust and confidence building for the long term. This meant that the team wanted local residents to

---

110 Susskind and Field, ibid; 154, 155
111 Susskind and Field ibid; 165

accept that interim solutions would be okay for the short term. And, the project team wanted them to trust that the team was advocating long-term solutions for them.

This aspect of trust and confidence building had several characteristics that drove communications and public engagement activities:

It would be important for the public to understand that project team members were technically and scientifically competent. We hoped they would trust the project team to make the right "what" decision. (e. g. "…we have come to know the staff and consultants at the G. E. Booth waste water treatment plant. They have engineering and technical competence and integrity and we trust them to make the right decisions…". We understood that public would want to have an oversight role. And, we welcomed this.

It would also be important for the public to accept the 'process' of resolving odour control issues in a trustworthy and credible manner. For many of our projects, accepting the 'process' is important, particularly if the resolution of the issue will be complex, and beyond short-term solutions. We wanted the public to understand that even though the G. E. Booth waste water treatment staff and consultants may not know what solutions are best today, they can trust the process for making the right "how" decisions about odour control.

We wanted the public to see that Region of Peel staff and expert consultants are trained and competent to make decisions. Particularly if they know the experts share their values, (eg. "…we know you will make the right decisions…you are balancing risks and benefits the same way we would…you are paying attention to our quality of life…".

The project team knew that trust would break down if the public felt the experts are compromising their professional opinion to satisfy one particular interest.

Fourth principle: Focus on process over substance.

This principle held that it would be more important for local residents to buy into the process of finding a solution than to accept the details of possible solutions. The project team felt that it was important for the public to feel that decision making processes were fair. Perceptions of fairness would dramatically influence public acceptance of odour control solutions. It was important for the public to see that staff and consultants associated with the G. E. Booth Plant also shared their value for a fair process.

Fifth principle: Perceived benefits matter.

The project team concluded that, if the public accepts that activities toward finding a solution would provide benefits to them or their neighbours in terms of cleaner air and less odour, they would be normally willing to accept short-term inconvenience. Furthermore, they would be willing to participate in a public consultation process involving their time commitment.

Sixth principle: Reinforce the need to make a decision.

In general, the Canadian public, and I expect members of the public around the world, are reluctant to make tough decisions. Given this we felt that it was important for Peel Region, the proponent and plant owner, to stress that the odour problem was not going to go away even though a lot could be done to reduce the odour problem. We needed to champion the position that the intensity of the odours will not go on any longer if solutions could be found through the study. The project team knew that once solutions were found, the climate needed to be created for making a decision.

Seventh principle: Comparative solutions.

This approach to trust and credibility building has three aspects. First, it is appropriate to go out to the public with some solutions in mind – perhaps a preferred solution. They generally do not trust organizations that say they are starting from a clean slate. It is most important to have the public understand that the motivation of the proponent and project team is to find a solution. Second, people will accept incremental solutions, if they are steps in the right direction toward an ultimate solution. Third and most importantly, the project team needed to communicate that there is no 'best' solution to odour control. There are only choices among 'better' solutions.

Keeping these seven principles in mind for any policy, program or project requiring public support will better equip proponents to building trust and confidence and avoid an angry public meeting. Implementing the three core dimensions of building trust and confidence involves: 1) our actions; 2) the public's perceptions of our actions; and, 3) the characteristics of trust and credibility that our actions create.

As a facilitator, I had the good fortune to work with some of Canada's finest water and waste water engineers and construction contractors. For a construction project of this size we were pleased to find there were few to no complaints and a high amount of community satisfaction. To this day, the Region of Peel works, engineering and communications staff continue to innovate and hold the spot of being among Canada's best.

In the following chapters, I present key lessons for building public support and ultimately achieving public accolades. These measures are further divided into distinct sets of actions that should occur: 1) before an organization seeks public approval; 2) while the organization is seeking approval; and, 3) staying the course and bringing a public issue to some form of resolution.

Investing in the Bank of Trust and Credibility

In April 2000, I was living in a community close to Lake Ontario, in a Toronto suburb called Guildwood. It was a lovely spring day. As I was outside doing yard work, I remember looking to the east toward another lakeside community called West Hill and saw a huge plume of black smoke. Being ever curious, I grabbed my bike and headed over to see what was going on.

West Hill had grown up around an industrial area of chemical companies and manufacturing, notably U.S.E. Hickson Products and Rohm and Haas Canada LP. The Hickson plant was in flames[112]. By the time I arrived, it was a five-alarm fire, sending plumes of black smoke over Lake Ontario. Fortunately, the wind was directing the smoke away from one thousand residents living nearby. Some homes were evacuated, but no one was hurt, although emergency responders were well prepared for a full-scale community evacuation.

The local news commented on the fire[113], saying "The Hickson factory, which made protective materials such as wood preservatives, cement sealers and

---

112 There was a second fire in 2003. http://www.insidetoronto.com/news-story/53389-sunday-blaze-at-fparticipanty-posed-no-risk-to-residents/

113 http://www.insidetoronto.com/news-story/28276-west-hill-caer-siren-to-sound-on-sept-25/

vehicle undercoating, had been there nine years. After the fire, many didn't want it as a neighbour."

Following another chemical-type explosion, now known as the Sunrise Propane Explosion, which occurred in the Downsview area of Toronto many years later, the media went back to community leaders who had experienced the Hickson Products fire, and reported as follows:

"Don York, president of the Manse Valley Community Association (local West Hill Community Association) said he thought any post-Downsview concern in his neighbourhood would quickly fade. Though he worries about the long-term effects of living with emissions - the community has lost some pollution-filtering trees to construction and will be losing more - York sits on the Toronto East CAER (Community Awareness and Emergency Response) Community Advisory Panel and said he's quite confident the area won't see another major incident like the fire at Hickson (now rebuilt and operating as Henry Company Canada Inc.). 'CAER members the panel meets with have always been open and honest,' York said, adding if a resident smells something strange, the companies investigate. 'They react very, very quickly.'"

How did the companies earn such accolades and avoid an angry, public meeting?

The reporter noted, Rohm and Haas, across the railway tracks at the south end of Manse Road, was also caught up in the emergency response. The company, which makes emulsions for latex paints and works with acrylonitrile, a dangerous chemical with some of the properties of cyanide, participates in the area's Manse Valley Fun Days and regularly sends its representatives out to the community, knocking on doors to inform new neighbours of their presence. "We do point out that we use chemicals, and that chemicals can have an adverse effect," said Rohm and Haas President Roger Hayward, adding that, no matter how comprehensive any plant's safety procedures are, warning sirens are a sound practice. "They're our equivalent of a smoke detector for the community." [114]

While there was concern about the fire from the local residents, both plants, Rohm and Haas and U.S.E. Hickson Products were back up and operating in

---

114 http://www.insidetoronto.com/news-story/28276-west-hill-caer-siren-to-sound-on-sept-25/

short order, without any public inquiry or massive protest to shut them down. They continue to operate peacefully as community neighbours to this day.

Its interesting to contrast the U.S.E. Hickson Products and Rohm and Haas experience with an issue that concerned another company, GE Hitachi Nuclear Energy Inc. located in a different Toronto neighbourhood. GE Hitachi was a uranium processing plant that operated in the Lansdowne and Dupont area of Toronto for fifty years.

The company sought and received renewal of their Canadian Nuclear Safety Commission (CNSC) license in 2010. Apparently, the license renewal notice alerted the local community to the fact that a plant was processing and shipping nuclear material.

A first community fact-finding meeting was held in November 2012. As is usual in Toronto, the panel of experts selected by the community consisted of people who were on record as opposing anything nuclear. The community became concerned. Over the next year, the issue escalated to the point where anarchists became involved, hijacking the community process.

*The former GE-Hitachi plant at 1025 Lansdowne Avenue.
Photo from Google Street View.*

Chris Riddell of the Torontoist[115] wrote, "Only recently has this operation come under scrutiny from neighbours, thanks to Zack Ruiter, a 29-year-old Trent University graduate and anti-nuclear activist, who had previously protested another GE-Hitachi plant located in Peterborough."

Niamh Scallan, a staff reporter with the Toronto Star wrote[116] as follows:

"West-end residents are looking for answers after they discovered that an unassuming building on Lansdowne Ave. is actually a nuclear facility licensed to produce nearly 2,000 tonnes of radioactive uranium dioxide pellets each year."

"The General Electric-Hitachi plant has been processing natural uranium powder into centimeter-long pellets that are assembled into fuel bundles elsewhere for Canada's nuclear participants since 1965. The shocking thing is that they can be there for so long and keep things so quiet," said area resident Dawn Withers.

"GE Canada spokeswoman Kim Warburton said the plant handles only natural uranium which is 'not dangerous' compared to its enriched counterpart. She said the company's sign is clearly visible. "GE-Hitachi is a nuclear business . . . it's on our website."

"In 2011, the Canadian Nuclear Safety Commission granted the GE-Hitachi facilities in Toronto and Peterborough a 10-year renewed license. As part of the process, the company testified in Ottawa that it had improved its public consultation process and made an effort to keep nearby residents informed.

"An operation that for decades has quietly shuttled radioactive material in and out of Toronto, GE-Hitachi's Lansdowne operation is now under the microscope as the number of residents set to attend the Nov. 15 community meeting — coordinated through a Facebook event — continues to swell."

"No matter how safe they say their production at their plant, there are risks," said Withers. "There are risks and nobody knew."

---

115 http://torontoist.com/2012/11/should-we-worry-about-lansdownes-radiation-station/

116 http://www.thestar.com/news/gta/2012/11/08/westend_toronto_residents_shocked_by_local_uranium_facility.html

Why is it that two chemical plants continue to have community support after a serious fire and partial community evacuation, while a plant producing nuclear fuel pellets loses the support of the community after fifty years of peaceful operation?

It all comes down knowing your community, being a good neighbour and maintaining a healthy account in "the bank of community trust and credibility".

Rohm and Haas had been building its community bank balance for many years. Everyone in the community knew who worked at the plant and the values they held. The company's president until 2006 was Roger Hayward, a PhD and chemist[117] who served as District Governor for Rotary International and was also on the Board of the Canadian Chemical Producers Association. Hayward was awarded the Governor General's Caring Canadian Award for his many years of community service.

The community knew who the president of the company was, what the company did and what the company stood for. Rohm and Haas had been active in supporting local school sports teams for a generation. They sponsored a community bus for disabled residents and, every time a local fundraising event was looking for a material or financial contribution, they were always there.

Like a bank account, Rohm and Haas had built up a high reserve of community support. True, when a neighbouring company experienced a chemical fire, there was a draw down for both companies, but it was not significant enough for Rohm and Haas to lose community support and acceptance.

For GE Hitachi, the challenge was not simply the fact that they were dealing with nuclear material. Cameco Corporation processes and refines uranium in Blind River. This facility and their Port Hope, Ontario plant has an excellent relationship with the local community. Indeed, whenever Cameco is challenged by outside activists, the company can always count on its communities to side with them and support their operations as good corporate citizens.

The challenges for GE Hitachi were: no community presence, a lack of transparency and a low or zero balance in the bank of credibility. Whereas Cameco had

---

117 http://www.clubrunner.ca/zonedata/22/html/756/WhitePages%2008-08-2009.pdf

(intentionally or not) built up a bank of community credibility from which to draw when needed, GE Hitachi found itself in the crosshairs with little or no trust and credibility to draw from when local activists came calling.

In order to maximize the chance of avoiding angry public meetings, it is imperative for companies, agencies and governments to be aware of their balance in the bank of community credibility. If the balance is low, they need to take steps to reach out to the community and be transparent about their operations and the associated risks. In this way, they will earn the confidence of the community, and hopefully not find themselves in the position of having to draw down on their social capital.

After the community issues arose in 2012, GE Hitachi formed a community committee and increased community outreach and communications. BWXT Nuclear Energy Canada Inc acquired GE Hitachi Nuclear Energy Canada Inc in December 2016. BWXT is continuing a strong commitment to involve the community and is transparent in terms of disclosure. The company has an impressive list of volunteer activities and they have a Community Liaison Committee,[118] a Public Disclosure Protocol and Indigenous outreach activities.

Two principles identified by Susskind and Field can be applied to guide how to build up the bank balance: 1) build a long-term relationship with the community and stakeholders, and 2) say what you mean and mean what you say. They state, "We should never make promises we do not intend to keep. Nor should we ask for commitments we know that others will be unable to honor."[119]

In summary, it is important to do a check on your balance in the bank of community trust and credibility. If the balance is nonexistent or low, you probably have some work to do by investing in the bank of community trust and credibility and build those long-term relationships before seeking a complex and potentially controversial public approval. Maintaining a positive balance in bank of community credibility is important for avoiding angry, public meetings.

---

118 www.bwxt.com/bwxt-nec/community/clc-committee
119 Susskind and Field pgs 40 and 41

Doing Your Homework

The first time that a project or plan proponent learns about who the audience is should not be when they are standing in front of them during an angry, public meeting.

I was asked to facilitate a small meeting for a nuclear utility over an operations problem that had caught the attention of the local community. The issue involved minor leaks of radioactivity that unfortunately indicated some larger management problems. The utility's failure to deal with the problem resulted in a need to consult with the community about a range of possible solutions.

The consultants hired by the nuclear utility, comprised of top Canadian health physicists and nuclear engineers (mostly PhDs). During the public meeting, they requested most of the time on the agenda to present a primer on nuclear energy, state why, in their view, the problem is minor, and why the public should accept their preferred solution.

The health physicist's presentation was long and allowed no time for questions. I could see members of the public grow increasingly angry over their inability to ask questions, provide comments or share their ideas about alternatives. I interrupted the scientist's presentation and pointed out that the public needed an opportunity to speak. After a brief and testy sidebar exchange between us, he reluctantly agreed to stop his presentation and take a comment or two. However, he firmly believed that, if the public didn't understand the basic concepts, they would not be able to provide the right comments.

The first question from the public was as follows: "…wouldn't it have been better to use a 't' test over 'lambda' when searching for the statistical presence of beryllium?" The second question was: "…what research protocols were used to assure yourself that the results were statistically reliable and not a matter of chance?" At that point, the scientist and the client asked to take a break. I was hauled into an office to explain who these people were and why they were asking such in-depth and complicated questions.

My client wanted to explain neutrons, electrons and other very simple concepts, hoping to keep the conversation with the public at that level. He asked me, "Don't they know who we are?" I responded, "Do you know who they are?" In fact, two of the local citizens were university professors with PhD degrees in the sciences. All of the residents had a minimum of a bachelor's degree, with basic minimum high school physics and chemistry courses under their belts. More importantly, several members of the public had read the three hundred-page technical reports handed out to them a week before the meeting.

The consultants had been prepared to present technical and scientific facts, but had done no preparatory research about the audience. Nuclear host communities are typically very well informed about the technical and scientific aspects of nuclear energy. Workers at their local plant are their neighbours, and local colleges and universities train students for this vocation. And, a few local people have been posing tough questions for many years, which has the effect of sharpening the minds of people in the community.

The same goes for people in communities in the vicinity of chemical plants, biomass facilities, hospitals, landfills, aggregate pits and other infrastructure facilities. They often have a high level of technical and scientific understanding. This is particularly true in Canada, where the percentage of residents with university and graduate degrees is high.

Other communities may be quite different. It should be no surprise that farming communities have specialized knowledge about impacts on agriculture. Yet change is happening in rural settings, as baby boomers with more resources and university educations are moving to rural areas of Ontario. Alternatively, there are residents in certain communities who have little information and perhaps have language difficulties, meaning that they are unable to grasp technical or scientific data.

The moral of the story: residents involved in community issues are often well educated, articulate, and sophisticated; they know how to do research and they know how to ask the right questions; and they don't appreciate being talked down to. These are the people I will often hear from when I facilitate angry public meetings.

Underestimating your audience can be the kiss of death. So, it is important to understand who the community is before planning to meet with them. I will discuss the issue of communicating science and technical matters in later sections of this book, as "internet experts" appearing at these meeting can be a particular challenge for facilitators.

When dialogue occurs between members of the public who have done their research and scientific and technical consultants, it can be wonderful and constructive. In contrast, when audience members don't have formal training, I can usually count on some residents passing themselves as authorities in the eyes of the community, which poses a problem when facilitating large angry public meetings because it confuses people. Knowing this, it helps to be prepared with a communications strategy in advance.

I have also facilitated meetings where members of specific cultural and language groups represented a large number of participants. To address this scenario, we include as part of our communications team, people who can translate questions and responses into Italian and Mandarin. There have also been many meetings where the majority of the attendees are seniors. Since baby boomers are aging and starting to lose their hearing, the act of listening and hearing needs to be emphasized.

In summary, the proponent speaking at a community meeting should learn about the community, its values and its aspirations well in advance, and scope the meeting accordingly. Doing your homework involves all disciplines on the project team, including those with expertise in the social sciences such as anthropology, sociology, economics, and philosophy. It can also involve special tools such as a Social Impact Analysis (SIA), a Community Impact Assessment (CIA) and a Stakeholder Sensitivity Analysis (SSA), which are discussed and presented in the Appendices.

Being Prepared to Discuss Ethics and Morality

In earlier sections I discussed some of the fundamental risk and rights issues that result in people showing up en masse in opposition. Their concerns may involve deep and difficult moral issues.

One thing that has always bothered me is how clients, be they companies, agencies or private citizens, back away when an angry member of the public makes a claim of being right because their actions are morally right. For example, 'I was able to ride my bike to the meeting so there's no moral basis for a new road'. People making these statements typically follow up this claim by accusing my clients of acting immorally, insisting that the moral high ground gives them rights that the other party, in their opinion, couldn't claim. The other party may be my client.

What my clients should be doing when encountering such a claim is to figure out where they stand in terms of their own moral position. If they conclude that they have a strong moral basis for their actions, then they should step up. If not, then they have a rocky road ahead.

Instead of backing away, both parties need to be circumspect and self-critical with respect to their own moral claims. They should be able and prepared to state clearly why they feel their actions have a solid moral grounding. Ideally, both parties should be brought together to examine the basis of each claim and work out whether one party actually has a compelling stronger claim.

Susskind and Field discuss the role of beliefs as a source of public anger stating, "arguments over principle are perhaps the most difficult to address…. People take their beliefs very seriously, and they want other to take them seriously as well.… Any attack on their fundamental beliefs will be seen by many groups as a direct and dangerous attack on the group itself. As we all know, some people are willing to die for their beliefs rather than be forced to compromise."[120] They suggest three ways of entering into the discussion: 1) acknowledge there are legitimate differences between you and those who oppose your ideas; 2) seek to understand the differences by entering into dialogue in a neutral setting; 3) seek outcomes that respect everyone's principles. While I agree, I recommend going deeper.

The examination of competing moral claims is ethics. Unfortunately, by the time all parties are at each other's throats, a dispassionate discussion of ethics is difficult. Moral assumptions underlie all public policy. For broad public policy issues where there is conflict, the conflict is at its heart a conflict involving competing moral claims.

Wise governments will call a halt and convene a commission, inquiry or special committee to sort out which moral claim should prevail. In Canada, administrative tribunals, essentially specialist courts, do a good job of hearing evidence,

---

120 Susskind and Field, op cit, p; 26 to 28

testing the public interest and sorting out these claims. Over the last few years, however, groups dissatisfied with their conclusions have successfully lobbied to get rid of these courts. (The respective emasculation and elimination of Canada's National Energy Board and the Ontario Municipal Board come to mind.)

Raising issues of morality in a corporate setting is difficult. Having corporations, governments, individuals and opposing organizations discussing ethics is much more difficult. But not impossible.

Early in my career in the late 1970s, our provincial electrical utility, Ontario Hydro, made the mistake of hiring six long-haired environmental activists from the Faculty of Environmental Studies at York University in Toronto. And, I happened to be one of those hired. It seems that the Chair of the utility had become impatient with people sitting in his office protesting a new 500kV high voltage transmission line. And, he heard that there was a Faculty in the same city that actually taught students environmental impact assessment (note – this is the 1970s). Perhaps they could inform the organization why people were fighting a transmission line, and do something about it.

Seeing women breastfeeding in his office was apparently the tipping point. The protesters pointed out that dropping a ruler on a map was not the best way to plan a transmission line route. The protection of farmland and the environment needed to be considered.

We were like kids in a candy shop, with a corporation of 30,000 employees to work with. My specialty was pointing out that the company needed to examine the morality of its actions. Only someone three months out of school would be cocky enough to suggest that they had a better idea of how to run the company than the directors, vice-presidents and senior staff of one of the world's largest electric utilities. It wasn't long before I became the problem.

"What do we do with a newly hired employee who is calling for us to examine the morality of our actions?" they asked. So, I got the call: "The Coordinator of the President and Chair's office wants to see you." Talk about a dry mouth and wobbly legs. Once in his office, I received a respectful cross-examination.

"What do you mean when you say that we need to do a better job in understanding the morality of our actions?" was one question he asked, to which I replied, "Well, from my perspective we are taking actions without having a good understanding of why. The moral and ethical underpinnings of energy decisions go deep. Most of what we are doing is, on the face of it, wise and right, but we are struggling to explain why."

"What do you suggest we do?" they asked. I replied, "We need to form a Social Responsibility Committee of the Board of Directors and have a thorough and deep discussion of issues facing us. And, we probably need to bring in people trained in philosophy, ethics, theology, as well as native shamans." Fully expecting to be fired, the response, to my astonishment was, "Make it happen." And I did.

As utility spokespeople, what we could do from that point on is to make decisions and articulate the moral basis of those decisions because they had been examined from a moral and ethical perspective. When someone presented a counter moral claim, there was no need to be defensive.

We knew the moral basis of our position, and we could state it clearly. With confidence, we could say, "Lets get together, role up our sleeves and sort out the competing moral claims relating to a particular public policy position." We sought people with opposing voices. And, in the early years, we learned that in a corporate setting, the philosophers and ethicists could help us think clearly. Not being afraid of the moral and ethical issues helped us to avoid angry meetings.

Our early work reached a pinnacle thanks to the activities of the Interfaith Panel on Public Awareness of Nuclear Issues (IPPANI).[121] Many of the faith groups were opposing nuclear energy, nuclear waste and nuclear weapons on moral grounds. In response, the nuclear industry said let's talk about the first two.[122]

IPPANI organized itself as a citizen jury, but a jury that drilled much deeper to understand the issues. The Panel's organizing committee brought together a broad range of faith groups, electric and nuclear utilities, anti-nuclear activists, pro-nuclear employees and policy makers. We had time to discuss risks, rights, truth, justice, sustainability, obligations to future generations and others as moral issues. Although the nuclear industry did not participate in the panel

---

121 IPPANI https://inis.iaea.org/collection/NCLCollectionStore/_Public/19/073/19073503.pdf

122 Canada is not a nuclear weapons state and the Canadian nuclear industry is not linked to this issue.

on nuclear weapons, at the end of the day, the report of the hearing panel was fair and well-received by all sides.

In terms of how all of this relates to an angry public meeting, I look for proponents being able to state: "We are confident of our decisions and actions. We've thought about the moral implications and believe that we are on solid ground. We are happy to have a dialogue with anyone with an opposing point of view."

How? The core of angry public meetings is usually a concern over some sort of change. The change is normally based on an agency, government or corporation pursuing their mission, i.e. providing electricity, housing the homeless, making a profit. Proponents of change need to be particularly clear that their mission almost always has a moral grounding. Using the example of the transmission line:

- Electricity is a public good.
- The source of the electricity is environmentally superior to other energy sources.
- The need for farmland is also a public good. Utilities can and would do a better job of finding environmentally acceptable transmission line routes.
- As a cheaper electricity source, getting the transmission line built would help millions of families.
- The utility is on solid moral ground advocating for the construction of a transmission line that has accounted for and avoided environmental impacts.

The ethical questions proponents and opponents need to ask are as follows:

- Is there a public good fundamental to the change? What is it?
- What are the competing moral claims? What is the basis for these claims?
- Are there risks? If so, would a reasonable person judge the risks to be acceptable?
- Are harms being created or avoided?
- Are residual harms after mitigation acceptable? To whom?

- Will future generations be impacted?
- In terms of environmental and social justice, is a harm or risk of harm sufficiently compelling that one voice, such as a rare and endangered species or marginalized individual, has a stronger moral claim than the broader society?
- If future generations had the information that all parties have today, would they judge that our actions are morally sound?

Since we don't know who the future generations will be, we have three scenarios to ponder. Firstly, people in the future will be vastly superior to today's generation (perhaps a society of saints and Nobel prizewinners?) In this case, a morally acceptable action would involve today's generation of lesser beings, minimizing risks and harms and spending great sums to protect future generation interests.

Secondly, people in the future will be a generation of misanthropes living in a world led by Hollywood reality TV types. Excuse me, worse. We would be foolish to waste money on minimizing risks and reducing harms, as they simply don't deserve our benevolence.

The third scenario is people in the future will be a generation of people just like us. Here, we would be on solid moral ground advocating that today's moral standards are a reasonable proxy for what could be an acceptable moral standard in the future. Personally, I lean to the third scenario.

If you've thought through your moral grounding, the moral positions held by alternative voices and made a choice, then you will be in a much better position to engage in dialogue with all parties and perhaps avoid an angry public meeting. I survived the trip to the Chairman's office and a Social Responsibility Committee of the Board was struck. Eight years later, I was the Coordinator of the President and Chairman's Office.

Using Common Sense

I have nothing against accountants – nothing, seriously. But it is a well-known fact that, when you put an accountant in change of a sensitive, social or environmental approval, the likelihood of public friction will increase. The focus becomes on dollars and the schedule, not on the people.

I can't count how many times I've been asked to facilitate an angry public meeting where the fundamental reason for the anger was that the proponent had not taken the time to listen. Variations on the same theme have involved proponents who are following a timeline where regulations don't call for engaging the public, so it doesn't happen. Or, there is a schedule or budget overly dictating how the proponent interacts with the public.

Common sense means that the accountant or engineer leading the approval needs to see the big picture. Forward progress toward project approval is understandable and necessary. But if the public sees that a project schedule or budget is over-riding their interest, they will be upset.

It is important to note the research of Susskind and Field on what they call the 'mutual-gains approach' and six principles for dealing more effectively with an angry public. Summarized here, they point out that the project manager interacting with a public already angry should:[123]

1. Acknowledge the concerns of the other side.
2. Encourage joint fact finding.
3. Offer contingent commitments to minimize impacts if they do occur; promise to compensate knowable but unintended impacts.
4. Accept responsibility, admit mistakes, and share power.
5. Act in a trustworthy fashion at all times.
6. Focus on building long-term relationships.

They state, "each of the six principles is related to and informs the others. Discounting one principle or another will likely lead to actions that contradict one another and exacerbate, rather than adequately address the public's anger."[124]

The success of public communications and engagement is just as important to the bottom line as engineering, scheduling and cost accounting. Few accountants have a ledger item stating, "cost of six-month delay due to protesters blocking construction crews". Even so, that's exactly what may happen in many projects.

---

[123] Susskind and Field, op cit; p. 13, 37
[124] Susskind and Field, ibid, p. 41

As facilitators, we prefer to be involved on the project team at the very beginning. When we are brought into the initial team meeting, I'm usually the only non-engineer and non-accountant. And I get the look that says, "Why are you here? Isn't your job to book meeting rooms and bring coffee and donuts from Tim Horton's?" Or, "Don't you do crowd control with the skill set of a professional wrestling referee?"

"We know when and how to engage the public. It's just an extra expense to have you on board."

My response to the project team is usually to tell them that their role is to do the easy stuff. They just have to work with numbers. My role involves the hard stuff – dealing with people. Although this attitude doesn't do much for building goodwill, at the end of the day public communications and engagement professionals will play their role in getting the project constructed on time and on-budget, often with public accolades.

To maintain common sense during the process, we will usually prepare a Public Engagement and Communications Plan. This will reflect, but not be driven by, the project schedule and budget. On numerous occasions, I've recommended that time be taken to expand some aspect of public consultation or engage with a particular group. Other times, I've suggested that a particular group is likely not interested and they probably don't need to be engaged, so the project can save some time and money.

The strategy and plan are part of big picture thinking about the policy or project. Sometimes, we will complete a Social Impact Assessment or a Stakeholder Sensitivity Analysis beforehand. These assessments provide us with great information about who wins, who loses, who benefits, who pays and who cares. All important questions to answer to avoid a large, angry public meeting.

Where engineering projects involve a "risk register", communications and public engagement risks are typically included. We ask the following questions:

- What are we trying to achieve?
- What does success look like?
- Which publics and stakeholders will be affected by the project?
- What are the issues that we can anticipate?

- What are the risks? Are particular risks more important than others?
- How do we avoid issues as the first priority? If they arise, how do we address them?
- How will we communicate and engage? Will the communications and engagement need to change over different parts of the approval or construction schedule?
- How does the public want to be engaged?
- Are we missing any stakeholders or members of the public?

This approach worked very well on a trunk sewer project in the West Vaughan area of York Region, Ontario, where a trunk sewer would open up many hectares of land for housing, employment lands and other urban uses. York Region has an intelligent and passionate environmental community. Residents had been successful in protesting and successfully lobbying for a conservation plan and a halt of urban development in a significant landform called the Oak Ridges Moraine. While the project lands discussed above were not in the Moraine, there was a chance that we could be caught up in the community's concerns about urban growth.

There were two other groups that surfaced as a result of our stakeholder sensitivity analysis. One was a group of residents who spoke Italian as a first language. Toronto has seen waves of people immigrating to the Vaughan area from around the world. Many Italian residents moved here as they gained wealth and purchased second and third homes.

A second group was public servant stakeholders. The trunk sewer would have to cross roads, provincial highways, regulated watercourses and rail lines. We knew that these people didn't come to work each day anticipating how to get a third party's trunk sewer approved. Their time was always tight and it would be difficult to get their attention, which could have resulted in the project approval delayed for a year.

We were fortunate to be working with two of the best engineers in the business: Shu He, Project Manager with the York Region and Don Cane, Project Manager with Hatch Engineering. Both individuals recognized the importance of getting the communications and engagement process right. Common sense meant that we had to develop a plan that would look at the project through

Who are these people and why are they yelling at me? | 103

a "sustainability lens". Most engineering projects conduct "value engineering" workshops designed to improve costs and schedules. We adapted this process by doing a sustainability assessment workshop, which was effective in pointing out how we could make the project more environmentally sustainable.[125]

Our second common sense move was to engage the Italian community. A newsletter and information materials were translated into Italian, so as to make the engagement process more inviting. A third common sense tactic involved giving regulatory stakeholders top priority. Where it has taken over a year to get their attention on other projects, I believe that engaging them early saved the project from lengthy delays.

As I've been involved with consulting and engaging the public for most of my career, I remember that the early days of public consultation and community engagement were overly characterized by confrontation. Project proponents in the 50's, 60's and 70s' generally didn't know how to consult the public and stakeholders. Or, they did it poorly. We often refer to a "decide, announce, defend" approach as typical of engagement at the time. Fortunately, common sense has prevailed over the years. Most well-financed and well-qualified professional teams have come to realize that community support is an important part of project management.

Many resident and environmental groups I work with have also realized that they can achieve better outcomes by sitting down and having dialogue with project proponents. Doing so creates less emotional drain and often can produce community benefits that they might otherwise not have achieved. The sort of confrontational politics that leads to pickets and protests, while effective from time to time, generally doesn't advance anyone's long term cause.

Preparing for the Unreachable Bar of Consensus

Achieving social license is not about achieving consensus. Yet, at some of the highest levels of government, that's what they are trying to achieve.

---

125 Hardy, D. "Sustainable Infrastructure, Implementing Sustainability Principles in a Wastewater Municipal Class Environmental Assessment", *Municipal World*, March 2014, Pgs. 7 - 10

I watched with interest Canada's Prime Minister Justin Trudeau digging a deep hole for himself over the construction of the Trans Mountain Pipeline, a project which underwent an environmental assessment and was approved. Bringing oil to Canada's British Columbia coast from the Province of Alberta, it was being opposed by the British Columbia government, which had no legal basis for opposing a nationally approved project.

A key problem faced by both the federal and provincial governments was that they both practice "identity politics", each drawing part of their power from people who were opposed to oil. Indeed, most of the opposition groups wanted the oil to be left in the ground, while the national public interest centred on exporting oil.

British Columbia Premier Ralph Horgan and Prime Minister Trudeau had nowhere to turn. Both wanting to satisfy opposition groups, they ideally desired some kind of consensus. Groups representing greens, local activists, Indigenous leaders and local municipalities would never agree. Consensus would be unreachable.

I recommend to my clients that they develop and stick to a strategy for addressing those people for whom the bar of consensus is higher than theirs will ever be. Reaching consensus is not about everyone agreeing, and it's definitely not about getting the loudest voices to agree with you. Even when you do want to listen to those with the loudest voices and address their concerns, as soon as you believe that you have reached agreement, another demand will be placed on the table. The question is why would a company[126] involved in public engagement related to oil even think about trying to reach consensus with a group dedicated to achieving their demise?

The strategy for addressing interest groups involves, at its heart, listening, but also the understanding that they do not necessarily represent the broader public interest. Pandering to more strident groups to determine if a consensus strategy can be found is akin to a cat chasing a laser beam. It will involve a lot of time, money and expenditure of political capital. At the end of the day, chasing

---

[126] As the pipeline was ultimately sold to the Federal Government, they find themselves faced with trying to reach consensus with those who will never agree.

Who are these people and why are they yelling at me? | 105

consensus with some groups won't work because the bar for reaching it with them will always be set higher.

When I'm facilitating an angry meeting, groups self-identify. The groups and individuals I'm referring to are often the loudest and most persistent voices, declaring, "You're not listening to us." Not all citizens groups, environmental groups or interest groups have the monopoly on wisdom or moral superiority. I have facilitated meetings where activist groups were opposed to public transit, new immigrants and people of certain faiths and ethnicities. In other meetings, groups were clearly working with the wrong set of facts. What my clients should be saying in response is, "We are listening, but we are not agreeing."

Needless to say, even thinking about trying to reach consensus with groups opposed to people of different skin colour, or blocking housing for the homeless is wrong. There are fundamental human rights issues at play. While these are probably the most extreme examples, there are many other issues where you would be wise to assume up front that you are not going to seek or get agreement. It isn't about isolating these groups. They still have a voice, but their forum is the media or the courts. Whether or not their opinions have weight can be decided through the electoral process or by a judicial decision.

One of our clients likes to triage issues in a smart way. Firstly, they ask, "Who will never agree?" Secondly, "Who will agree to learn the facts and either agree or disagree with the client's perspective on the basis of the facts?" Thirdly, "Who agrees?" Their public engagement efforts are strictly focused on the latter two groups.

Another challenge to reaching consensus is people in a meeting who believe that reaching consensus means reaching one hundred percent agreement. Or, having the audacity to believe that consensus means agreeing with them. Even if there's one loud voice left at the end of the meeting, people would argue that consensus has not been achieved. My view is that consensus is not about reaching complete agreement. It's about most people agreeing, with issues held by outlying voices explainable through facts.

What's important to know is that many issues, particularly those that are scientific or highly technical, can't be decided by a show of hands as a way of finding consensus. I would typically make sure that people know who is making the decision (normally government or a regulator) and what steps need to be taken or studies completed before a decision can be made.

In summary, a strategy for addressing the bar of consensus is required. Otherwise you find yourself in a meeting where the loudest, angriest voices demand that the only social license is the one that involves agreement with them.

Practicing Horizontal and Vertical Consultation

Horizontal and vertical consultation means consulting people, groups and agencies above and below where the client sits in the organizational chart and other organizations for whom the client relies. For example, vertical consultation may occur with senior regulators or junior staff. Horizontal consultation may occur with a broad cross section of people, regulators, agencies and stakeholders.

As both a facilitator and an urban planner, on some rare occasions I end up being both the presenter and facilitator. I don't like playing both roles at the same time because being an expert on one hand eliminates my ability to be a neutral facilitator on the other. It confuses people. In a public meeting where there are likely to be angry people, the chance of things going wrong increases. That's exactly what happened in a small town on the Niagara Peninsula in Ontario.

We had completed a study of future land uses in a particularly picturesque part of the town. I was on my feet in the process of presenting options. The audience was made up of the Chief Administrative Officer (CAO), my client (a department head), several politicians and about sixty residents with very long faces. About half way through my presentation, the CAO and my client left the meeting room. When they returned, the CAO was looking at me waving his hand sideways under his chin. In any language, that means "stop talking".

As a consultant, it's not unusual to get fired. You're often hired to take on difficult assignments that no one else wants. Occasionally, we are thrown into a jumble of thorny issues where there will be winners and losers. I always work hard to help my clients avoid being on the losing side. Frankly, I'd rather not be on the losing side either. Being fired at ten minutes into a presentation has got to be some sort of record. Why did it happen?

The next day, I called my client - in part to ask what happened, in part to see if they would be open to discussing the "getting paid" part of the assignment. Apparently, my client gave approval for my presentation without talking to the mayor, politicians or the CAO. Without my knowledge, the residents were complaining loudly and wanted nothing to happen in that part of town.

Making sure that the people above you are informed and that they give consent is an example of vertical consultation. It also extends to personnel below you in the organizational hierarchy, since these are the people who often will have responsibility for implementing the results of a decision. Sometimes the need to consult well with staff and internal stakeholders in an organization has more bearing on the outcome than consulting well with members of the public. Indeed, on occasion I've been hired to do internal corporate facilitation where corporate departments were at war with each other.

When scoping a consultation process, the following vertical consultation questions should be asked:

- Who above me and who below me (in the corporate or bureaucratic hierarchy) needs to be informed? When?
- Where is organizational buy-in required?
- Who is making the decision?
- Who needs to comment and who needs to give permission?
- Who needs to see and approve a presentation in advance?
- Who will implement the results of a decision and needs to have a smile on their face when you tell them what they are supposed to do?

There is also a need for horizontal consultation. Typically, a wide range of regulators, government departments, agencies, authorities and crown corporations will play a role in approving projects. While each will have an established commenting or approval role, I recommend developing and implementing an engagement process for them as well, particularly for complex and controversial projects. That way no one is left out, we've heard issues that they might have in advance, and we've given them a heads-up that we are going to need their attention.

In some cases, the regulator will simply listen and provide no comments. In others, they will be forthcoming about the issues they will be watching for and provide comments throughout the process.

Engaging these individuals in the way that they want to be engaged is important. The typical way of consulting horizontally is to strike a Stakeholder Advisory Committee. This group is limited to and includes people representing agencies and approval bodies. Where an environmental assessment study is being conducted, it's normal to meet several times at key benchmark stages.

I've had a few clients over the years ask why we need to engage the agencies. My response is as follows: "When do you want to hear the difficult questions? Now, when changes can be made, or after you've spent millions going down a path that may or may not be approved?" Neither the public nor interest groups are invited to sit on the Stakeholder Advisory Committee, as they will instead participate in a Community Advisory Group. However, I always inform the public that a Stakeholder Advisory Committee has been formed.

Staff representing agencies and approval bodies tend to clam up if they are mixed with the public. If members of the public are sitting at the same table, they will often ask how the agency is going to regulate the proponent well before that question is relevant. They will also push agency and approval body staff to regulate in a way that supports their interest. How and when the public engages with agencies and regulators is normally clearly defined by acts, laws and regulations. The public normally has ample time to provide input.

Getting the engagement process right for agencies and approval bodies is important. As in the public process, they are looking for integrity, transparency and competency. What's often missed is the human side of horizontal engagement. While their representatives have set parameters for what they can say because their authority is regulated, they are also human beings with families who live in communities, and they have personal points of view. If risk, health and rights issues are wrapped around a project, they will also be trying to draw conclusions about the right course of action based on their values.

Questions germane to a successful horizontal engagement include:

- What agencies, governments or regulators need to comment on the project or program?
- Are they approving or simply commenting?
- How do they want to be engaged?
- What are the key benchmarks that guide when engagement should occur?
- What information will they need, and when?

As a footnote to my experience of being fired during my presentation on future land uses in a Niagara Peninsula community, I was hired again by the same municipality several years later.

Personifying

This is one piece of advice that I always give to my staff and clients: they need to pay attention to their actions leading up to a meeting and the impressions the community has of them during a public meeting.

While people will normally try to understand what is being proposed through the information provided by a proponent or via the internet, it's the people associated with a project who make the biggest impression and convey the most information. People personify projects and give them an identity.

During one particularly difficult landfill project, the community saw my client and spokesperson for the project as being so untrustworthy that conflict was the only option. I ultimately fired the client. Consultants can tell the client they are no longer working for them. I've rarely done this. When I have, there was no other option.

For other projects, where the relationship between the community and the proponent was very bad before I got hired, I pleaded to start the project over so that we could get it right.

I pull my hair out when the spokesperson for a proponent at a meeting has no personality and struggles to make a cogent argument for why the project is worthy of community support. The public sees what I'm seeing in the first minute. I work hard for my pay cheque during those meetings.

In contrast to this scenario, we were hired to work with staff from the Portlands Energy Centre (PEC), a 550-megawatt natural gas electrical generating station on Toronto's waterfront, shortly after it had been approved and constructed. The project was located in an area that consistently elects left-leaning environmental advocates as their politicians. It wasn't surprising that the community strongly opposed the construction of the plant as well as any other form of energy that produced air emissions.

Upon being retained, I was struck by the high quality of the personnel at PEC. The original plant manager, Curtis Mahoney was one of the most forthright and honest clients with whom I'd had the pleasure to work. He approved a series of changes at the plant to make it one of the greenest in North America. In order to "walk to talk", Mahoney was famous for his marathon no-emission bikes ride to work. PEC staff were supported by strong and progressive directors from Ontario Power Generation and TransCanada Pipelines.

At PEC today, community engagement is a continuous process which includes a Community Ecological Committee (CEC), on-site environmental initiatives by environmental non-governmental organizations (ENGO's), and a "Doors Open" each year welcoming hundreds of residents to learn about the plant. All CEC records, including statistics on the plant's environmental performance, upsets and answers to community questions are posted on its website to insure transparency.

Residents came to know that PEC, as the only generator of electricity in Toronto, is also consistently achieving low air emissions. What is perhaps more important is that PEC staff are known to the community. Through their actions, the community knows that the plant staff care about their neighbours. They know that PEC staff pride themselves on producing power reliably and efficiently, doing so in a clean manner that meets or exceeds provincial environmental standards. The community trusts PEC for telling the truth, giving them unfiltered news – good and bad – and caring about their relationship.

Proponents need to be aware that projects have a personality. They need to understand what that personality is and that it needs to be earned, nurtured and truthful. Ideally, to avoid community anger the project should have a positive personality that the public can appreciate and relate to.

Who are these people and why are they yelling at me? | 111

Almost to a fault, the project teams I've worked with always want to do the right thing. Living in communities with their families, they recognize what it means for a community to be concerned about matters of health and the environment. I caution clients when, as technical experts, they tend to structure their communications around corporate speak and matters that they are professionally qualified to discuss. Sure, you need to share facts and get the message across, but what the community wants is to see and hear who the team really is.

I'm not suggesting manipulation, dishonesty or some contrived way of establishing a bond with the community. When you try to deceive people, things ultimately go wrong. Many years ago, I sat in on a Council meeting in Atikokan, Ontario to hear a presentation by a federal civil servant who, it seems, had never before left Ottawa, the nation's capitol.

Atikokan is a wonderful northern community that I grew to like over the years. Ontario is a very large province, with two time zones and different northern and southern cultures. Apparently, one of the civil servant's colleagues advised that the civil servant should drop the suit and tie and dress more like the locals when making his presentation in the Northwestern Ontario town. His colleagues said it would help him to establish rapport with the community.

The civil servant came to Town Council wearing cowboy boots and a Stetson western hat. As Atikokan councillors were being who they were, it wasn't long before they began referring to him as "Tex". As I expected, the civil servant who recommended this style of dress wasn't aware that the councillors were poking fun at him.

Telling the community who you are requires spokespeople and technical staff to engage the community - well in advance of tough decisions, and continuously thereafter. Community trust and credibility needs to be earned as discussed earlier.

When looking at the yourself and the project through the eyes of the community, questions to consider include:

- Who is speaking for the project, program or policy?
- What are the values shown by the project team to the community?

- Are the most technically competent people in front of the community?
- Can technical team members be trusted by the community?
- What is the persona of the project and your actions? "Sincere, honest, caring, competent" or "get an approval at any cost and be prepared to fight it out"?

Chapter 5:
Great Design: Implementing a Sound Community Engagement Process

Susskind and Field, raise the simple question: why should we care if people are angry? I'd add, and why should we design a sound community engagement process designed to successfully interact with the public. Writing from an American perspective, they observe two important outcomes of not adequately addressing the public's fears and anger:

"First, a continually angry public undermines American competitiveness in the international marketplace. That is, it can sap the productivity of corporations and government agencies who must spend inordinate amounts of time and human capital rehashing every action to defend each decision they make. Second, angry public contributes to the erosion of confidence in our basic institutions. When important decisions must be made, especially in times of emergency, no one will give the relevant decision maker the benefit of the doubt if the public's trust is eroded."[127]

"When anger is directed, in a blunderbuss fashion, at the way in which government operates, civil society quickly erodes."[128]

The following Engagement Framework developed by HSAL (see Figure 5 – HSAL Engagement Framework) helps to define how to best engage the public. Four different approaches can be considered and selected when designing and evaluating the engagement programs or processes. One or more desired

---

127 Susskind and Field, op cit; pg. 2
128 Susskind and Field, op cit; pg. 5

Figure 5 HSAL Engagement Framework

	Inform/Awareness	**Involve/Engagement**
Description	• Provide information to a community or stakeholder group to create awareness or share updates. • Communities absorb and retain information for possible involvement or action. • Communities acquire new information, provide input, and inform the entity sponsoring the engagement.	• Communities exchange information and ask questions • The engagement sponsor establishes the initial terms of the involvement/ engagement • The clients' and communities' decisions are informed depending on information shared.
Outcome	• Well-informed individuals/ communities and increased community awareness of key issues. • Client/ proponent receives informed input.	• The proponent/ client and the communities have gained new insight from one another. • Approved plan/ study/ program /project with support from the communities.
Client/ Proponent Relationship with Public/ Stakeholder	"We will provide information and support."	"We need to understand your views and seek to inform our decisions based on the input received."
Communication	One-way	Two-way

Who are these people and why are they yelling at me? | 115

laborate/ Empowerment	Partner/ Formal Relationship
ommunities participate in collaborative ction to achieve a mutual solution to a oal. oles and responsibilities are established y both the client and the communities. he client may or may not be the convener. ommunities may empower others, lentify community needs and aspirations, nd take action to implement change here necessary.	• Both the proponent/ client and communities exercise equal power and/or authority. • The proponent/ client and communities work together to make change happen and build capacity. • Both engage in joint-learning, decision-making and actions. • The proponent/ client and communities develop formal long-term relationship where each party is responsible and may bring resources.
he proponent/ client and communities' utual goals are attained. ollaboratively developed solutions.	• Partnerships are developed. • Formal agreements. • Joint action by both parties.
will work jointly with you to derive a ually acceptable solution."	"We share equal authority and decision-making toward a common goal and agree to work as partners."
versational	Consent/agreement based

approaches are selected in the design stage based on the engagement goal(s). In the evaluation stage, the success of the program or process is assessed against the outcome(s) of the chosen approach(es).

The involvement of the public and stakeholders in designing the engagement programs or processes is vital to ensuring success and buy-in. Their involvement in designing the evaluation adds to the evaluation process.

The HSAL Engagement Framework is based on the International Association for Public Participation's (IAP2) Spectrum of Public Participation (see Figure 6)[129] and HSAL research.

The IAP2's Spectrum of Public Participation is another tool to help engagement practitioners define the public's role in any engagement processes. Although the IAP2 Spectrum is used internationally by engagement practitioners, it has limitations, which makes it less effective for some engagement programs or processes. Recognizing these limitations, the IAP2 completed an engagement process to seek input from engagement practitioners from Canada, America, Australia, and New Zealand on the Spectrum[130]. The results from the process are being considered to determine if modifying the Spectrum is appropriate and what a modified Spectrum would look like.

---

[129] IAP2 Spectrum Review: Summary of Engagement Process, IAP2 Spectrum Review: Summary of Engagement Process, March 2017. Accessed Online: June 7, 2017.IAP2's Spectrum of Public Participation.
[130] IAP2 Spectrum Review: ibid

Who are these people and why are they yelling at me? | 117

Figure 6 IAP2's Spectrum of Public Participation

	INFORM	CONSULT	INVOLVE	COLLABORATE	EMPOWER
PUBLIC PARTICIPATION GOAL	To provide the public with balanced and objective information to assist them in understanding the problem, alternatives and/or solutions.	To obtain public feedback on analysis, alternatives and/or decision.	To work directly with the public throughout the process to ensure that public concerns and aspirations are consistently understood and considered.	To partner with the public in each aspect of the decision including the development of alternatives and the identification of the preferred solution.	To place final decision-making in the hands of the public.
PROMISE TO THE PUBLIC	We will keep you informed.	We will keep you informed, listen to and acknowledge concerns and aspirations, and provide feedback on how public input influenced the decision.	We will work with you to ensure that your concerns and aspirations are directly reflected in the alternatives developed and provide feedback on how public input influenced the decision.	We will look to you for advice and innovation in formulating solutions and incorporate your advice and recommendations into the decisions to the maximum extent possible.	We will implement what you decide.

The IAP2 Spectrum and the HSAL Engagement Framework provide a common language and/or terminology for those designing, implementing, and evaluating engagement programs or processes. The HSAL Engagement Framework adds to the IAP2 Spectrum in the following ways:

1. In some instances, the IAP2 Spectrum is viewed as a top-down perspective of organizations that believe it has the ability to give power to participants. Many organizations have non-mandatory engagement programs where the vision may be the opposite; it may be that the public has the capacity to be engaged in decision-making without the organization as a convener. In some instances, the public will be at the centre of the power structure, engaged in providing advice, action and advocacy.

2. The IAP2 Spectrum is tilted towards getting to a decision. While some organizations must undertake mandatory engagements that are oriented to decision-making, the majority of their engagements might be non-mandatory, involving multiple stakeholders and bodies working together to bring about change through civic discourse, community-building and collaborative decision-making[131].

---

131 International Association for Public Participation. IAP2 Spectrum Review: Summary of Engagement Process, March 2017. (p. 2). Accessed Online: June 7, 2017.

3. In the IAP2 Spectrum, different levels of public engagement are identified. 'Levels' can be misinterpreted as higher levels of public participation with empowerment being more desirable and lower levels being less desirable. Instead, the HSAL Engagement Framework sees each engagement approach as having its own merits regardless of where it is on the Framework. An engagement program or process can have a mix of the approaches to engagement.

I am paid well to facilitate large angry public meetings. However, when I'm standing at the front of the meeting hall with two hundred or more angry members of the public waiting to take a bite out of my client, I wonder how we all got here in the first place. So, it is important to have well designed and implemented community engagement and communication programs.

Sometimes public anger is inevitable. A project needs to proceed or a policy needs to be approved and my client needs to make a tough, unpopular decision. They know that they are going to take it on the nose. But for most other projects, well thought-out and well-executed communication, citizen engagement and public consultation programs based on the theory above will take some of the sting out of a meeting or might help to avoid an angry meeting in the first place. Indeed, I've heard members of the public say, "We strongly disagree with the decision, but we do compliment the government agency or company for the community engagement process they've used to inform us and listen."

Normally, when I hear those comments, I know that, at least part of the meeting will be productive. There are many good books on how to design effective communication, citizen engagement and public consultation processes. However, when I've had a chance to evaluate whether a public consultation program has been designed to succeed, the criteria in Figure 7 are helpful in delivering best outcomes for the community and the project proponent[132].

How do we know when the community engagement process is sound?

---

[132] Public meetings are almost always centred on hearing from the public before a decision is made or a project is approved. However, not all community engagement is centred on decisions. For example, the reason for community engagement might be to engage people in a park clean-up.

Who are these people and why are they yelling at me? | 119

Figure 7 Evaluation of a Community Engagement Process

Criteria	Indicator	Sample Measure
Transparency	Members of the public and stakeholders can see all aspects of the process as it unfolds, including the input of other stakeholders.	Open Houses and Newsletters inform the public of the progress of the project. Information obtained from the public and stakeholders is listed on a website.
Traceability	The public is able to review the steps in the decision-making process to determine how the proponent and/or the consultant made decisions. The public is aware of how their input was used during the decision-making process	Reports document how decisions are made. Reports provide lists of issues raised by the public through multiple public consultation opportunities. Proponent states clearly whether the comment has been used or rejected and why.
Legitimacy	There is a clear rationale for the project. Private companies, government departments, elected officials and authorities can communicate it clearly.	Information distributed to the public includes a "purpose statement". The proponent is open to discussing all options and alternatives suggested by the public.
Accountability	The public knows who is making the decision and people making the decisions are on hand to explain them.	Decision-makers are present at public consultation events and they engage the public. Decisions are explained during engagement activities.
Inclusiveness	The process is open to anyone interested in participating. The proponent sought out and engaged people who they expected would have an interest.	Community Advisory Committees and other engagement activities include a mix of people with differing opinions. The broader public has access to the process through Open Houses or other ways of participating.
Timeliness	The process allowed participants enough time to effectively participate in a process.	Information is received from key stakeholders and members of the public before key decisions were made.

Public consultation practitioners are professionals, and they may be professionals in another field such as land-use planning, communications or facilitation. Many will be members of the International Association for Public Participation. The following principles can also be used as a framework in the design stage for developing a successful community engagement program.

Transparency

Much of the community engagement process involves the transaction of information that is shared with and sought from the community. I firmly believe that the information received from the community helps the proponent to make better decisions. The public consultation program designer needs to ask, "How is the transaction going to occur? Will the public see the proponent as an honest broker? Will decisions and information leading to a decision be transparent?"

Transparency issues arise when the public senses that information is being hidden or that they are not getting the full truth of the matter. Anger manifests if they feel that decisions are being made behind the scenes or that the proponent is ignoring the official decision-making process.

I always feel a sense of trepidation when we are asked to engage the public at a point when other engagement efforts have failed. Sometimes I discover a long and tortured history of a project. Or, I need to dig to find the real reasons for sour relations between a project proponent and the public.

For one assignment, we were about three months into a rural infrastructure project when I got the call from a professional who had been involved with the project for a long time. "Now that you're hired, I thought you should know what's really going on", he said. "Are you sitting down?" Many of our assignments come with issues. One of the sayings around our office is, "There's always something we don't know".

It turns out that a former senior official in a decision-making capacity had decided to take money from an infrastructure vendor at the same time as they were in a position to steer the decision toward purchasing the vendors product. Being on the public payroll at the same time as being paid by a private sector vendor is, to put it mildly, disconcerting.

The public caught wind of the conflict of interest. The senior official was fired, lawsuits ensued and local politicians were voted out of office in the next election. Yet the infrastructure project was needed. And so, as the public consultation firm, we found ourselves engaging a very suspicious public.

In the design of a communications and community engagement process for this troubled project, transparency would be essential. Beginning with our engagement plans, everything was open to the public and put on the project website. All meetings were open to anyone, and the notes from internal project team meetings discussing technical and design matters were available to the public. A wide-open public process was used to evaluate whether one infrastructure technology was being preferred over another.

Despite our efforts, we ended up having a final open house and a large, angry meeting (attended by about two hundred and twenty-five people) after all. But much of the anger was dissipated by the team because the process was so transparent. The engineers, biologists and economists had a very high level of integrity, and the public saw that.

The question of whether there was anything being hidden came up in several very loud and emotional questions, to which the project manager responded, "We have nothing to hide. We have no reason to do so. We've done our very best to make sure that you are seeing the same information that we are working with. It's that information that is forming our recommendation."

In the end, our client concluded that the project, including the public consultation process, was a success.

Traceability

There are a few killer statements that project spokespeople make at public meetings. For example, when the public asks how a proponent came up with a recommendation, the response is usually as follows: 'We applied our professional expertise and that's the recommendation."

I work with many planners and engineers. When they apply their expertise to a project, their recommendations are usually well thought-out, and internal team members, the client and political decision makers have usually been at the same table to trace each step in the decision.

However, in an age when passionate people become internet experts, the public may be using the same facts to arrive at a different decision. Friction arises if they are not able to trace how the planning or engineering decision is different from their decision. "Trust us, we are the experts" no longer applies. Furthermore, if a member of the public has provided a comment that they feel is important to steer the decision in one direction or another, and their comment is not acknowledged, they will feel ignored.

There are two aspects of traceability. Firstly, it means that a member of the public can trace the facts and steps used by the project team to arrive at a decision. The names of the members of the Steering Committee and Project Team are made available to the public, so that they know who is making the decisions. Usually, there is a decision tree showing the steps in the process and the name of the ultimate decision-makers.

Traceability is achieved when we: 1) clarify and communicate the steps in the decision-making process; 2) present the factors being used to make a decision; 3) point out whether any factors are more important than others and whether they have been weighted so as to tip the decision one way or another; and, 4) how public input was considered.

Frankly, being clear about the decision process is usually just as important for internal technical team members as it is for members of the public. A very good example of traceability is the decision-making process that led to the clean-up of low-level radioactive and marginally contaminated soils in Port Hope and Clarington, Ontario, which was the result of wartime radium and uranium processing. My company was hired by both municipalities to provide peer review and technical support services.

We led a large technical team charged with peer reviewing technical reports from Atomic Energy of Canada (which later enlisted Canadian Nuclear Laboratories as managers) as the proponent. Both the public and the municipal engagement process involved dozens of technical reports circulated for comments. Several steps were required before the proponent could have approval of the clean-up from the Canadian Nuclear Safety Commission.

The proponent made sure that both the steps in the decision-making process and the details of the evaluation process were clear. A particularly useful tool

Who are these people and why are they yelling at me? | 123

was the use of a "Comment and Disposition Table". After a fifteen-year approval, design and construction process, there were literally tens of thousands of comments. The proponent took care to answer each and every one.

While the municipalities (our clients) didn't always agree with every comment, everyone knew why and how particular decisions were being made. The "C & D Tables", as they came to be known, were also useful to regulators tasked with tracing how the proponent reached certain decisions. (Refer to Appendix 2)

A second aspect of traceability has to do with members of the public being able to see that their comments have been noted and that the proponent has either accepted on rejected them. The proponents, be they decision-makers or expert advisors, may or may not have to agree with members of the public. However, whether or not they agree, and why, should be clear.

Problems arise when the public is asked for comments, but they become concerned that no one is listening to what they are saying, and when the public cannot "trace" back the notes of an engagement event to see if their advice has been considered or not.

Some of the best listening and traceability practices to incorporate traceability into a community engagement process include: live recording of notes; independent note-takers whose notes are made public; tables listing specific public comments; and a website containing public comments and responses.

We have found it very helpful to show traceability by placing public comments into a note template indicating whether or not the comments have been accepted, an explanation of why some comments have not been accepted, and which comments are being explored that may or may not be accepted. By the end of the public process, the expectation is that most of the arrows will be in the Yes or No columns, as follows:

Figure 8 Tracking Public Comments Template

What we heard:	Yes	No	Exploring
Comments on the Terms of Reference			
Clarify the section regarding 'sustainability'.	✓		
Merge physical analysis with social analysis		✓	
Add a Glossary	✓		
Review cumulative impacts			✓

Legitimacy

The US Environmental Protection Act (NEPA) was passed January 1970. The Province of Ontario passed the Environmental Assessment Act in 1975. The Canadian Environmental Protection Act was passed in 1988 and Canadian Environmental Assessment Act was passed in 1992 and updated in 2012. A new Impact Assessment Act (Bill C69) was passed in 2019. In the early days, project teams were scrambling to figure out what the Acts meant for them and what they were supposed to do. I appreciated a simple explanation from a colleague at the time, Charlie Wolf[133], who said that two words are key to unlocking a complex environmental approval process: "Think rationally".

Whether or not a proponent is thinking rationally underpins the public's concern about the legitimacy of the environmental assessment process and in parallel the legitimacy of meetings called within these processes to hear from the public. Most of these processes now include a "scoping step", which forces the project proponent to think through a "problem statement" and "consider alternative methods and means" of solving the problem. But it wasn't always that way.

Some of the earliest and largest meetings I facilitated involved the siting of landfills going through the environmental assessment process. While the social sciences struggle to be as quantitative and predictive as the physical sciences, it

---

133 http://villagehealthworks.org.onexcale.net/media/in-the-press/charlie-wolf-dies-at-81

is almost an indisputable sociological fact that if you are proposing a new landfill beside a small rural community, you can predict with one hundred percent accuracy that public anger will occur.

Most of the landfill proponents that we worked with at the time (private and public operators) struggled to explain why a landfill was needed. Since this was a time before modern recycling programs existed, they found themselves at a loss to answer why a recycling program wasn't a better policy. Energy from waste and waste reduction were suggested, but those options were not considered at the time.

Thus, the central problem of how to site a landfill was that the project was scoped too narrowly, undermining the legitimacy of the problem statement, which should have been, "How do we manage materials we create?" Without opening the process up to larger, common-sense questions, the public saw the process as illegitimate. As a result, most environmental assessment acts around the world today include 'problem definition' and 'scoping' stages to address the legitimacy issue. Because this issue of legitimacy is now commonly addressed, there are fewer large angry public meetings associated with these approvals.

Accountability

Occasionally, I work for residents' groups fighting city hall. Since these people usually don't have enough money to hire consultants, I get paid in cookies, pieces of local art, food and hugs - lots of hugs. On one occasion, I worked with a small group of homeowners fighting a landfill site in a brand-new community in Markham, Ontario.

I shared with this group an explanation of the environmental assessment process, how decisions are evaluated and what they could expect in terms of studies to be completed. When wrapping things up, as I was putting on my shoes at the door, I asked the homeowner what he thought about the highway interchange scheduled to be built in the field beyond his back-yard fence. "What interchange?" he replied.

Shoes came off. Back into the meeting we went. For some reason, the residents didn't realize that they were living beside a future 400-series highway[134]. At this point, the project decision couldn't be reversed, and they couldn't find who was accountable for the decision.

As a related example, we were asked to facilitate a public meeting involving a new 400-series highway being built close to a community of newly-built homes in Caledon, Ontario. Apparently, none of the lawyers for the two hundred homeowners informed their purchasers that the highway was being built through their community. Or, so it was said.

In this case, we were hired to work with provincial civil servants, mostly engineers and transportation planners without any authority to decide. While the decision had been made by the Minister of Transportation, the civil servants were responsible for making recommendations, but not accountable for making the decision. For most of the meeting, I had to field screaming protestations about the absence of a decision-maker to hear public comments.

From my experience, provincial and federal government community engagement programs are particularly difficult in terms of accountability issues because people never quite know who is deciding. Is it a Minister, a senior staff member, Cabinet, the Premier's office, the Prime Minister's Office?

Often the public is concerned that someone may have a back door to the decision-making process. Regrettably, in Canada and in the US, this is a legitimate concern. The question is, who is accountable?

Federal and provincial politicians who ultimately make decisions almost never show up to an open house or a community meeting. As a result, the civil servants can't help but come with baggage. When residents want to vent about a wide range of wrong-headed policies, corrupt practices and politically-motivated decision-making, the civil servants are the only ones who they can yell at.

As a facilitator, my focus is on the project at hand, and I encourage the public to focus their comments thusly. When residents ask why politicians aren't at the

---

134 In Ontario 400-series highways are the widest and can be over 16 lanes at certain locations. These are like to US Interstate I90, and 290, 390 and 490 city highways.

Who are these people and why are they yelling at me? | 127

meeting, the civil servants would like to be frank, but can't. What they would but never say is, "The Minister of Transportation has already made up her mind and showing up tonight will result in negative press."

When I know that accountability is an issue, I try to make sure that the other measures of a good public engagement process are working, hoping that the public "gets" the politics and is kinder to the civil servants and their consultants. I do what I can to help. When spoken language is constrained, body language helps.

Some accountability questions to ask include:

- Does the public know who is making the decision?
- Does the public have access to this person?
- Can the recommendation to the decision-maker be distributed to the public?
- Are there other factors influencing the decision that the public is unaware of?

Inclusiveness

Issues of inclusivity go deep. Much has and will be written about appropriate engagement with Indigenous people, and there's much to learn. As I don't have enough knowledge of this topic, I have not addressed it in my writing. That being said, there are some universal issues to do with inclusion:

- Are you engaging the right people?
- How easy is it for all relevant people to want to be engaged?
- Have key groups and individuals been left out?
- Are some groups having an overly large influence on the decision?

Natural justice[135] states that affected members of the public have a fundamental right to be heard fairly. Normally, community engagement programs are geared

---

135 In English law, natural justice is technical terminology for the rule against bias (nemo iudex in causa sua) and the right to a fair hearing (audi alteram partem). While the term natural justice is

towards any member of the public who wants to participate, but there are often people in the community who should be involved. Sometimes the community engagement process should be geared to specific groups such as the homeless, youth, the poor and people of certain ethnicities. The question is how to figure out who to consult and how to hear from people fairly. Missing certain groups may result in rising anger.

Sociology, economics, political science, geography and anthropology are helpful disciplines in sorting this out. On occasion, I've engaged cultural heritage specialists, political scientists and social scientists to advise on whether or not we are consulting the right people. Social Cultural and Socio-economic Impact Assessments and a Stakeholder Sensitivity Analysis are tools and methodologies that are helpful in identifying people who will be affected and those who have an interest in the policy or program seeking approval.

The community engagement process should be open to anyone interested in participating. The proponent should seek out and engage people who they expect would have an interest. Community Advisory Committees and other engagement activities should include a mix of people with differing opinions. To make sure that I get it right, I will state to the community at the beginning of most engagement processes, "Here is who I think should be consulted. Is there anyone else you can think of?"

I cringe when I see a community engagement process that is designed not to be inclusive. While its intent is to avoid conflict, sometimes the design actually undermines the communications that should occur in a democracy. Typical examples of this include using an open house format (one of the least successful community engagement techniques), narrowly notifying people, and scheduling a community engagement event on a date and time when most people can't attend. I have actually had clients who interpreted poor community attendance as indicative of people not concerned about the project, and therefore a measure of success.

---

often retained as a general concept, it has largely been replaced and extended by the general "duty to act fairly". https://en.wikipedia.org/wiki/Natural_justice

Unfortunately, municipal and provincial acts and regulations often prescribe the timing and method of community engagement. For example, Ontario's Municipal Class EA Process[136] recommends an open house at key stages of a study. On the bright side, most of my clients view this technique as the minimum activity and conduct much more engagement.

Timeliness

When I get philosophical, I view the work I do as repairing the rips and tears in the fabric of democracy. When the fabric is torn, a large, angry meeting is inevitable. The most gaping hole occurs when the client or the project proponent makes the decision about a project, plan or policy before asking people for their comments.

Even a fifth grader can see that, if you have already decided, or are too far along in the decision-making process before you ask for comments, there is a fundamental denial of natural justice. Democratic decision-making is not about standing still or waiting until the last person agrees for consensus to be reached. Not everyone will agree and it's foolish to think otherwise. Most people understand that society is not static. Communities change, and not all changes will go their way. Broad general agreement is usually acceptable. But people see right through processes where their comments have no consequence.

Most people that I've met at large public meetings understand that, unless elected, they as individual citizens are not empowered to make decisions for other members of society. They also understand that government agencies and departments have the authority to make decisions, as do corporations, if they are acting lawfully.

The public also correctly recognizes that, if a government agency or company is going to make a decision that affects them, they have a right to be heard before the decision is made, understanding that the decision may or may not go their way. Nevertheless, the democratic process is legitimatized by listening to people before making the decision.

---

136 http://www.municipalclassea.ca/manual/page1.html

Some of the worst meetings I've facilitated are those where the client has either made the decision in advance of asking for public input or, where the decision is so imminent or obviously fixed that the public sees the timing of the process as fundamentally unfair.

On project teams, my role is to usually suss out whether decisions have already been made, then shine a light on decisions to come. Once I can figure this out, I can develop the communications and community engagement process that needs to occur before those decisions are made.

These internal meetings are never easy. Too often I've found that my recommendation to roll back decisions - to a point where it is legitimate for the public to comment - is not welcome. I am good at reading faces. There's a look I get that means, "You ass, who invited you onto the team?"

Typical timeline problems occur in the following situations:

- The public isn't given enough time to provide comment.
- Time for commenting on the proposed decision is out of sync with the complexity of the issue and the amount of time needed for appropriate dialogue, i.e. "This is a complex matter and we need more time to comment".
- A schedule has been developed unilaterally by the proponent and is seen to be either closing the doors too early, shutting people up, or going on too long, wearing people down.
- Recommendations for developing acceptable timelines are ignored.

Power Balance

While these criteria are helpful for designing a sound community engagement process, an additional consideration has to do with the power balance and how it is defined and implemented through the engagement process.

Essentially, the proponent of the project needing public approval has some power but needs to hear from the public. The public participates with the expectation that, in a democracy, they have some power, but it is up to either the proponent or a government approval body to make the decision. In the latter

Who are these people and why are they yelling at me? | 131

case, the government body has the power because the public has given it to them via the ballot box.

In the design of community engagement processes, there are many ways of defining the power relationship. The proponent needs to get it right. How the power balance sits, comes down in part to how the proponent defines "engagement", a word that is commonly used differently by different individuals or groups because there is not a single widely accepted meaning.

In effect, there are different perceptions of what activities constitute engagement. Public friction arises when the proponent is using one definition of engagement and the public another. Furthermore, it occurs when the proponent has got the power balance between them and the community wrong. For example, if an approval needs a lot of public buy-in and the proponent is saying, "We want to hear your ideas but we will make the decision" instead of "We would like you to partner with us", public concern will result.

Engagement is defined as a process whereby the proponent shares information, seeks input, and/or encourages involvement by the public and/or stakeholders on matters important to everyone. The process could be as simple as providing information and seeking feedback. Or, it could be as in-depth as engaging in a two-way dialogue, sharing ideas and asking questions. It could also involve power-sharing or the proponent giving their decision-making power to the public. The degree or level of engagement would vary depending on the intended engagement goal(s).

The HSAL framework discussed above helps in understanding the definition of engagement and required types of engagement. (See Figure 5). The framework is characterized by four different engagement approaches to consider when designing the engagement programs or processes. During the design stage, one or more desired approaches are selected based on the engagement goal(s). In the evaluation stage, the success of the program or process can also be assessed against the outcome(s) of the chosen approach(es).

The involvement of the public and stakeholders in designing the engagement programs or processes is vital to ensuring success and buy-in, particularly if the issue is contentious, and the comments add value to the process.

In 2018, we were hired to help secure community approval for a homeless shelter in an existing community. A successful communications and community engagement process was designed and implemented, and everything rolled out as planned. The client representing a non-profit agency helping the homeless received excellent community comments, and there was no angry, public meeting.

I asked my client at the end of the process how things were going. "Not well," was the reply. "The local Councillor was expecting an angry public meeting and that didn't occur. They think we did something wrong and now want to extend the community engagement process." Aaargh!

In summary, designing a sound community engagement process can help to avoid having an angry meeting. Good design means that key criteria are considered. There is a good understanding of the necessary proponent-public transaction, and the power relationship is right.

Chapter 6:
The Dynamics of Large, Angry Public Meetings

Facilitators who work with small groups need to be aware of group dynamics. This part of facilitation involves knowing where the group is at when helping them to set goals. It also involves helping individual members of the group to achieve a successful outcome. The dynamics involve managing meeting structure, working with individuals who aren't participating or are participating too much, helping the group to find its "aha" moment, reach consensus on next steps and then draw the group to a close.

The facilitator of a small group has an opportunity to interact with each individual member of the group and can expect to work with them over several meetings. Participants, possessing an excellent knowledge of the issues and subject matter informing choices, will typically have a personal or professional interest in achieving the goals identified by the group. In essence, the facilitator is normally hired by the group to work for the group.

The dynamics of large, angry public meetings however, are very different. And so is the interaction of the facilitator with members of the group. In this scenario, it is impossible for the facilitator to know who is present and what each person wants from the meeting. While all participants will see clearly who the facilitator is and what they are trying to achieve, the facilitator will only be able to interact with a small number of participants, within a large group, over a short period of time.

In large public meetings, the people who end up speaking may or may not represent the views of the large number of people attending. Indeed, I will always have comment forms available so that we can hear from participants who either don't want to speak in public, have an opinion that is contrary to that of the most vocal people, or are intimidated by those with the strongest voices.

Although the agenda is set by the client, for some meetings I will do an agenda check, intended to identify if the public wants to add agenda items.

Most of the people attending large public meetings do so for the right reasons. They feel strongly about an issue based on the information available to them so far. They decide that it is worth the effort to give up their precious time to learn more about the matter being discussed. By being present and stating their opinion, they have an opportunity to influence the direction of a decision.

While a decent public consultation process will provide lots of opportunities for obtaining information and commenting, for most people the meeting will be the first time that they will have access to the facts related to a decision, to the client and to the experts. Very few of the interactions important to small group facilitation can happen with large groups. This is because I will be speaking to but I won't be able to engage in one on one conversations with most of the participants.

Although advanced preparation helps, I won't know how participants are divided up in terms of being supportive, neutral or opposed to my client. Unless I watch group dynamics carefully, I also won't know if the members of the public providing comments and asking questions represent the views of most of the people who will not speak. I always keep in mind that not everyone in the crowd is opposed to the position of the client. Many public participants will be seeking information so that they can develop their own opinions.

Participants may also include public officials and the media, as well as agency, regulatory and political representatives, and people who are just curious, looking at the event as a form of entertainment. Not so long ago, public executions and bear baiting drew large crowds. Whole families would gather in town squares because of the entertainment value and a morbid curiosity. I realize that this may be an extreme comparison, but it's important to understand that not all people in angry public meetings hold the subject matter and issues near and dear to their hearts.

The job of the facilitator is to rewrite, script and remove the entertainment value from a large meeting and ideally ensure that people leave the meeting more informed than before they came - all within a typical two or three-hour timeframe.

In order to deliver the best outcomes at a large, angry public meeting, it is important to understand the sociology and psychology of large groups. These

Who are these people and why are they yelling at me? | 135

meetings have a dynamic and intensity of their own. There are stages of group process. In addition to considering the normal dynamics that smaller groups go through, it is critical for the facilitator to understand what stage the group is in and then help move the group through each stage of the process.[137]

I am usually most active during the "storming stage". That's what I prepare for the most - either avoiding it (if possible) or managing it for the best outcome if it occurs. There are six stages that I expect the group will go through, and need to be managed by the facilitator: 1) Forming; 2) Norming; 3) Storming; 4) Performing; 5) Reforming; and 6) Closure.

The Forming Stage

For every one of my meetings, I lead my client, their consultants and specialists, my staff and others on a "mental walk-through" of the meeting that's about to happen. Usually this is done up to a week before the event, or at least at a point where we have enough intelligence that we know who's attending and what issues will be raised. I envision how the meeting will unfold and have each member of the team take the mental journey with me.

It's a narrative I do about what is to come.

I usually start in the parking lot outside of the venue. What do people see when they get out of their cars and come to the entrance of the meeting hall? How do they get in? Do they see welcome signs and directional arrows posted in advance? Are the signs professionally made and friendly?

While the next questions may sound absurd, I raise them because the issue has happened on several occasions. Did anyone remember to unlock the door to the meeting hall? Do we have the cell number of the caretaking staff, or at least the person with the key? I once facilitated a medium-sized meeting in an Ontario town on the subject of a waste water master plan. No one had unlocked the door to the meeting hall. As dozens of people showed up, my client was scrambling to find someone with a key. Having members of the public waiting

---

[137] See original 1965 theories on group process by Bruce Tuckman 'Forming, Storming, Norming, Performing Team-development model (and Adjourning), www.tuckmanforming normingperforming.com Also see Alan Chapman, 2001 - 2007 www.businessballs.com

outside for a meeting to begin doesn't instill confidence in the professionals at the outset.

When people come into a meeting hall, they immediately have questions that need to be addressed. Where do I go? Do I have to sign in? Who are these other people also attending? What am I supposed to do? How do I get information? Who do I talk to about my issues?

Continuing our mental journey, I advise clients to think about how they would greet someone as a visitor to their home. I suggest they apply this approach to members of the public coming to the meeting. Friendly staff should be at the registration table as well as at the entrance to greet people as they arrive. Their role is to explain what the meeting is about and ask if there are any questions or concerns that can be discussed before the meeting starts.

Staff will also tell participants that there will be presentations and an opportunity for them to ask questions and provide comments. As a lesson learned, it's important to make sure that there are no long lineups at the registration table. "Waiting line road rage" can occur – not a good way to begin a public meeting. If several hundred people are expected, I will typically make sure that there are multiple registration tables attended by staff.

This part of the mental walk ends with assessing the state of mind of members of the public before the meetings begins. Have they been given information (a brochure or fact sheet) that will address likely questions in advance? Have they provided an email address or other contact information to receive ongoing information? Do they know who the decision makers are? Have these people been pointed out? At this stage, I am usually part of the greeter team, telling participants that I'm an independent facilitator, and that I'm eager to hear from them.

The active involvement of trained staff as greeters has a secondary benefit: it allows them to determine the level of public interest or anger and inform me and the staff team before the meeting occurs. We facilitated a large public meeting in rural Ontario over a project that would cost each household tens of thousands of dollars. As my staff welcomed residents and helped them to sign in, several people responded rather impolitely, to say the least. (One member of the public told my staff to "'**** off" at the registration desk on the way into the

Who are these people and why are they yelling at me? | 137

meeting.) On hearing about this, I had a much better idea of who I was going to be dealing with during the meeting.

The mental journey also includes determining how people will be seated (discussed later), the locations of fire exits and other matters relevant to managing the lead-up to the start of the meeting. (Discussed in more detail in the Chapter entitled, Safety and Security.) The journey ends at the beginning of my initial remarks to meeting participants.

The Norming Stage

This stage of facilitating a large public meeting is centered on a primary question in the minds of the public: "Now that we're here, what are we supposed to do and how are we supposed to act?"

People attending a public meeting will bring their attitudes, values and feelings, and they will come with either more or less factual information about the matter at hand. A set of group norms - accepted ways of behaving in a group - are either brought to a meeting or take form at the meeting. Some norms help a group to get through the later storming stage. Others will make the "storming" stage of a meeting more intense.

Often people will have a pre-conceived image of what to do at a public meeting through the news media. In this case, the norm being formulated is influenced by television images of people standing up during a meeting waving their fists and lined up behind a microphone stand. Residents anticipate that there will be a panel of experts at the front of the room portrayed as red-faced punching bags taking the wrath of the public.

When anger intensifies, normal group behaviour involves joining with others to show these feelings. (They think, I see others doing it. So, this behaviour is totally acceptable.) This group norm could involve yelling, talking out of turn and, at times, saying rude remarks or engaging in minor acts of civil disobedience. Sometimes the storming stage is short and members of the public will engage in constructive dialogue. At other times, emotions build and the group never leaves this stage. As discussed in earlier sections, my role as an extreme facilitator is to move the group into constructive dialogue.

It often happens that leaders not previously identified will emerge. These (formal and informal) leaders will vocalize and implicitly claim leadership as they speak. They will be watched by each member of the public as to whether there will be an alternative tone for the group. Meetings do not typically begin in the storming stage. They evolve into it. In general, groups will not move to the next stage until they are ready. My job at the outset and throughout the meeting is to set the tone through my presence and lay out the ground rules. Essentially, I suggest the desired 'process' outcome.

Much can be done in the Norming Stage to move the group into the Performing Stage and avoid or shorten the Storming Stage. In the Norming Stage, the role of the extreme facilitator is to lay out expected behaviours and sometimes enforce behaviours. Effectively, my role initially is to spell out desirable norms by first establishing my role as an independent facilitator, then bringing the desired norms to the group. (The topics of presence, independence and neutrality have been discussed in the earlier Chapter, The Extreme Facilitator.) The presentation of ground rules, discussed later, assist me to establish group norms.

It is not unusual for people watching my actions to see me as a sort of referee amongst them, waving yellow cards in the air as required. In reality, I am content neutral, but they see that I'm exercising process judgement over the course of the meeting to insure fairness.

In the tougher meetings, people see clearly what's going on, knowing that the facilitator is keeping them centred on dialogue rather than allowing them to engage in less desirable behaviours. In fact, I will often have people come up to me after a meeting to thank me for keeping the process under control. With the norm of civility consistent over the course of the meeting, people often comment as follows, "I thought this was going to be a bloodbath tonight, but you kept things under control. I was glad I attended. I learned and I had an opportunity to share my views with someone who listened."

Setting the tone in the Norming Stage is also important. Other practitioners and I refer to this as the act of "confronting the power conflict". When you know that an angry public meeting is going to happen, it should be obvious why. Often the public may believe that the proponent doesn't know why they are angry, so they view their role at the beginning of the meeting as telling the proponent how they feel.

I discussed the need to start positive and friendly earlier. In order to further set the tone and reduce the temperature somewhat, my role up front is to state the obvious, "I can see there are a lot of people here tonight. Thank you for giving up your time to be here. This meeting is about a tough decision that has to be made. The proponent knows that many of you have strong views about each of the options. In a democracy, hearing from you helps to improve decisions. I know that you want to state those views tonight. My role is to make sure you have that opportunity."

And so, the norm is established. The public is aware of the fact that the independent facilitator knows why they are at the meeting, how they should share their views and what the normal behaviour is while they are sharing those views.

The Storming Stage

As its title implies, the Storming Stage is a meeting situation where people are usually animated and emotional. "You haven't treated us fairly!" they say. "You are acting unethically! Your facts are wrong! We don't want what you are selling! Our rights are being violated!"

Even though members of the audience may be at odds with the position of the proponent, either because they disagree with what they've heard or they don't yet have the information necessary for agreement, this stage is often a very creative time. It is also a time when the most hostile activity will occur. People will yell, cat call and applaud frequently.

My clients always want me to help them get past the Storming Stage and on to a stage where they can begin to either have constructive comments or reasonable dialogue. Sometimes the group will get to this stage and stay there, which doesn't make for a rewarding evening for the proponent but will certainly be a learning experience. If the group stays there after all the information has been provided, there are usually other issues at play or bigger decisions that have to be made. The proponent and the facilitator should have a good idea of this potential process outcome before the meeting even starts.

There are a couple of actions that can be taken to move people through the Storming Stage. First, and most obvious, is to acknowledge what the people are saying and agree with them. I've had clients see the writing on the wall and say,

"You know, your right. We can do a better job." Since most angry meetings are about tough decisions, agreeing would be the simple solution, but not necessarily the responsible one.

Secondly, we acknowledge the anger and make sure that everyone who is angry has a chance to vent. At this point we are looking for next steps, asking. "Were there stated alternative decisions that need further examination? Was there simply an agreement to disagree, with both parties taking the issue to another forum? Is there an extension to the public consultation process that would deal with concerns, such as striking a committee or having another public event where the issue raised can be discussed?" If people can sense during the Storming Stage that there is a way to advance their interests, then the door to the Performing Stage is open.

Thirdly, we recognize that people are not leaving the Storming Stage, we are skipping the Performing Stage and working toward the Closure Stage. I find my interpersonal relationships with members of the public fascinating during the Storming Stage. Instead of asking questions of the client or the project proponent directly, they will often turn and direct questions to me.

"The experts are not listening to us, but you are," they say. "Help us get them to listen." I know that the client is listening, but there's no requirement for me to agree to get them to listen. That's not my job.

Other times, when I'm listening to the answers given to the public, I will notice that the client either hasn't understood the question or overlooked part of the question. I will know that the member of the public has perceived this by their response. Before having them raise the issue, often with anger, I will intervene with the client and point out that they didn't completely answer the question. While the client may sometimes be taken aback by their facilitator asking them questions, the public will see that the process can be trusted. That's usually more important to the big picture.

The Performing Stage

This stage is characterized by people coming together for a common cause during a meeting. The group (and perhaps the proponent) concludes that all issues have been discussed and goals have been set, and that they should be

Who are these people and why are they yelling at me? | 141

working together with the client to achieve them. Top of the group's mind in the Performing Stage is, "This is how we really want to spend our time."

I facilitated one meeting where people were opposing a new highway interchange required for safety and to alleviate congestion. The members of the public were all drivers. While they were concerned with the social and environmental impacts of the interchange, they seemed to also understand that it was needed to improve their lives and the lives of other people. However, a number of homeowners whose properties backed on to the proposed new interchange were not happy campers.

More than three hundred and fifty people attended the public meeting. The client did a very good job of presenting the need for safety and transportation efficiency. The Storming Stage was brief, with several loud comments such as, "Why here, why now and what's the impact on me?" The client was well prepared, answering questions from the public with sensible "street" logic. The audience got it.

The client then reached out to the audience, saying that they could really use more public input on the details of the project design and asked people to join a committee. Many hands went up and, except for some grandstanding at the end by a local politician who wanted people to stay in a storming mode, the meeting ended well. In terms of performing, the meeting participants knew what needed to be done. Offering recommendations on how the decision should advance, they were willing to volunteer their time to work with the proponent. The project turned out much better as a result.

The Reforming Stage

When it is part of a loud and angry public meeting, the Reforming Stage occurs towards the end. The meeting process so far has led to several steps being identified and accepted by the public, with ensuing comments such as, "Is there a better way that we can work together in the future?" This characterizes the public and client working as a cohesive group.

From the perspective of the facilitator, the process involves the confirmation of next steps. My role is to telegraph what the reforming stage looks like. I might say, "Okay, we've had some strong views stated. We've also heard some ideas that we all seem to agree need further attention. Several of you have volunteered, so let's find a time to meet again. And, lets meet in the following way."

The next activity, which likely will not involve a new Storming Stage, is bringing the group together for a smaller committee meeting. The group structure has been reformed and the process continues in a constructive manner.

The Closure Stage

You've probably seen TV clips of city council meetings that have carried on until the early hours of the next morning. Politicians have asked for input on a contentious item and found themselves with an exceptionally long list of people who want to speak. No one wants to turn anyone away. Yet, all meetings need to close. Preparing for closure is important.

I have run into the most difficulty when many members of the public want to stay in the Storming Stage. After several hours, many people indicate that they want to speak, and it looks like the meeting will have to go on for another hour or more. The implication is that my clients are going to have to be yelled at or put on the hot seat for another hour. Other than people being satisfied that they have been heard (which is important) there are usually few new ideas that come forward in the late hours of a meeting.

When I'm facilitating a normal meeting, I plan for an intentional close down process, technically called the "cool down" period. The Closure Stage can last five to ten minutes for small groups, and up to an hour if it happens to be a conventional workshop or a conference that lasts for several days. It is a time for letting go and, if the workshop was particularly meaningful, a time to say goodbye to friends.

Groups have a life. The purpose of closure is to help participants think through and collect their thoughts about what they've accomplished during the meeting. In a workshop setting, I ask participants to share what they've learned. I also ask them to share the common direction they thought they were headed, going over actions and agreements that were reached.

The Closure Stage is also a time when the group can set a new direction. I will ask the group for final comments, encouraging them to share the common direction they felt they were headed towards, and agreements reached. The end of the meeting also gives participants an opportunity to evaluate how they thought the session went. At times, I will also ask them to provide feedback on how I did.

In contrast to small group processes, planning for closure during large and angry meetings involves several stages: ending the meeting, getting people out safely and assessing next steps. The client needs to decide whether or not they want to make closing remarks or sum up what they've heard, but their observation on the value of the meeting to the decisions that have to be made is imperative.

A checklist of matters to address at the closing stage of the agenda includes:

- Reaching agreement with the client before the meeting on how and when the end of the meeting will occur.
- Making sure that there has been a reasonable time for members of the public to express their opinion.
- Communicating why and when you are ending the meeting.
- Giving notice that the meeting will be ending at a certain time.
- Pointing out that we are now ending our time together, and gauging public reaction to this announcement.
- Setting up the room and the microphones so that, when the time comes to end, it's easy to do.
- Ending the meeting by wishing people a safe journey home.

Towards the end of the meeting, there are several signs I look for that indicate people are ready to go. There is a noticeable decline in the number of people who want to speak, with no new people wanting to ask questions or provide comments. Points are being repeated. Some people are already leaving, and it's getting close to the end time of the room permit.

When meetings are in the performing stage and things are going well, you want to make sure that you continue to get the best ideas from the public. Alternatively, there may be a large issue that the client needs to address. If the meeting ends too early, they will miss the opportunity to hear what people want to say.

During a large, angry public meeting, it is important to give early notice that the meeting is about to end. When we are at the scheduled end, I will usually announce that we will either need to take an extra half hour or that the meeting will be ending in half an hour. I will then give a fifteen-minute notice. If I'm lucky, the public has followed along and I'm leading them through a cool-down stage. It helps if I state that the client and the experts will be available after the meeting for one on one discussions.

The public will want to know the next steps. Normally, this involves the client announcing when meeting notes or reports are going to be available and whether or not there will be additional meetings. The client also needs to thank everyone for spending their evening with them.

At this stage, particularly if we are beyond the storming stage I may ask, "Will anyone be very upset if we end the meeting?" It's a serious question, and I will look for a response. If I receive a comment, I will ask the person to state their objection, "Is there anything else that needs to be said before we break?" This question ensures that, if there is a big issue that has been missed, we know about it.

When the meeting ends, there may be hangers-on. Most people will not want to spend a late evening listening to other people talk, and when I announce that the meeting is coming to an end, they normally want to go home. If there are people who still want a public forum for their comments, I will point them to the project team and ask, "Is what you are about to say something that requires everyone attending the meeting to stick around and listen to you, or can you state your comment directly to the expert or the client one on one?"

Generally, most members of the public will see this process for ending the meeting as fair, and the meeting will end at the scheduled time. There are, however, a number of reasons why the end could be complex:

- The client, experts and the public agree that there's nothing else to discuss.
- Members of the public are undertaking actions that are unacceptable to the client, and there's no benefit to continuing.
- Other unanticipated circumstances such as a fire alarm going off or the simple matter of cleaning staff insisting that you leave.

In summary, the end of a meeting, just like the beginning, needs to be carefully planned in order to achieve the best outcome.

Chapter 7:
Setting the Stage: Preparing for the Meeting

There are many ways to engage large numbers of people without having to convene a large public meeting. Each technique has its strengths and weaknesses. Whether or not to use these techniques versus having a public meeting requires answers to the following questions: What sorts of comments and opinions are being sought from the public? Where is the proponent in the decision-making process in relation to the public's ability to influence outcomes? What is the level and direction of public upset?

If the process is open, seeking a range of opinions on matters to be decided in the future, it is better to convene a process that stimulates public thinking and gathers ideas. An alternative meeting structure would work well in a situation where the client is developing a Transit Master Plan, for example, and public comments are sought on alternative routes and modes of travel; meaning that the decision is wide open and that the proponent could choose equally between similarly beneficial options. Another example is where a proponent needs to assess the impact of a new power plant and wants comments on what environmental effects they propose to study.

In terms of community impact and response, if large numbers of the public are generally neutral or supportive of a decision, an option other than a large public meeting would be preferred. As an example, an alternative way of convening large numbers of people would be preferable in a situation where a new hospital is desired by a community and the proponent needs to understand what architecture best meets the community's needs.

The three alternative techniques I've use with success are Spider Facilitation, World Café and Roundtables.

Spider Facilitation

When I tried to explain Spider Facilitation to my spouse, I described it as speed dating. Her immediate response was, "When were you speed dating?" After a half an hour of marital discord had passed, I finally had a chance to explain that this is a process whereby you generally start with one on one interviews, then work it up to large group consensus.

My company worked on the 2010 Vancouver Winter Olympic and Paralympic Games bid with Jon Spalding and Bruce Gillespie of REWERX in Vancouver, British Columbia. The technique they chose to engage many residents and stakeholders was Spider Facilitation - for good reason.

There's a group of people around the world who oppose spending money on any large games and expos, so Bruce and Jon had to consult the residents of British Columbia on key matters; in particular the residents of the 22 'Olympic communities' in the Sea to Sky corridor. Against this backdrop, holding a large, meeting to hear from people opposed to the Olympic Games would result in only one point of view being heard.

In sum, Spider Facilitation roughly involves the following steps:

1. **Convening people and presenting questions that need their input.** The facilitator develops a list of key questions in advance to probe issues important to the client and the community. The questions are usually prepared in consultation with key stakeholders, and/ or by talking to a cross section of spokespeople from the various interests to determine what the presenting positions are. In the case of the proposed Olympic Games, the questions were designed to query the significant opposing positions[138]. Alternatively, when we used spider facilitation to develop a tourism vision in Burlington, Ontario we focused the questions on what the broad vision could be as well as potential impediments to achieving the vision. So, the questions need to centre on the problem or opportunity at hand.

---

138 Thanks to Jon Spalding for adding to the text.

The questions are confirmed in the initial plenary, with the group adding to them or adjusting them. When the questions are well designed there are no changes.

Technically, it is better to start with an even number of questions. Since part of the process involves pairing off, four to eight questions are ideal. For example, "What do think are the two most important benefits the games should deliver for average people? If there is one legacy benefit the 2010 Olympic Games should deliver, what do you think it is?"

2. **Numbering off the group.** If there are four questions, the group numbers off one to four. If there are six questions, number off one to six and so on. Each individual owns one question. The person is responsible for obtaining the input within their small group on that question. For example, person number one would be interviewing the other five group members about the two most important benefits.

3. **The Interview Process.** The first group of six people then starts an interview process with other group members. The next group of six does the same until there are many groups of six engaged in interviews. Like a reporter, the person who owns question one interviews the person who owns question two. The person who owns question three' interviews the person who owns question four, and so on. As a facilitator, my role is to make this part of the process as simple as possible.

Figure 9 Pairs Interviews

4. In pairs, each set of participants have three to five minutes to introduce themselves, ask their question and receive a response. The other person then has three to five minutes to interview the other person on their question. Notes are taken by each reporter and, as a final part of each interview, each person repeats what they wrote down to confirm with the person interviewed that what they heard was accurate.

The first set of pairs interviews will last up to 10 minutes, and time is tracked. At the ring of a bell, a new set of pairs convenes. The person with question one will interview the person with question three. The person with question two will interview the person with question five, and so on. After the final round of interviews, the result is that every person has been introduced and has had a chance to share their opinion on every question. And, have their comments read back to them so as to confirm accuracy.

Figure 10 Round Table Comparison of Like Questions

5. **The Round Table.** Once all the interviews are completed, question owners of like questions convene at a round table. For example, question one owners are at one table and question two owners convene at a different round table until all the people owning the same question are together at the same table. This stage is facilitated by someone with a flip chart and someone else recording. Usually, the group nominates

or volunteers a recorder and facilitator. Up until this point the process facilitator has had very little substantive involvement in the discussions, other than to prompt and encourage the participants to probe each question and keep time.

The first person debriefs on the common response to their question and responses that were not as common, but "keepers" nonetheless. If there are fifteen "question one" owners at the table, the views of seventy-five people are being presented on that particular question. If there are one hundred and fifty people participating, I will usually split up the tables into two tables of fifteen, resulting in the group hearing one hundred and fifty opinions on that question. I find that in any group there are many common ideas. Once the first 3 or 4 people have debriefed, the remaining people normally confirm or add to earlier views.

My colleagues, Jon Spalding and Bruce Gillespie encourage the groups to use numerical criteria to identify 'keepers'. For example, more than 80 percent of the interviewees identified or supported the point. They encourage groups to recognize creative genius and identify ideas or points that may not be widely supported, but that the group of interviewers recognized as a solid or valuable perspective. They call those ideas the 'Silver Bullets'.

6. **The Plenary.** The round table process usually takes forty-five minutes to an hour. Once the round table debrief has occurred, each table debriefs back in plenary, reporting on the most common comments and the "keepers". At that point, the large groups reflect on and discuss the responses to the questions and confirm that what was being reported is a reasonable and accurate group consensus.

Figure 11 Reporting out in the Plenary Session

7. The advantages of Spider Facilitation over large public meetings are as follows: everyone participates; loud opinions are brought forward and ideas are discussed immediately; the process works well for managing the emotions and tone of the gathering. Colleagues Spalding and Gillespie note, "we have always believed that the process is one of forced consensus and that is very valuable as a way of identifying what people agree on. Often this is good enough."[139]

Disadvantages include: community leaders or opinionated grandstanders don't have the opportunity to present their positions until the end of the process, doing so against a backdrop of a fair, consensus-building procedure; people with predisposed strong positions may not want to participate; while Spider Facilitation is effective, it is a complex process, and the facilitator needs to know what they are doing.

---

139 Spalding, Jon, personal correspondence, 2 April 2019

World Café

A search of "spider facilitation" on the internet mostly yields information on how to insure a healthy ecosystem for wolf spiders. There is, however, a lot more information online about world café.[140] The World Café Community Foundation (www.theworldcafe.com) is a good source.

When I bring together large numbers of people to participate in a World Café session, the goal is usually to facilitate public discernment over a particular issue. It's a good technique for developing community strategies, but less effective when emotions are running high or there's conflict between a community and a client. In other words, World Café works for brainstorming community options and hearing comments on a plan or policy decision in the early stages. It's not good at all if there's a single, pressing issue that's on the minds of the public.

The World Café Community Foundation sets out steps that are helpful.

Step 1: The design step involves thinking strategically about what you want to accomplish with the group. The facilitator and the client need to think about goals, who's going to participate and the desired outcomes.

Step 2: The second step involves creating a hospitable space. A venue is set up as a series of small café-style tables with four or five chairs at each table. I usually start with a plenary discussion, setting out questions or subjects for discussion using a PowerPoint presentation. While I would normally have discussed the initial questions with the client ahead of time, I will ask the participants if there are other questions I've missed. Questions can be added to or amended at this time.

People who have additional questions that we may not have thought of are welcomed to speak to the whole group and make a case for their question being be assigned to a table. I once facilitated a World Café to hear public comments on the social, economic and environmental changes required for a community to plan for the growth created by an energy development.

About one hundred and twenty-five people attended the event. When the floor was opened for other questions to discuss, an individual came forward with

---

140 http://www.theworldcafe.com/wp-content/uploads/2015/07/Cafe-To-Go-Revised.pdf

the issue of the high cost of municipal dog licenses. He felt very strongly about it. Out of respect, we assigned that individual their own table and encouraged anyone who wanted to talk about dogs to join him. Few people did, but he felt respected.

Step 3: The third step is assigning an issue or subject to each café table. People who want to talk about a specific issue go to the designated table with others who share the same interest. Normally, these are the more popular issues and thus, the more desirable tables. For this reason, I will call for three rounds of visiting tables during the café. If people can't visit the table on the first round (because there are too many people), they can visit on the second or third round. As a fourth step, everyone is engaged.

Step 4: Step four involves connecting the various perspectives. Participants are encouraged to doodle ideas on a sheet of paper at each table as they discuss their ideas with others, so that subsequent table visitors can see what others have written. A table ambassador stays at each subject table. While participants hear the views of others as they travel from table to table, the ambassador also notes ideas as they become deeper and richer with each round.

Step 5: In the fifth step, patterns of ideas and insights are connected. First, we hear from the ambassador on the matters being discussed and the ideas that have come forward. Then we hear the ideas of others on the same subject. It is important to not have the ambassador have the final word, as the process is designed to be democratic and interactive.

Step 6: The sixth step involves the debrief, where the insights and discoveries are shared with the group and discussed.

The advantage of a World Café process over a public meeting is that it allows everyone to participate. Subjects and issues can be added depending on what's important to the public. Compared to spider facilitation, the loud and passionate voices are heard early, and a forum is created to discuss those views. A wide range of subjects can be discussed over several hours by a large number of people.

The weakness of a World Café is that it equalizes subjects and issues. If there's a strong and dominate public issue that needs to be discussed, such as the need to help youth at risk for example, it may be seen to be on the same plane as the issue of lower-cost municipal dog license fees.

Roundtables

In my view, Roundtables are the next best technique for hearing from a large number of people. The method is relatively straightforward, involving people seated at tables of eight or ten. In some instances, I will break people into quads - four people speaking together - or pairs. This style of meeting may be preceded by a presentation by the client providing background information.

When using Roundtables, it is important to develop meaningful questions for participants to discuss. Normally, the same three to five questions are given to each table. Table members are asked to assign their own facilitator and note-taker. After an hour of prompting participants to go through each question and comment, there is typically a debrief, and the meeting ends.

Figure 12 Roundtables

In terms of the method's weaknesses, I find that locally-appointed facilitators generally do a lackluster job, with only one or two of the questions discussed. To address this problem, I will often mix the questions up numerically, so that some groups will start with number five and others with number three.

Roundtable meetings are more difficult to facilitate because people are spread wider across the meeting room. If the issue is pressing, the meeting will still include people who want to grandstand or otherwise put an exclamation point on an issue. Thus, when frustrated people finally get a chance to speak in public, the final plenary session can be very active and angry. On the other hand, everyone has had a chance to participate, and comments have been heard on specific questions.

Assuming that the process has evolved so that the facilitator is not using alternative ways of engaging a large number of people, my role shifts to that of the designer of a large public meeting. Using the analogy of a play, there are two fundamental tasks that I complete to achieve a successful outcome: write the script and direct the play.

In terms of a script, there's a story being told, and the media will often be present to cover the story. There's also a plot. It begins with the audience receiving the information it needs to know in order to understand what is going to be said and what their role is.

The plot moves along through dialogue in several acts. First there are presentations by the client and the proponent, both of which have a beginning, middle and end. Next, various actors comprised of members of the public play their part in moving the story along, often with conflict and drama. There are always complications. The play ends with a climax, usually in the form of closure activities.

There's a stage, and there are rehearsals where people have to learn their lines. There are props such as flip charts, display boards and power point presentations. And, there's a director or conductor. That's me. As an extreme facilitator, there are basically four tasks that I need to accomplish in order to choreograph a successful outcome: write the script, get the stage ready, manage the rehearsal and manage the "chalk talk".

Choreographing Successful Outcomes

Facilitation theorists and professional facilitators all acknowledge the need to write, script, choreograph and otherwise design a custom process for the meetings they are facilitating. The most important first step is being clear on what you and the client are setting out to achieve. This involves asking the fundamental question of what they want to get out of the group. For example, I often say to my client, "One way or another we've brought a large number of people to this venue. Why? What are the questions we want to ask them? What are our goals?

Who are these people and why are they yelling at me? | 155

On occasion, I need to be clear with my client about my role and the design and structure of the meeting. Most importantly, my client needs to understand that facilitation is not about mediation, although they may believe that this is my role because they would like the support of a calmer and understanding public as an outcome of the meeting.

My client may be looking for me to provide some sort of mediation service, or to structure the meeting in a manner that's conducive to mediation. But, facilitation is not mediation or conflict resolution.

Schwarz[141] provides an excellent comparison between facilitation and mediation/conflict resolution. Among a long list of comparisons, three stand out as being important in the context of large, angry public meetings:

Figure 13 Mediation vs Facilitation Comparison

TYPE OF INTERACTION	COMPARISON
Mediation	Parties can't, but want to, settle a conflict.
Facilitation	Helps a group to improve the process for solving problems and making decisions.
Mediation	Mediator is brought in after parties have reached an impasse. Parties need help from a third person.
Facilitation	Facilitators are brought in early. Parties know there might be an impasse and they want to learn how to avoid the impasse.
Mediation	Works with a small number of people.
Facilitation	Works with the whole group.

---

141 Schwarz, R., 2nd edition. P. 57

Occasionally, I will work with a client who hires me with the expectation that I will help them make the public listen. Facilitators are not there to exercise authority or make people listen. Kellerman and Bolger stress the importance of the client and facilitator understanding that the facilitation process is not about control. Even though the client may want the facilitator to control the group, the facilitator needs to understand that they are there to serve the group, and that they have been given permission by the group to play this role.

The group consists of the public and the client. Ground rules are not laws. They are guidelines, invokable by the group, that the group has agreed are important for achieving dialogue. According to Ghais, the role of the facilitator is to help the client and the public to hear themselves, not for the public to hear the client.

I once facilitated a very large and hostile meeting where the client saw my role as insuring that the public would not clap for a favourable comment, to which I explained, "I can discuss my expectations for civil behaviour, but there's no rule I can invoke that says, 'thou shall not clap.'"

In a public meeting, a script also forms a contract with the client and, occasionally, with the public. Occasionally, as a way of building trust, I will meet with citizens' groups ahead of time and lay out how I'm proposing to facilitate a meeting. The agenda is my contract with the citizens and the client on how I will deliver the meeting.

It is important to my client to be clear with the transaction. The transaction involves communications flowing between the client and public and vice versa. Schwarz[142] states that ineffective contracting results in problems. Being clear on the purpose of the facilitation role is important for three reasons: 1) it states the conditions of how we will work together; 2) it confirms whether or not we want to work together; and, 3) it develops the trust that allows the facilitator to facilitate.

What can be achieved through the design and structure of a large, angry public meeting?

Although clients sometimes don't want it, meetings discussing the design and structure of the meeting can be productive in their own way. To understand

---

142 Schwarz, R., 2nd edition. P.237

what can be achieved from the group, the facilitator needs to, as a priority, help their client to step back and identify what they want to get out of a meeting. Clients I have worked with who have discussed meeting structure gain a clear understanding of their expectations. Together it helps us do a much better job of managing public interactions for desired outcomes. I use the following criteria for defining an acceptable minimal outcome from a large, angry public meeting:

- Did members of the public learn from the information presented by my client?
- Did my client learn from the comments provided by the public?
- Given that listening to the public is about making better decisions, did the client present alternative decisions? Were those alternatives accepted, improved or rejected for good cause by members of the public?
- Was there an opportunity for members of the public to learn from each other? Were diverse and alternative viewpoints shared during the meeting? Were dissenting voices heard?
- Could members of the public assess their own opinion in the context of listening to the opinions of others?
- Did meeting participants reach the 'reforming' stage? Was a clear way forward accepted by the group?

If, by attending the meeting, members of the public were able to learn and understand the parameters of a decision, then the meeting was productive. Actions occurring after the meeting can then help the group to move toward the goal of making decisions in the public interest.

Writing the Script

Much of our work occurs on the outskirts of the City of Toronto, a region with five regional governments[143] known by its telephone area code as "the 905". Within the 905, the population of the Greater Toronto and Hamilton Area (GTHA) is about 6.9 million (2016 census), representing twenty per cent of

---

143 City of Hamilton, Halton Region, Peel Region, York Region, Durham Region and City of Toronto.

Canada's population. This area, with one of the strongest economies in North America, has experienced significant growth pressure including the need for new roads, housing, schools and water and waste water infrastructure.

The Region of Peel has the largest population in the 905, with about 1.4 million people (2016). At that time Peel was growing rapidly, especially in the local municipalities of Brampton, but also in Mississauga and to a lesser extent Caledon.

In 1996, the ownership of the South Peel Facilities, which comprised two water treatment plants and associated feeder mains and reservoirs, and two wastewater treatment plants and associated trunk sewers were transferred from the Province of Ontario to the Region of Peel.

Investment in these key facilities, while continuous, really had not kept up with the need and as such Peel recognised that upgrades would be required at each of these facilities. A Water and Wastewater Master Plan was undertaken to determine the capacity required at each of the facilities in order to satisfy the growth for the following 20 years. Upon its completion, the Region selected consultants to undertake Class EA studies to define the social, environmental and economic impacts of plant expansions and consider potential mitigation measures. The KMK Consultants Limited team, which included Hardy Stevenson and Associates Limited, was selected for developing the Lakeview Waste Water Treatment facilities.

The plant had a history of complaints from the neighbourhood regarding foul odours, and these were increasing in number and frustration as the loading to the plant had increased over the preceding years. The facility also utilised a technology known as Zimpro which was problematic and particularly odourous. The number of complaints were sufficiently numerous that Peel had a hotline to respond and record these.

Very early in the EA process KMK recognised that Zimpro capacity was a bottleneck causing raw sewage solids to back up and turn septic thus releasing foul odours to the atmosphere. The prevailing southwesterly winds then sent the odour into the community.

We were asked to develop a communications and community engagement plan and begin community consultation for the Environmental Assessment of the approval and expansion of the Lakeview Waste Water[144] and Water Treatment Plants. Local politicians were strongly opposed to the project due to its potential impact on the community.

To develop a strategy for obtaining political and community approval, we worked closely with Mitch Zamojc, Commissioner of Public Works, who led the development of the strategy. Key members of the Works Division staff team included Mark Schiller Director of the Water Division, Sandi LeFaucheur, Coordinator and Anne DeCraemer, Communications. Deborah Ross and Bob Fleeton at KMK, with Joan Lockhart-Grace of Hardy Stevenson and Associates Limited were members of the consulting team.

Understanding the need to synthesize engineering and communication, the public/private team performed with great skill and creativity. The script could have been premised on muddling through the acrimonious situation that characterized the existing relationship between the Region, politicians and the community, but it didn't.

The team analyzed the situation based on a community profile that we conducted, as well as technical reports. As a desirable alternative to more odour from old thermal-oxidization and open aeration tanks and clarifiers at the plant, we noted that the new facilities would modernize the plant and significantly reduce odour. The reduction of odour would result in a significant improvement to the quality of life of residents.

We knew that we had to do a much better job of communicating, but we needed to reset the relationship. So, we changed the story. Realizing that the only way to move ahead with the approval was to start building trust, we called for a community meeting in south Mississauga. About one hundred and twenty-five people showed up. I was the facilitator.

The first words out of the mouth of Mitch Zamojc, Commissioner of Public Works, were, "We have failed you and I need to start with an apology". I was proud of the integrity and sincerity that Mitch showed that night. He spoke of the need for the Region to do a much better job at communications and said he

---

144 Now called the G. E. Booth (Lakeview) Wastewater Treatment Plant https://www.peelregion.ca/pw/water/sewage-trtmt/lakeview-trtmt.htm

wanted the community to partner with the Region to strengthen their relationship and create long-term positive improvements to their quality of life.

The sincerity of his apology was recognised and appreciated by the crowd. Commitment was made to keep the community involved and informed. Zamojc demonstrated his, and the Region's commitment by authorising an immediate expenditure of $10 million to implement a bypass to the solids handling problem. He also authorised introduction of chemicals to selected pumping stations and the main trunk sewer to inhibit the formation of foul odours such as hydrogen sulphide.

Through this commitment, the Region was able to significantly improve the quality of life of residents, reduce complaints and allow the EA to proceed. The Zimpro process was taken out of service as part of the plant upgrades, all within a project capital cost of over $300 million.

Setting realistic expectations was important. Mitch pointed out that construction would be disruptive, but when the expansion was completed, odour would be reduced. He talked about forming a community liaison committee and a stakeholder committee and conducting community polling so that the community would have hard data documenting whether the Region was succeeding or failing. Open houses and regular newsletters would keep everyone up to date.

The residents listened carefully and accepted the Commissioner's mea culpa. The script involved the Commissioner, taking ownership of the problem, apologizing deeply to the community and promising to take action immediately. Questions asked by the Commissioner to the community included, "How do we best communicate with you? Are the proposed community engagement methods acceptable? What's the best way of getting you the information you need? What does an ideal relationship mean to you as we move through the EA and construction?"

The Region of Peel committed to and ultimately delivered an excellent communications and community engagement process that possessed integrity and sincerity. The communications plan, called the "Clear Scents Plan" won an award[145] for its effectiveness. The Environmental Assessment was approved.

---

145 Dalton Penn Communications Award of Merit

Four years later, the project came in on time and on budget, with very few public complaints.

Whether or not there was going to be an angry meeting in south Peel that night started with an understanding of the background information, facts and issues. The agenda at the initial meeting focused on building trust and seeing the project through the eyes of the community. The team was transparent, and efforts were made to establish a long-term positive relationship.

If we had kept to the old script, an angry public meeting would have involved: a failure to acknowledge the obvious odour problems; a failure to take responsibility; a panel of presenters passing the microphone; people standing behind a microphone in the aisle; presenters showing very little understanding of the community and local issues; a lack of sincerity and sensitivity to community remarks.

Instead, the new script was centred on:

- Acknowledging a start point that was uncomfortable for the team, but necessary.
- Truth-telling, transparency, integrity and sincerity.
- A goal of achieving best outcomes.
- Partnering with the community.
- Creating an agenda best geared to achieving dialogue.
- Managing roles and behaviours so as to influence outcomes in a positive way.

Suzanne Ghais refers to this stage of extreme facilitation as the "design stage of a custom process"[146], occurring early when a facilitator is first retained. Comparing the process to an architect building a custom home, the facilitator:

- Works with the client group to agree on purpose, goals, and outcomes of the facilitated process.

---

146 Ghais, S. op cit, p. 32, 33

- Draws on a wide range of possible group activities, techniques and processes to design the details of a process that will meet the agreed-upon goals.
- Recommends that this meeting design will meet these goals for this group.
- Makes adjustments to the agenda and techniques up to the start of the meeting.[147]

There are four considerations involved in "getting the script right": an in-depth understanding of the group and its circumstances; agreement with the group on the purpose and goals of the process; a knowledge of a wide range of techniques and activities; and creativity."[148]

In terms of the story line for the script, a desirable outcome for a large, public meeting could involve members of the public:[149] identifying desired options for a decision or action; expressing how they wish to narrow and evaluate options; identifying proposals for how all parties could achieve their outcomes; recommending ways to get past deadlocks; and developing action plans for moving forward.

The Facilitator's Agenda

As stated earlier, the important work involved in facilitating a meeting actually occurs before the meeting. A key part of the script is the Facilitator's Agenda, a detailed meeting plan or choreography that focuses the team on the outcomes they want and the road they will take to get them there. The Facilitator's Agenda also plays an important role in clarifying the relationship between the client, the project team and the extreme facilitator.

A Facilitator's Agenda is:

- A detailed agenda documenting who speaks when.
- The 'script' that describes how the meeting will unfold.

---

147 Ghais, S. op cit, p. 32, 33
148 Ghais, S. op cit, p. 33
149 Ghais, S. op cit, p. 132

Who are these people and why are they yelling at me? | 163

- A way for the proponent to see and understand what the facilitator is going to do and say before they do so.
- Documentation and approval in advance of what the facilitator will do to keep the meeting under control. Specifically, "Who does what if someone acts out? Does the facilitator have permission to throw someone out? Does the facilitator have permission to suggest alternative methods of achieving dialogue during the meeting?"
- A guide to how the facilitator will manage the conversation around issues that the proponent does or does not want discussed.
- An understanding of issues germane to the discussion and those that have nothing to do with the matters on the agenda.
- Specific directions on what happens after the meeting occurs.

The Facilitator's Agenda is created days or weeks before the meeting. It scripts what the proponent will do and say, the timing of what happens when (e.g. what power point slide should be on the screen at what point in the agenda), the timing of presentations and the agenda. It is a script for the role of other participants and the document that guides logistics, safety, handouts and other information provided to the public.

In terms of the "business" of facilitating, the Facilitator's Agenda also becomes a series of draft agreements and contracts between the facilitator and the client on how the meeting is expected to unfold. Suzanne Ghais describes it as follows.

"It is the process of negotiating agreement with the clients about what they can expect from your services, and what you will need from them to fulfill their expectations. It sets you up for success, because it allows you to participate in defining success, and it helps the client group understand its role in ensuring success."[150]

Ghais states that the Facilitator's Agenda is an iterative series of agreements that clears up what is implicit, spoken but not written, and written.[151] All members of the proponent team - politicians, consulting professionals and others - are

---

150 Ghais, S. op cit ppgs 102, 103
151 Ghais, S. op cit p. 104

expected to review the Facilitator's Agenda, understand their roles and agree before the meeting.

The Facilitator's Agenda allows the facilitator to concentrate on the dialogue with the public instead of worrying about the structure of the meeting or looking over their shoulder at how proponents and consultants are responding to the process. It also allows the client and project team to anticipate what the facilitator will say. The last thing I want to hear as a facilitator is, "I really wish you had not said that or that you had handled matters differently."

As a neutral party, the extreme facilitator is often able to talk to everyone before the meeting, including members of the public opposing the client. For meetings anticipated to be prickly, I like to meet with residents and the proponent independently and in advance. Doing so allows me to ask very important questions of each side, such as, "What are the assumptions that you are bringing into the meeting? What are the beliefs and behaviours (norms) serving as your start point? What outcome from the meeting are you are looking for? Is there a better way of achieving your desired outcomes?"

Suzanne Ghais[152] provides a strong list of sample questions to pose to the client before the meeting that lead to a better understanding of what the client wants to get out of the meeting, including:

- What are the major issues you need to confront or problems you need to tackle?
- Where are you weak?
- What are the obstacles you are facing?
- What prompted you to seek a facilitator?
- What do you hope the public meeting will achieve?
- What are your greatest hopes and fears in the process?
- What is your vision of an ideal outcome?
- What demands are being placed on you from outside?

---

152 Ghais, S. op cit, pps 61 to 66

- What external conditions affect the problems you are facing?
- What concerns do you have about the process we're undertaking?
- Have you worked with a facilitator before? What was the experience like? What was helpful? What was unhelpful?
- Are you looking forward to the process or dreading it and why?
- What advice or suggestions do you have for me as a facilitator working with this group?

A critical question needs to be asked when preparing the Facilitator's Agenda: "Is there a better way of organizing the meeting to achieve your outcome?" If the extreme facilitator can achieve dialogue around important questions before the meeting occurs, there is a better chance that the meeting will include more "meaningful dialogue" than angry yelling. Not all community dialogue requires a meeting, however. As discussed earlier, workshops, kitchen table meetings and other forms of community engagement are also good ways to share information.

A sample of a Facilitator's Agenda appears in Appendix 3. Creating this document basically involves taking the short Public Agenda and expanding each section by adding details. It's a Word Document using the Table format with the header giving all of the critical logistics information: meeting title, date and location; parking and loading areas; disabled access; names of team members; cell phone numbers of key contact people (e.g. custodian with keys); and time of arrival.

The next rows of the table document all of the preparatory steps (the "don't forget"' list). These are the items the team needs to consider before the meeting. For example:

- Room booked?
- Room set-up approved?
- Security contacted?
- Post-meeting clean-up timing confirmed?
- Did we bring the "public agenda"?
- Were directional signs printed?

- Were directional signs posted?
- Door unlocked? When do we have access?
- PPT reviewed and approved?
- Power point projectors in car?
- Screen booked or brought?
- Handout materials agreed on and approved? AV equipment booked?
- Name and contact information for the AV technician
- Fire alarms checked and fire doors unlocked?
- Extension cords?
- Sign-in registration list printed?

The next part of the Facilitator's Agenda involves introductions. I am almost always the first on my feet, identifying myself as the independent third-party facilitator so as to seek and confirm my authority. I will then go through about five minutes of introductory remarks including:

- Welcome – thanks for spending part of your evening with us.
- As an independent third-party facilitator, I don't have a stake in the outcome. I do this for a living.
- The purpose of the meeting: why the team has asked you here tonight.
- The agenda.
- Introduction of speakers and guests, particularly politicians and senior officials.
- The ground rules.
- When I will ask the public for comments and how long on the agenda they will have for comments.

Before the Facilitator's Agenda is completed, the team and I will go over it during a series of conference calls or face to face meetings. We will know what's going to be presented and by whom. We will rehearse the Power Point presentations

Who are these people and why are they yelling at me? | 167

(see later discussion about Rehearsals). And we will lengthen or shorten each presentation to insure the public continues to be engaged.

Long presentations are killers. It is very hard for me to get the public to listen for more than twenty minutes. If the presentation needs to be longer, I will find a way to break it up into ten-minutes segments.

I ask all of my clients to rehearse their presentation for timing before the meeting. Large numbers of angry people will not wait an hour to be allowed to present their comments or questions. On very rare occasions when my client hasn't rehearsed timing and has gone way longer that is acceptable and people in the back of the room are throwing their shoes, I've cut them off. But this rarely happens.

Before the meeting, we will prepare a list of the tough questions that we can expect.

The team meets to consider the questions and what the acceptable answers will be. This is called the "Frequently Asked Questions (FAQs)" list. It is important to establish in advance who will talk, when and for how long, and equally important to predetermine who will answer which questions. At this time, I will be fully aware of which public comments are on the agenda and which are not. For example, I've had the occasional meeting in the middle of an election campaign and a question will be asked purely to score political points for a candidate. This is never part of the agenda.

The final part of the Facilitator's Agenda deals with closure. While the topic of meeting closure is discussed elsewhere, its important that the project team knows how closure is going to occur. More than once I've asked a client who's had a pretty rough night to thank the very people who were beating him or her up. It's the last thing they want to do but, as professionals, they need to. When I know that this is a problem for the client, I usually give them a few minutes before I close the meeting to allow themselves to clear their heads, find a happy place psychologically, smile and thank the public.

The public will always want to know the next steps and what will be done with the notes we took during the meeting. While I discuss Closure group dynamics earlier, closure questions to address include:

- Who thanks people for attending?
- How do you thank people for attending?
- Is there more than one person doing the thank you?
- Who else do you need to thank?
- Will the person closing be doing a brief summation of public comments?
- How will members of the public contact the team after the meeting ends?
- What happens if they have additional comments during closure?
- What happens if a small group of people still want to talk?

The Stage

People arriving at a meeting venue may be concerned if they think the facilitator sees them as actors on a stage, as they would with expert presenters. For me, a 'stage' analogy is a good way to conceptualize how people are going to be organized and how they will interact with others during an angry public meeting. Even though they are different people, I routinely see the same acts and actors in different meeting halls in different communities.

Setting the stage begins long before the meeting starts. It includes all aspects of venue planning including how people are seated, audio-visuals and logistics. As other facilitators'[153] do, I typically have an eye for the comfort of the participants and clients, making sure that they have water, food, light, fresh air, proper temperature, decent chairs, tables (if required) and space to move around. I will also consider the needs of people with disabilities, which also applies equally to the client and specialist groups. The client and their consultants will often be hungry and thirsty and need to hang up coats and store bags and equipment.

Figuring out how people should be seated is an early task. Most of the meetings I've facilitated occur in community centres, hotel ballrooms, municipal council chambers, school gymnasiums or sports arenas where the ability to be creative with how people are seated is limited. There are factors, such as fire codes, limits on the number of chairs and the physical layout of the venue, which can't be

---

153 Ghais S. op cit p. 156

changed. Despite these constraints, choices can be made that will lead to the best outcomes.

It is a fact that the set-up of a room makes the people at the meeting more or less angry, and how people are seated allows more or less meaningful dialogue between the client and the public. Doyle and Straus state, "Where you meet can affect the way a meeting will work. A good meeting room won't guarantee a good meeting, but a bad meeting room can contribute to a bad meeting."[154] They recommend that the room be selected that fits the group based on high and low estimates of attendance. A lot of people in a small room creates excitement. A few people in a big space will feel intimidated and will not be able to hear other people speak. They conclude by suggesting that the facilitator select the space for the effect wanted.[155]

Returning to the 'stage' analogy, there are many good books on how to set up entertainment stages. Playwrights have been experimenting with stage set-ups since the time of the Romans and Greeks. It is useful to draw from this experience.

The Architecture of Democracy

In the context of a public meeting, staging has been referred to the "architecture of assembly"[156]. I instead refer to it as the 'architecture of democracy'. Adrian Seger provides great insights about room set-up, stating, "A room setup implies and influences what happens at meetings" and observing that room setup can, "… ultimately affect the quality of democracy, sharing, and the equality experienced by participants". He identifies five types of room set-up: opposing benches, semi-circle, horseshoe, circle and classroom.

Stating, "Architecture sets the stage for our lives; it creates the world we inhabit and shapes how we relate to one another." Seger also cites research

---

154 Doyle and Straus, op cit p. 187

155 Doyle and Straus, op cit; p. 187

156 The architecture of assembly Monday, April 3rd, 2017 by Adrian Segar https://www.conferences-thatwork.com/index.php/event-design/2017/04/the-architecture-of-assembly/#more-10038. Read the rest of this article at: https://www.conferencesthatwork.com/index.php/event-design/2017/04/the-architecture-of-assembly/#more-10038

by Max Cohen de Lara and David Mulder van der Vegt, which declares, "In a time in which democracy is under increasing pressure in different parts of the world, it is time to rethink the architecture of assembly."[157] In order to maximize the transaction of information and create an opportunity for constructive dialogue, some room set-ups are preferred and others should be avoided.

Classroom and Auditorium Style Stage[158]

The classroom and auditorium style set-up usually consist of a raised rectangular platform stage at one end of a room with the audience sitting in rows facing the stage[159]. The stage may be raised or simply a spot at the front of the room where presenters are standing. While classroom and auditorium seating are common, it is not necessarily the best set-up for large public meetings.

When several hundred people need to be seated, it's impossible to get them all in the room efficiently, and its very difficult to be creative. This type of seating is the best way to show information on a screen, with all eyes pointed to the front of the room, but it sets up an "us" on stage and "them" in the audience relationship. I strongly resist putting clients and consultants on a stage or even on an elevated riser at the front of the room because it creates a, "we are above you" perception among the audience. If the public and the client are jointly making a tough public decision, I want to show symbolically that everyone is at the same level and that every view is important.

---

157 Max Cohen de Lara and David Mulder van der Vegt, "These 5 architectural designs influence every legislature in the world — and tell you how each governs ", The Washington Post, March 4, 2017 http://www.parliamentbook.com/book; also see https://www.wired.com/2016/09/beautiful-book-reveals-architectures-impact-politics/

158 Carnegie Mellon University, Graphics on various seating styles. https://www.cmu.edu/conferences/facilities/meeting/uc/room-styles.html

159 http://www.theatrestrust.org.uk/discover-theatres/theatre-faqs/170-what-are-the-types-of-theatre-stages-and-auditoria

Figure 14 Classroom Style Set-up

If possible, I prefer to slant the seating to create a herringbone chair arrangement. Doing this allows people to see who is talking on the other side of the room as well as their facial expressions and body language. They may perceive that not everyone in the room has the same opinion. Seeing and hearing other points of view creates the understanding that decisions are not dependent on the point of view of single members of the public. Instead, they will see experts at the front of the room who are also commenting on how a complex problem may be solved or the alternatives available to solve a particular public issue.

The classroom style is generally not as safe for large crowds as other room arrangements. It's harder for people to get into or out of rows, and also difficult to bring a microphone to the middle of a row without stepping on people's toes. And I will often see people standing along the wall of a meeting hall rather than venturing to the middle of a row to occupy vacant seats.

Figure 15 Auditorium Meeting

The auditorium style is easier to move people into because there are one or more rows between sections of seats. It's also easier to bring a microphone to someone and in an emergency, to move people out of their seats and onto a safe location. The herringbone style has the advantages of the auditorium style, while also allowing members of the public to have a better perspective on who's saying what.

Semi-Circle or Thrust Stage[160]

I prefer the Semi-Circle set-up for seating, which has its roots in the Thrust Stage. The Theatres Trust in the UK describes the Thrust Stage as follows, "As the name suggests, these setups project or 'thrust' into the auditorium, with the audience sitting on three sides. The thrust stage area itself is not always square but may be semi-circular or half a polygon with any number of sides. Such stages are often used to increase intimacy between actors and the audience."

---

[160] Theatres Trust, What are the types of theatre stages and auditoria? http://www.theatrestrust.org.uk/discover-theatres/theatre-faqs/170-what-are-the-types-of-theatre-stages-and-auditoria

Figure 16 Semi-Circle or Three-Sided Stage

When a meeting is going well, the Semi-Circle allows the public to see the presenters' body language and facial expressions. Intimacy between the professionals and the public is desired. As the meeting unfolds, the public, the client and the professionals are all acting out roles. If someone has a point to make, they are closer to the other members of the public. Symbolically, the Semi-Circle allows me as facilitator to bring them closer to the people making the decision, which is important.

However, this room set-up also creates a "bear pit" because the professionals are still on an elevated platform and separated from the members of the public. It is also more difficult to pass microphones into the audience, as you need to pass the mike across the row to someone in the middle.

Circle or Theatre in the Round

The Semi-Circle has its origins in the Theatre in the Round. It is effective because no one's point of view is impeded, and it creates intimacy among the client, their experts and the public. When I've facilitated meetings in this format, members of the public tend to be more reserved and thoughtful in their comments because the client or professional proponent and other members of the public are physically closer to them.

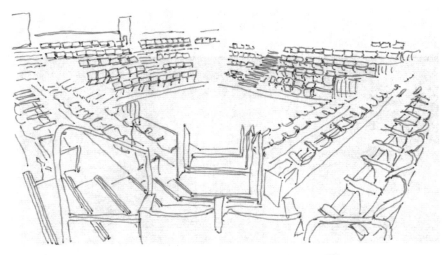

Figure 17 Four-sided Stage and Theatre-in-the-Round[161]

Professional presenters and the client are seated with the public until they are called up to speak. Once they are on their feet, though, it's also a bear pit. A member of the public may express a strong opinion or provide an emotional response but, after making the statement, there's nowhere to hide. They are going to own their opinion and wear it until the end of the meeting.

With a Semi-Circle arrangement, it is almost impossible to show PowerPoint slides or other information. Although it makes it easier to hear people without microphones, it is more difficult to move mikes (and myself) around the room during the meeting.

Horseshoe or U-Shaped

The Theatres Trust describes the U-Shaped style as follows, "… a central performance area enclosed by the audience on all sides. The arrangement is rarely 'round'; more usually the seating is in a square or polygonal formation. The

---

161 Theatres Trust, op cit

Who are these people and why are they yelling at me? | 175

actors enter through aisles between the seating. Scenery is minimal and carefully positioned to ensure it does not obstruct the audience's view."[162]

The U-Shaped style is excellent for promoting dialogue in smaller groups. I've used it frequently for meetings where I expected anger from a smaller number of people representing their interests or those of stakeholders. This style allows me to walk up to people talking so that I can hear them or emphasize a point. It's an easy style for the presentation of audio-visual information. It is ideal when there is conflict because there's no separation between the members of the public, the client, the professionals and the facilitator. However, there's never a hall big enough to have several hundred people arranged in this setup.[163]

Figure 18 U-shaped

---

162 Theatre's Trust op cit.
163 https://www.cmu.edu/conferences/facilities/meeting/uc/room-styles.html

Roundtable

This seating style has worked very well for many larger meetings. (I talked earlier about meeting agendas that were structured based on a roundtable format.) There are many advantages of Roundtable style seating. It is easy for most people to see and hear. I can easily get microphones to them, and walk among the audience. When tent cards are placed on the tables, it allows me to call on people wishing to speak by name.

The Roundtable style also allows for work assignments during the meeting that involve people talking in small groups. I can pose questions, have each table talk about their collective response and then, after fifteen minutes, report out to the larger group. An example of a question I would ask might be, "The project proponent and staff have identified three alternative solutions to the problem. Should they have considered other solutions and, if so, what are those solutions?"

The key consideration in selecting the stage for an angry meeting is to have the public as much on stage as the client and the professional staff. Everyone will have a role to play and many members of the public will have acting parts. Advance planning needs to go into choosing a stage set-up that maximizes communication, dialogue and thoughtful deliberation on important issues.

The Parts of a Stage

Each stage has components that contribute to the outcome of the meeting. Thinking about each component and how it contributes to the performance adds a second layer of complexity. Before and during the meeting, these parts of the venue need to be planned.

Front of the House

Every angry public meeting has a "Front of the House". This is where people come in from the parking lot and transit stops to a registration area. We put a lot of effort into wayfinding signage, so that meeting participants don't have to wander around aimlessly trying to find the meeting room. This can be an issue for meetings in larger convention centres or hotels. For this reason, we put up

Who are these people and why are they yelling at me? | 177

welcome signs with the name of the meeting (Meeting to Discuss this Topic Tonight) and arrows pointing the public in the right direction.

The Front of the House normally includes a registration desk or, for large meetings, several desks. Desk staff need to be friendly and astute. Their job is to welcome the public, ask them to sign in, answer preliminary questions, explain the agenda, give them handout information, and occasionally "bling" and comment sheets. They then direct members of the public to the meeting room.

If there is an Open House component of the meeting, we will inform the public which information boards have subject content and who to talk to for specific questions. As discussed earlier, this is the area where the prologue will be occurring. People sitting at registration will be hearing initial comments and getting initial reactions from the public and provide initial responses to questions and comments. It's a place where people will also be: recognizing and talking to their neighbours; waiting for other people to arrive; seeing and talking to politicians.

The Front of the House is a component of the meeting that needs to be carefully managed. This is the first exposure many people will have to the client and vice versa. Challenges at this stage could include: people not wanting to register; initial exposure of the client to anger being brought into the meeting; ensuring that people have support material and people not wanting information; and minor initial acts of civil disobedience.

If not well managed, the front registration time is the first opportunity the client has to "piss off" members of the public. We ask people to register because we want to send them project updates, such as the date of the next meeting and documentation to regulatory authorities on how many people attended.

As an example of one challenge we experienced, we noticed that the registration sheets signed by two hundred people had disappeared from two tables. A member of the public had taken them without our permission for the purpose of obtaining people's names and contact information so that they could organize everyone in attendance to oppose the client.

For many years, we adjusted the sign-in process by taping down the registration sheets. We realized, however, that people signing in would still have access to names (and, now everyone is able to photograph the sign in sheet.).

Today, we have people sign contact information cards containing a permission request and deposit them into a ballot-type box. By providing us with their contact information, people give permission to have photos taken, receive email alerts, and have their comments on matters being discussed collected and quoted according to Privacy and Freedom of Information legislation.

Centre Stage

During the meeting, presentations take place and the client and consultants successfully (or not) answer questions and respond to comments in an area that we call Centre Stage. I will usually do a final check of seating before the meeting starts to make sure that people at every seat can see the presenters at the front. As the facilitator, I start at Centre Stage. My clients move to Centre Stage as they begin presenting, sometimes staying in this place all evening.

Rather than using a panel-type set-up involving talking heads sitting at a table, I encourage each speaker to come up to a single microphone, make their comments and then return to where they are sitting. So as not to distract participants and allow them to focus on individual speakers, support staff and expert consultants are typically seated off to the side but still at the front of the room.

As the question and answer period opens up, I will typically roam through the audience - upstage, left stage and right stage. As we start to reach a Storming Stage when some vocal and emotional people wish to take over the meeting and shift the conversation to a different part of a script, I'll firmly be at Centre Stage. Centre Stage might move into the audience involving audience members engaging in conversation amongst themselves or several grandstanding speakers controlling the script by asking heated questions of the client and consultants.

Backstage

There are two other important parts of a stage that are sometimes overlooked in planning. A team consisting of clients and their staff, consultants and their staff, and my company will add up to fifteen or more people on site to manage the meeting. Each of us will bring printed materials, coats, purses and other personal items that can't be left in the meeting room. And, if staff are at the venue at 5:00 PM for a 7:00 pm meeting start, they will be hungry. For these reasons, a Backstage area is usually designated to accommodate staff belongings, serve as a small eating area for an order of pizza and serve as a safe space for socializing before each person takes their role in the meeting. The Backstage may be a kitchen area, coat room, side meeting room or other such space.

Another stage is an audio-visual Control Booth or area, which can take different forms. Its configurations range from a dedicated place at the side of the room where technicians control microphones, to a sophisticated Control Booth housing high-priced AV equipment, technicians and translators. Sometimes, when a meeting needs to be bilingual (English and French), a translation booth is set up at the back of the room. For the meeting to be a success, I need to be able to see the people working audio-visual and communicate with them at all times.

Audio-Visual Equipment

Large meetings simply cannot occur without audio-visual equipment. The quality of the equipment is an important contributor to the success of a meeting. People in the back row need to hear what's going on as much as people in the front row. When I try to explain to a client that I need professional equipment and skilled technicians, I usually get push-back: "We didn't budget for it. Can the old equipment we have on hand do? Why do you need so much equipment?"

During a meeting I was facilitating in a high school auditorium, the client told me that they were going to ask students to set up and manage the school's audio-visual equipment. The equipment was old and inadequate, and the meeting happened to be one of the most boisterous and disorderly I had experienced that year.

The students continually had difficulty in getting the microphones to work, to the point where members of the crowd started complaining and blaming me for the bad sound system. In between taking questions, I was trying to figure out how I could help the students. I could see that they were becoming upset about not being able to get the mikes to work properly – so upset that they left in the middle of the meeting. And so, I needed to explain to the audience that this was the best we could do. I felt sorry for the students. This was likely the toughest experience they ever had earning volunteer hours.

A colleague of mine, an excellent facilitator, shared a similar experience that she had with faulty audio-visual equipment. Rural meetings discussing proposed landfill sites are always chaotic, with local residents often enraged to the point of threatening violence. Her setting was a rural school gymnasium. The issue was the location of a landfill site in the community that would take garbage from another community. The Public Works Department staff and politicians needed to determine whether or not it would support the landfill location.

In the week leading up to the meeting, all the local politicians were being intimidated by a growing chorus of anger. The whole community was invited to the local school. My colleague and her crew met with several politicians in advance, who insisted on being the ones to start the meeting. This is not the way any facilitator likes to have a meeting started, as things can get out of control in the first minute, before the facilitator is introduced and begins to do their job. That's why I insist on being the person introducing the politicians. If they get into trouble in the first minute, I am able to step in and bail them out. If politicians begin and things get rough, I have to get past the new issue raised by the audience of, "Who are you and what right do you have the tell us how you are going to run the meeting?"

In rural towns, there usually isn't a dedicated audio-visual company nearby where new sound equipment, screens, LCD projectors and microphones can be rented. You are at the mercy of using antiquated equipment, which usually works poorly, or renting equipment from a local disc jockey (DJ). DJ equipment is fine for a dance at the local Legion Hall, but not adequate for the demands of a large angry meeting.

In my colleague's rural meeting scenario, a local DJ tried to get his equipment to work for about an hour before two hundred and fifty angry people arrived. In addition to microphone feedback problems, loud pops emanated every so often from the speakers – not good to hear in contentious meetings because they sound a bit like gunfire. (Being the veteran of many public meetings, it's not unusual to hear this sound – the popping, not the gunfire.)

The politician in charge of Public Works bravely decided that he would be the one to welcome people and explain that Council was facing a tough decision about the landfill. Known in the community to be in favour of the landfill, he was greeted with outbursts and cat calls. About a minute into his remarks, it was obvious that the councillor knew that he was in trouble. I've seen this hundreds of times: no longer smiling; reddening face; hesitations in remarks responding to each outburst; begging the crowd to be allowed to speak.

At that very moment, the audio-visual system let out one of the largest pops my colleague had ever heard. The crowd pulled back their heads in unison, wondering what the sound was. Within a split second, someone screamed, "Don't shoot me! Stop! Please don't shoot!" With the councillor on the floor face down in a spread-eagle position, microphone still in hand, my colleague knew that this was the time for her to step up and take control of the meeting.

Wrangling Microphones

"Is this working? Is this working? Hello?"

Unfortunately, these phrases are all too common at public meetings. The way that microphones are handled has a lot to do with whether the meeting is a success. When TV crews cover a large angry meeting, they want to get a shot of people lined up at a single microphone in the middle of an aisle, shaking their fists at a panel of experts or yelling at a politician.

That doesn't happen at my meetings. Because microphones are necessary with large audiences, my staff and I pay a lot of attention to training how to move them to people asking questions and providing comments. I insist on providing FM portable microphones (no cords) for the client and consulting team, as well as for staff bringing microphones to people asking questions. Sometimes I will have up to six microphones live at the same time, and I will wear an FM lapel version that allows me to move around.

Several issues can occur when microphones are not well managed. People in the audience who are holding the microphone will often not let go until they've asked every question on their mind and heard every response from the team. "Hogging the mike" means that, during a ninety-minute meeting, with twenty or more people wanting to speak, one person who won't let go of the mike will take up to ten minutes of the allowed time, making it very difficult for everyone else on the list to speak.

Most people don't know how to speak into a microphone, as some microphones have a two-second delay before their voice is heard. Other mikes require you to speak right into the top of the mike. People will switch a microphone off thinking that they are switching it on, or they may accidentally mute the device. Concluding that the microphone doesn't work, they may abandon it entirely, so that no one hears what they are saying.

My staff are trained to bring a microphone to a member of the public, and they know how it works. They go to the person next on the speakers list according to my instructions. They will stand next to the person until it's their time to speak and try to hold on to the microphone as they speak. They are trained to stay with the person and help to cut them off should they hog the microphone or grab it and take too long.

Cutting someone off is the most sensitive part of staff training. As I work with the client, consultants and staff up front, my microphone staff will be working beside the person in question. We use a lot of body language. If someone is taking too long, I will start making closure remarks.

I would like to say, "You've said enough. We've heard you. You're going on way to long." But I try not to be rude. Instead, I will tell the person that I have understood what they've said and would like the team to respond, reminding them that there are other people who also want to speak. This usually causes the speaker to begin summarizing their comments or talking faster. At the same time, my microphone wranglers are trained to start crashing in on the speaker's person's personal space, taking steps closer (without touching them) until it's almost indecent, while continually whispering "thank you". When the speaker takes a breath, my staff will put their hand out to take the microphone back, signalling to them that they are finished. When the microphone is moved toward the staff member, they take it away from the speaker.

While this training may sound like a small detail during a large public meeting, it helps in avoiding prolonged grandstanding with a few individuals dominating air time among several hundred who may also want to speak.

Knowing What's Happening Next Door

It is particularly important to know in advance what is going to be occurring in rooms adjacent to the meeting venue. On one occasion, I forgot to do this when preparing to facilitate a meeting in a hotel banquet room involving about a hundred seniors and environmentalists concerned about electromagnetic effects related to a local cell tower.

As it turns out, someone else had planned a stag party in the next room for a player on a hockey team, which I wasn't aware of until the night of the meeting.

The rooms were only separated by a thin bi-fold screen. My meeting and the hockey stag began at the same time. At first, it was quiet enough to hear the speaker in my room and the questions and comments of participants. But, after about a half an hour and the first round of beer at the stag party, things got louder, and we could hear the voices of young men greeting other young men arriving with laughter and boisterousness.

About fifteen minutes later, there was loud applause as the groom arrived. After I gave my first apology for the noise on the other side of the screen, I could hear the voices of women and young men cheering. To my relief, things quieted down until I heard a man yell, "Ride 'em cowboy!" At this point, my audience was clearly annoyed and embarrassed. Hoping to bring their attention back to the meeting, all I could think of saying was, "I'm sorry. It looks like they're having a rodeo in the next room. Apparently, the horse has arrived." As tension was relieved in the other room, I was hoping it would be relieved in my meeting room as well.

Doyle and Straus pay more attention to creating the right atmosphere and understanding what's happening next door. They state that "If you want to solve a problem or accomplish a task, you can try too hard, you can be too tense or uptight.... There is a special in-between state – not too relaxed and not too tense – when ideas begin to pop and lots of work gets accomplished."[164] Temperature and lighting are important. They state the janitorial staff are also part of the team as they will know how to adjust the lights, heat and turn down the Muzak if its blasting in a hotel. Seek out or make rooms as soundproof as possible so as to keep interruptions to a minimum.

---

164 Doyle and Straus, op cit; p. 194

The Rehearsal

It is important to do a "dry run" rehearsal before a large public meeting, particularly if the project is large and a lot hangs on the outcome of the meeting.

A rehearsal involves the project team, the facilitator team and the client team getting together on someone's turf about a week before the meeting to run through the logistics and presentations. It allows the presenters to fine-tune their remarks, adjust the presentation, develop a list of answers to difficult questions and, in the absence of pressure, think through responses.

It is always important for the lead presenter to have integrity, be articulate, allow some openness and vulnerability and make the public aware of the proponent's values. The lead presenter needs to be good on their feet during the question and answer period. The last thing I want to see on the night of the meeting is a presenter who is dry, talks in techno-speak and has little ability to relate to the audience.

For some clients, the meeting could be the most stressful part of their careers to this point. The chief spokesperson should also know when members of their team will be answering certain questions. The team will assign key individuals to answer specific questions beforehand, so that what is left to chance is minimized.

A thick skin is usually helpful during a large public meeting. Most of the teams I've worked with are committed to the success of their clients and the solutions that they believe will work. I do my best to remind them that we've asked the public to comment on the project for a good reason: they may have ideas that will improve the decision. When hearing those ideas (the good ones), the lead presenter needs to be prepared to say that his team will consider the suggestion. This may involve starting a Citizen Liaison Committee, doing additional study or inviting citizens on a tour of a facility or site, so they can see why they are making the recommendation.

Because the public will always let you know if they disagree, every presenter needs to be prepared to not take loud applause and other comments personally. They have a job to do and information to share, and their job description may include being yelled at. The rehearsal allows the team to bond and lets the speaker know they have psychological support.

Some rehearsal questions could include, "Are you presenting all the information you need to? What material is to be presented in the formal part of the meeting and what should be left for questions and answers? What are the tough questions you're going to get? Are there gaps in your presentation? Is the presentation running too long? Who will be answering which questions?

The rehearsal also allows the team to do a mental walk through the evening, asking these questions: "What are the behaviours we expect? Are politicians coming and what role will they want? Where do the support team members sit? How are the chairs laid out?"

I know I'm going to be a pariah among male engineers, but I can always count on one question coming up in a pre-meeting rehersal: "What should I wear?" Yes, I've had eight male engineers sitting around the table, on the clock, discussing their wardrobe for the evening. My answer is usually, "Dress one step up from what you expect members of the audience to wear." (It usually takes several minutes to explain what "one step up" means.)

The Chalk Talk

The first part of choreographing a successful meeting ends with a Chalk Talk. For those of you who've played little league hockey, baseball or soccer, you'll remember the Chalk Talk delivered by your coach just before going onto the field of play. The talk delivered by the facilitator is much the same. I will run through the agenda, remind the team about safety, the potential tough questions and how to answer them, confirm how I will be directing comments and questions that will need answers, go over how to deal with hostile questions (acknowledgement, calming, mirroring responses), and thicken skins by building comradery.

The most important part of the talk is reminding the team to speak truthfully and firmly. Their job is not to give an opinion that will be liked by the crowd, but to give an honest and straightforward professional opinion. I tell the team that, if there's a truth that has to be said, they should say it. Vague responses and shifting responsibility inflame public anger. The team may be in front of two hundred and fifty people who are insisting that "black is white", but it is their role as professionals to say no. It is my job as facilitator to allow them to give honest and professional opinions without getting beaten up.

Susskind and Field provide three definitions of public anger, that when understood, assists the engagement of people who are angry. As a way to prepare the project team as part of the Chalk Talk, rather than write-off or avoid the emotion of the angry person:

1. 'Focus on finding the cause or perceived threats that underlie their anger as a problem-solving process.

2. Assume the anger is legitimate so as to force ourselves to empathize with and acknowledge the concerns of the other side rather than devaluing or downplaying the emotion.

3. View the person who is angry as defending themselves rather than attacking you. The natural tendency of the listener is to look for ways of easing pain.'[165]

The Chalk Talk is normally a "stand-up" meeting involving the client, consultants and the facilitator staff. If security personnel are hired, they also need to be included. On the day of the meeting, clients and consultants will typically be working on presentation boards, finalizing a PowerPoint and dealing with other last-minute changes up until the time they leave their offices. When they arrive at the venue, they will be going all out to make sure that everything is properly set up before the public arrives.

A Chalk Talk is a pause that's needed to collect thoughts, make sure that everyone is on track, and to eat. I recommend that it occurs at least forty-five minutes to an hour before an open house or meeting is scheduled to begin. That way, the whole team can gather before registering early arrivals.

Typically, the Chalk Talk is supported by printed out Power Point notes (for easy viewing) handed out to all the participants (See Appendix 4). These handouts are always collected after the talk so that a copy is not inadvertently left on a chair in the meeting venue. A second handout contains a list of expected questions and answers. Sometimes I will number both as a method of document control. Eight Q and A sheets were handed out and eight were returned to me.

---

165 Susskind and Field, op cit; p 20

Because the public meeting is usually a part of an open house or occurs afterwards, I include information that will be helpful for the open house as well. During an open house, my clients will most often be talking to people one-on-one. (Good one-on-one skills ensure that the open house portion will help prepare the way for a productive meeting afterwards.)

The Chalk Talk is structured to achieve the following:

- **Introduce the client team that will be part of the meeting.**

  In my world, it's not unusual for members of large project teams to work together for years without ever meeting. The evening's public meeting may be the first time some of the specialists work together face to face.

- **Remind the client and the professionals about what they want to get out of the meeting.**

  This will include information that the team wants from the public, areas of the presentation to be highlighted and information that needs to be presented to the public in the clearest manner possible. The facilitator will also remind people that while there may be difficult questions and comments, it will be the role of the project team to be as professional, respectful and thick-skinned as possible (but not insensitive).

  Note-taking will be important. The team will be coached to write down as many of the informal public comments as possible. Formal comments will be gathered by designated note takers. Active note-taking is an important way for members of the project team to show that they are listening to the public. Taking notes while listening to someone helps the person speaking let go of stress. 'I had something to remember to say. I said it. The person heard it. Now I can move on to the next point I wanted to share.'

  Doyle and Straus provide great insight into the role of the note taker. So much so that I don't want to overlook the symbiosis between a note taker and facilitator for a successful meeting. They assert that groups need a memory. For some groups it could be a recollection of what they said when they last met. For example, when I facilitate a series of meetings, I will always recap what happened at the last meeting. For other groups, it is to remind them what they said minutes ago. Do you remember this fact? Do you remember that we discussed this already? The note taker as recorder of group memory helps the group in several ways:

1) Helps people keep an open mind. People tend to remember only what is important to them. By referring to other ideas the note taker helps to keep minds open.

2) Helps people release tension and move on. The note taker and notes help people let go of energy. Many times, people have a point to make during the comment period and can't move on until they have made that point in public and had it recorded. The note taker helps with psychic release. 'My point was remembered by the group because it was recorded. Now I can get on to my next comment.'[166]

3) Provides a physical focus of the discussion. The note taker occupies a space in the meeting that can be pointed to.

4) Helps with accountability. For example, here are some of the tasks and actions that the public raised and the client agreed to. The notes are seen to be an accurate summary of what we will remember.

- **Review the Open House and meeting agenda.**

While the agenda will be developed long before this point and reviewed at the rehearsal, there may be members of the public who were not part of the public conversation who will need to absorb information about how the meeting will unfold before it begins. The Open House part of the Chalk Talk centres on welcoming people, helping them with way-finding and providing them with information, such as who to talk to and which information boards to read first.

- **Remind people about safety and security.**

If security staff are on hand, they will deliver this part of the Chalk Talk. If not, the facilitator will present this information.

---

166 Doyle and Straus, op cit, p. 43, 44

- **Instruct the team on effective communication.**

  I will always take the time to coach the team on interpersonal relations and dealing with difficult people. This part of the Chalk Talk helps with team-building and reminding everyone that they may be discussing matters with angry people, but they are not alone.

  A reminder of how to control language is essential. As stated earlier, it is important to say "yes, and" instead of "but". Killermann and Bolger elaborate this point, stating: "'And' and 'but' serve similar functions grammatically. And, generally speaking, we can exchange one for the other without noticing much of a difference in meaning. But when disagreeing with someone, the difference between 'and' and 'but' grows to a canyon. Whenever someone makes a statement, connecting your response to theirs with 'and' builds on what they said; connecting your response to theirs with a 'but' negates what they said. 'And' recognizes their truth and adds yours on top of it or alongside of it; 'But' negates their truth and replaces it with yours. It's a matter of picking your battles.[167]

  It is difficult to agree with a member of the public who has drawn strong opinions based on few facts or their unconventional view of the public interest. When the team member points to larger public interest objectives that need to be addressed, it moves the conversation to a higher level. This helps to keep the conversation positive because the subject matter has been shifted to a position that both parties may be able to agree with.[168]

  For example, a person may be opposed to a cell phone tower because of electromagnetic effects. But they may support a higher objective of using the tower and EMF fields to communicate with 911 EMS services if there is an emergency. Members of the team might respond, "Yes, I understand your concern about electromagnetic effects. And, I wonder if you would agree with me that being able to have cell phone access 911 is important?"

---

167 Killermann and Bolger, op cit. P 46

168 Eugenia Cheng, 'The Art of Logic in and Illogical World', Basic Books, New York, 2018 does an excellent job in describing how conversations can respectfully be walked up and down so as to achieve dialogue.

Killermann and Boyle state that, when you are in total disagreement with a member of the public, the objective is to listen to the person in a healthy way. "I hear you. I see what you are saying. Your voice is valued," enables discussions that foster more genuine curiosity instead of predatory listening, where folks are just waiting for their turn to attack an idea that's put forth, instead of truly considering its merit." [169]

Another communication lesson in the Chalk Talk is reminding the team how to address emotional responses. Team members need to know how to avoid trigger words, defined as "a stimulus that invokes a disproportionately negative response"[170]. These are words that are intended to hurt, sometimes spoken on purpose, sometimes because the person is unaware of how their remarks are being heard.

As an example, I was in a meeting where a member of the public was truly concerned about an effect of a project that would never occur. Rather than responding with a fair and respectful answer, the expert pointed out that the question was "nonsense". While he may have been correct, the expert's answer was hurtful to the point where the person will remember how they were treated by the project team that night until their dying day. As the facilitator I asked for and received a public apology from my client to the member of the public.

Killermann and Bolger[171] list the following indicators of emotion: a shift in body language, a change in tone of voice and a change in the speed of reaction.

Effective methods for dealing with emotions include:

- Showing empathy by letting the person know that you can see their emotion. Saying something like, "I can see that you are upset" allows them "confirm or correct that emotion" [172].

---

169 Killermann and Bolger op cit; p. 60
170 Killermann and Bolger, op cit; p. 95
171 Killermann and Bolger, op cit; p. 116
172 Killermann and Bolger, op cit; p. 118

- Validating the emotion: "It's OK to feel that way." Killermann and Boyle state, "The first time a participant shares something emotional, it is especially important to validate their emotion, and that it is ok that they brought that emotion into the space." [173]
- Exploring the emotion: "Tell me why you feel that way."
- Integrating the emotion: 'Would you like to tell me more about why the subject matter being discussed makes you feel this way?' If they say "no", leave it alone. If "yes", then listen.

Another lesson in effective communication involves coaching the project team to listen. I once facilitated an in-house meeting for a large agency involving about two hundred employees. Several of them were confrontational, suggesting goals and programs that obviously no one else agreed with. In fact, I could see from the body language that most of the participants were getting annoyed, slapping their foreheads in disbelief that the idea was being raised and shaking their heads.

For this assignment, we were asked to write up a report on consensus recommendations and unconventional recommendations but keeper ideas. Following up a year later, I found that, indeed, the recommendations of the few confrontational people became the new program that was worked on by everyone.

- **Determine how the transaction of information will occur during the presentation and during the question and comment period.**

Part of the job of the professional team in the presentation portion of the meeting is to educate the public by presenting the facts as they know them, with the expectation that many people are there to listen and learn. In the question and answer portion, the facilitator will lead the discussion of who is responding to which questions, who is playing the role of gatekeeper directing questions to the right person, and who is going to be wrangling mikes in the audience.

---

173 Killermann and Bolger, op cit; p. 119

As stated earlier, it is important for the facilitator to have a good understanding of the topic being discussed. This will allow the facilitator to help direct questions to the right experts and, more importantly, assess which questions are on-topic and which are not. Some projects are very complex, with issues raised by the public being satisfactorily addressed years earlier. The client team will fault the facilitator if they have to answer old questions, as it wastes public time and their time.

The list of Frequently Asked Questions will be reviewed. Team members are reminded that if they can't answer a question accurately, they should, instead of improvising, direct the member of the public to the person who can accurately answer the question.

- **Explain how the facilitator will run the meeting.**

The final part of the Chalk Talk determines the agenda for the meeting portion, what happens if someone is acting out, what time the meeting will end and how. The client is reminded to thank people for coming at the end of the meeting.

The Chalk Talk has always been one of the most important, albeit brief, components of setting the stage for a large, angry meeting. It is the final opportunity to bring a team together and remind them what they want to get out of the meeting and how to act during the meeting. When all team members know that they are working together, the interaction with the public is much better. The public expects to see a professional team when they come to the meeting and the Chalk Talk helps to make sure that this occurs.

Chapter 8:
Safety and Security

Screaming, yelling, chanting, loud applause, interrupting, heckling and insults can all be part of large, angry public meetings. These behaviours are a sign of a healthy democracy. However, when the pitch of meetings reaches a crescendo, all but the thick-skinned and crazy people become intimidated. I believe that I fall into the later category.

We were asked to facilitate a meeting in the mid-2000s in Richmond Hill, a GTA suburb. The issue was a proposed transmission line along the route of a formerly abandoned right-of-way. As this route was in an urbanized area, concerns from residents about electromagnetic health effects had been in the media for many weeks. My client and I expected a large turnout, so we booked the largest convention hall we could find.

On a warm spring evening when suburban homeowners would normally have been outside on their decks, over seven hundred very angry people showed up. I knew it was going to be rough night when I was asked to break up a demonstration in the parking lot half an hour before the meeting began. The demonstrators, a small group of about a dozen people including children, were chanting and intimidating other residents as they entered the hall. The homemade simplicity of their signs indicated to me that they didn't have the same experience as the professional protesters I've had to deal with.

Wading into the midst of the fray, I introduced myself as the independent facilitator of the meeting and told the protesters that they could come in, but couldn't bring in their protest their signs. Because the signs were nailed to hockey sticks, I felt that they were a safety hazard. I was also concerned about objects being hurled at my clients or other member of the public.

"What gives you the right to tell us what to do?" they demanded, to which I replied, "I'm hired to make sure that everyone gets a chance to share their views, and I'm not going to let you bring the signs in. And, because I'm running the meeting, I see the signs as a safety risk." The people insisted. "And what if we do?" Fortunately, a police cruiser was parked at the entrance to the parking lot with an officer directing traffic. I pointed to the officer and said, "I'll bring the officer over and ask him to charge you with creating a disturbance."

I wasn't sure if the officer would or could lay a charge. Even if he came over to help, I expected that his comfort zone had more to do with traffic than arresting a mob of protesters. But I felt that I had to up the ante a bit to show the protesters that there are consequences to actions. I did have some authority under the Trespass Act[174] to ask people to leave, as we had the rental contract for the property. During the planning of the meeting, I had made sure that the venue was private rather than a public venue. If a meeting hall is public, people will claim that, because they pay taxes, they own the building and have a right to be there. At the same time, I had my fingers crossed that my threat would work. As it turned out, the protesters backed down and put their signs back into their cars. Then, I welcomed them into the meeting.

The protesters ultimately got back at me. Their questions during the meeting had to do with my "bullying" in the parking lot. "Sorry, but I felt the signs were a security risk," I replied. "I understand how you feel. Thank you for the comment." As I did so, I actually saw a smile on the face of my client, since I was taking more flak from the public than they were. The Germans have a word for what my client was experiencing - "schadenfreude" – which means feeling joy at the pain of others.

Although my client's plain-clothes security staff were present, I had asked them for uniformed police presence. As it turned out, the uniformed police left before the meeting to handle the traffic, and never returned. I was out of luck.

Once the protesters finished with me during the early part of the meeting, it became obvious that my client was doing very little to effectively communicate with the audience. Their efforts to 'stay on message' aggravated the situation by showing little empathy for the views of the public. They responded to simple

---

174 "While trespassing is usually defined as the unlawful entry onto the private land of another, it also includes performing an unlawful activity on the land and refusing to leave when told to do so. " https://www.legalline.ca/legal-answers/trespassing-on-someones-property/

Who are these people and why are they yelling at me? | 195

questions in techno-speak. They had no sensitivity to avoiding trigger words. Disagreeing with my suggested friendlier room set-up, they sat on an elevated podium as a panel. To my amazement, instead of wrapping up the meeting after the scheduled two hours, they actually wanted to continue to have people yell at them.

I learned after the meeting that someone in government had put pressure on my clients to advance the project. As professionals, they knew that the project was a bad idea, and they were in favour of a better option. They actually agreed with the residents, and an angry, well publicized public meeting seemed to be just what was needed.

In the middle of the most vocal and emotional part of the meeting, I spotted a member of the public with quite a worried look on his face. He was very persistent in getting my attention. "Sir, I'll get to you in order," I said to him. I returned to the fifteen people on my speakers' list while, at the same time, trying to control unsolicited comments including one from a woman who was holding her three-year-old child above her head yelling, "You're going to give my baby cancer!"

Then the worried looking member of the public stated, "Mr. Facilitator, I need to talk to you now!"

Needless to say, managing questions and comments with a crowd that large was a challenge. It offered no time for having an intimate conversation with a member of the public.

"Sir, I'm a bit busy."

"Lady, please put the child down. You in the back, it's your turn to speak," I said.

And then, a startling exclamation from the worried person:

"Mr. Facilitator, the man over there just threatened to kill me."

This got my attention. The resident handed me his business card. It was the Provincial Member of Parliament, pointing to a rather disturbed, obese and disheveled person who looked quite threatening.

In the middle of managing the list of people wanting to speak, I now had to deal with a death threat, so I signaled to one of my staff wrangling microphones to join me. "Where are the plain-clothes security guards?" I asked. "They're in the back room," replied my staff member. "What are they doing there? Go get them," I said.

It took about two minutes for the security guards to come to the side and front of the room, where the potential incident was going to occur. Why they decided to sit in the back room I'll never know. Perhaps the actual role of providing security wasn't in their job description. By the time they arrived, I had placed myself between the potential murderer and the politician. Frankly, I had no idea what I would do if the person lunged at the Minister with a knife.

Despite this serious incident, the meeting went on. I announced that I was now going to take a few questions from the back of the room. Fortunately, the next two speakers turned out to be grandstanders. Their comments were long, and I let them go on. The security guards finally arrived, giving us a chance to talk. They were both ex-police, fit, tall, and showing the maturity of people in their fifties.

"Glad to see you. I want that man thrown out. He's threatening to kill the Minister," I said.

"We can't," they replied, to which I asked why not. "Our job is to observe and report any crimes," they said. "And, threatening to kill the Minister isn't a crime?" I asked. "Not yet, as he hasn't taken a step in the Minister's direction," was their response. "Ok, here's what I want you to do," I said. "Stand in front of the guy. If he takes out a knife and lunges at you to get to the Minister, I want you to observe and report that."

On that spring evening in Richmond Hill, I was not impressed with the security personnel. But, I did make friends with the Minister. By ten thirty, only half of the residents remained. Completely ignoring my client's request to keep going on, I called the meeting to an end.

How do you plan for matters to get worse? When thinking about managing an angry public meeting, the most important consideration is safety and security goals. When I return from facilitating a particularly large and angry meeting and get back to the office, the first thing I'm asked by my staff is, "How did it go?" My immediate response is always, "No one got hurt."

I realize that a lot more was accomplished at the meeting, as I'm sure that all the parties learned from each other. But the substantive outcome doesn't matter. When you have several hundred people show up at a meeting, there is a parallel dynamic. It is important that people express their views, but they need to do it in a manner that is safe. If you are facilitating a meeting where someone gets hurt, you are the one holding the microphone.

When you have hundreds of people showing up, you need to shift your expectations of a successful outcome. With safety and security paramount, the goal is to make sure that everyone comes and leaves safely. Among a group of five hundred people, some will have heart conditions, substance abuse problems, mental illness issues and tendencies to act out civil disobedience in violent ways. It would be nice if everyone was fair-minded, peaceful, open to hearing new ideas and seeking consensus, but only someone completely naïve would think that every meeting is going to end with everyone singing "Kumbaya". When emotions are raw and people are yelling, the meeting can be quite intimidating, particularly for people in the audience.

Generally, there are four steps that I take in preparing for a safe meeting:

1. Develop a safety checklist.
2. Go through procedures with my staff, event venue staff and the client. Add a procedural check with police, security and bodyguards as required.
3. Do a mental and physical walk-though of the venue ahead of time that identifies things that can go wrong, and make adjustments.
4. Adapt as the meeting unfolds and issues arise.

The extent of your preparations will vary. Canadian safety goals and security issues are somewhat different than in other countries. Given the mass murder in Toronto in April of 2018 however, that's changing. When preparing for a safe meeting, I tend to over-prepare, worry and become quite anal. Contemplating what would I do if I was preparing for a safe meeting in the U.S., I scale back in a manner that reflects the intelligence we receive and the local circumstances.

For example, I was facilitating a small meeting in the City of Pickering, Ontario regarding a rather uncontroversial issue: the remediation of a stream to prevent residential backyards from eroding during and after floods. The meeting was open to all residents of the city, but we only expected a few homeowners to show up. What could go wrong?

About five minutes before the meeting began, a resident walked into the registration area with a large bowie knife in a leather sheath strapped to his thigh. When I noticed this, I alerted the client, who brushed it off as a local resident who enjoys walks in the bush and brings a knife with him.

Being a keen observer of my surrounding environment, I noticed that we were in fact not in the bush, but in a municipal council chamber. As my health and fitness goal does not include being on the receiving end of a large knife, I informed my client that I was not going to allow the meeting to start if someone in the audience had one.

My first action was to find building security, which turned out to be an elderly, retired gentleman who chose the job to supplement his pension. "Can you instruct him to remove his knife or leave?" I asked, to which he replied, "No." When I asked why not, the gentleman said, "My job is to make sure doors are locked and no one gets in at night."

That wasn't going to work, so I asked my client, who knew the individual, to tell the "bushman" that the facilitator is having a "hissy fit" and doesn't want to have the knife in the hall. Effectively, I altered the client-facilitator relationship so that I was the person to take the blame, and the client could save face. Fortunately, the bushman was a reasonable person. He locked his knife in a car, and the meeting went smoothly.

The Active Assailant

In the United States, and increasingly in most countries, the security focus in angry meetings is on an individual referred to as an "active assailant", described by the U.S. Department of Homeland Security as not only a shooter, but anyone seeking to harm people in a confined area.

The FBI reports that most active assailant attacks end before law enforcement arrives, either because the attacker or a victim stops it. In large, angry public meetings, the facilitator is the person on their feet and in control. While most of us think of active assailant incidents in schools (due to media reporting of school shootings), most mass shootings - 43 per cent[175] - occur at conferences, which brings large, angry meetings into play. Therefore, meeting facilitators and their staff, security personnel, and clients need to know how to react. Suspicious people and objects need to be reported, and an emergency action plan needs to be developed and communicated.

My staff and I practice situational awareness. When working together, my staff need to keep their eyes on me no matter where they are in the room. I'm the one who's looking at people's faces from the front, seeing reactions and selecting who will speak next. I know who is upset and who looks like they are going to act out. We use simple non-verbal queues, such as hand signals, facial looks, gestures, head nodding and others, as a way to communicate and guide our actions. While I'm at the front, my staff are situated at the sides, beside people yelling and at the back of the room. They will see behaviours that I won't.

The police recommend three actions that the public can take when there is an active assailant: run; hide; and fight. Running is the best option because most people will be under stress and will have difficulty thinking clearly. They can figure out that running is a sane, immediate option.

I see this stress response happen when I'm facilitating a meeting and a fire alarm is pulled. When this happens and I'm on my feet, people become suddenly quiet and I'm immediately looking at three hundred "deer in the headlights". I have their full attention. No matter how rancorous they've been up to that point, they will count on me to be prepared, know what to do and tell them what to do.

Playing dead or freezing is the worst decision you can make when confronted by an active assailant. Running down a hallway or hiding in a washroom is also not a good strategy. Getting out of the building is a good option but, if you can't exit, go to the safest room – a room that is lockable or has doors that can be blocked. Lights and cell phones should be turned off, and everyone should keep calm and quiet. While a safe room may work for clients, staff and consultants, it can't provide refuge for hundreds of people. The goal is to get them out of the building and out of harms way.

---

175 FBI Quick look: 220 active shooter incidents in the United States between 2000 and 2016: Location categories.

Fighting, a last resort, is something that few people would envision doing. If the situation gets to this point, however, their lives will depend on it. In the spring of 2018, Waffle House customer James Shaw Jr. decided to fight an armed assailant in Tennessee and prevented further casualties by taking a high-powered gun from him. Fighting can work, but your odds of not being harmed are only 50:50.

Creating chaos can also help. If everyone in a room is moving and yelling, it forces the active assailant to make choices amongst people who are fleeing or fighting back. Weapons for fighting back can include keys, shoes, purses, canes, pens, chairs or other items that might be in a room.

Security Guards

When we are planning for a large, angry public meeting, my staff and I will visit the venue to check it out beforehand. This is also a good time to talk to local security guards who will be present. (Smaller venues usually don't have a security guard.)

Local security personnel at a hotel, arena or conference centre are good at dealing with single unruly individuals. While some may possess good de-escalation skills, they are just not trained to deal with the angry meetings that we are hired to facilitate. They are more broadly trained in matters such as theft and vandalism prevention.

Venue security personnel are not trained to deal with angry mobs. Nor should they be asked to remove individuals who are acting out. Most security guards I've worked with acknowledge that they don't have the authority to deal with civil disobedience. They will call the police. More than once they have told me that, if they knew that civil disobedience was going to happen, they would not have rented us the facility in the first place. That being said, I count on them to do what they do best - to keep general order through their uniformed presence.

Municipally-hired security guards, including permanent city hall security staff, tend to be better-prepared and more responsive. As an example, I was asked to facilitate a meeting in Hamilton, Ontario over an issue of sewage waste backing up into the basements of about three hundred homes and institutions such as day cares, schools and businesses. As it turned out, causing a foot of smelly, liquid, fecal waste to back up into basements was an excellent way to piss-off a whole community.

A door to door engagement strategy might have been a better way to deal with the issue, but the City wanted to bring everyone together to discuss what they were going to do to make things right. The meeting was held in an old school auditorium in the oldest part of the city with the oldest and least effective sewage infrastructure. A sewage backup had occurred during one of those rare but intense summer thunderstorms, and the meeting took place a week afterwards, when summer temperatures were high. With no air conditioning, the school auditorium was unbearably hot.

Fortunately, Hamilton's mayor brought uniformed city security with him. (They are usually very well-trained.) I began by welcoming people, acknowledging the problem and the high temperature in the room, and laying out the ground rules. Once I finished, the mayor, a person of Italian descent, began his apologies and committed to making things right. About ten minutes into his remarks, I noticed the security guards converging on three rather rough-looking individuals with lots of tattoos wearing black leather jackets. Apparently, one of them had directed a particularly nasty racial slur at the mayor.

In about two seconds, the uniformed city security guards grabbed the perpetrators and threw them out the door. While their removal was quick, the process was loud and violent. The guards had no qualms about breaking bones. In fact, one of the rough guys was actually off his feet when he was thrown against a crash bar. I surmised that the security guards had done this before.

I didn't hear the racial slur and threat to the mayor. The city guards did, and acted. Rather smugly, I took the opportunity to remind people that we had agreed to show respect to each other. Witnessing how the agitators were manhandled by city security, the rest of the crowd was exceptionally polite during the rest of the meeting.

Police Presence and Plain Clothes Police

I rarely have uniformed police at a meeting. While their presence announces that the client is serious about civil behaviour, it also sends the message that the client is not in a mood to reach consensus. Most corporations and governments don't want to be associated with an image of a strong-armed presence. If matters have become so serious that uniformed police are required then, in my opinion, the client has larger issues, which need to be resolved through the ballot box or legislative means.

Whether or not you have uniformed police involves choreographing what you want out of the meeting. I want people to be able to say what they need to say without fear that there's somebody watching their behaviours. A uniformed police presence might mean that people will be somewhat constrained in their views and their actions. Uniformed police put boundaries on behaviours.

That said, we were facilitating a meeting in Niagara Falls and having uniformed Niagara Regional Police at the registration area was needed. The issue had to do with a proposed housing development in a treed nature reserve. The nature reserve and field were always proposed to be future housing, but local housing developers and real estate agents hadn't bothered to tell homeowners. Most of the homes up to that point had been marketed as being beside nature. The new homeowners were surprised and angry to find that newer homes would require removal of this amenity.

The project team informed my colleagues and I that there had been serious threats against the new developer and several email authors of these threats hadn't even bothered to disguise who they were. We discussed whether to wait until these people surfaced during the meeting and throw them out if they were misbehaving. But we came to the conclusion that since we knew who they were, we would have the officer stand at registration, and for everyone to sign in before being allowed to enter the meeting so that we would be able to put a face to who was threatening. That way we could deal with them before they became disruptive.

This worked, but instead of barring them from the meeting we took them aside and asked them, in the presence of the officer, how they were going to state their views at the meeting. They saw that we were serious and they behaved well. During the meeting, there were several strong questions on why the meeting had to have a police officer present. We explained the threats and that seemed to work in placing the situation in context.

Who are these people and why are they yelling at me? | 203

Plain clothes police are another matter. I've had many meetings where plain clothes security officers work closely with me, most often when there has been a death threat, a bomb threat or earlier civil disobedience. On occasion, I've even placed trained former police officers on my staff, giving them the job of handling logistics and wrangling microphones in the crowd. While it isn't difficult to spot a fit six-foot, six-inch person, most people aren't looking at who's holding the microphone for them. Their presence remains undisclosed. If asked, I will be honest, saying, "Staff holding the mikes have training in policing and security. These are their skills. That's who they are."

Being honest with the public is important. We were once asked to facilitate a hockey rink-sized meeting involving people who were concerned about the City of Toronto's efforts to find a community that would accept its municipal waste. The proponent, the Interim Waste Authority, concluded that a community in Durham Region east of Toronto would do just fine. Several other regional communities were also candidates.

The fact that Toronto was proposing to ship its waste elsewhere instead of finding ways to deal with it locally, was a social justice issue not missed by people in surrounding communities. As the site selection process advanced, the project team began to receive death threats. When a public meeting was scheduled, I advised local community leaders that it would be large and loud. Asking for (and receiving) support from Durham Regional Police, six officers were assigned to the meeting.

The dynamic was interesting. The officers had not worked with a facilitator before. Normally, I connect with the local police department or Ontario Provincial Police before the meeting to give them a heads up on what's going on. This time, I had to do it on the fly. When the police officers asked me what I do to keep matters on track, I gave them a five-minute primer on setting ground rules, active listening and keeping a fair process. I told them that my role was to manage the meeting in an orderly manner, and that I would likely not need them.

The police officers wanted to know what they should do if things got off track. One of them asked, in jest, if they would be required to shoot anyone. The question got a good round of laughter from the other officers but, just to be safe, I responded with a firm "no". As the meeting began, the residents, noticing uniformed police, questioned whether their presence was really necessary. "Is it?" I responded. They replied "no". I asked the police to leave, and the meeting was one of the more successful large meetings that I had facilitated.

The fact that police and security wear a uniform does count. (The fact that they are armed may count as well.) It shows people that everybody's pretty serious about how the meeting will go. However, their role and mine are fuzzy. If someone is committing a criminal act, they know exactly what to do. But, if somebody is being vocal and somewhat disorderly, that person, in my mind, hasn't reached the tipping point where they're causing a disturbance. Because you need to hear from people who are emotional during a public meeting, intervention from the police at this point is premature. When someone threatens or acts out a threat, however, they cross the line. I lose my ability to manage the meeting. The police decide and act on their decision.

Overall, local municipal and Ontario Provincial Police forces have excellent training. They've had to deal with "alt left" radicals at G20 meetings, so they know what the worst looks like.

Bodyguards

Canadians have an image of themselves and their fellow citizens as being peace loving, polite, well-mannered and compassionate. Indeed, it's a well-known fact that Canadians know more than thirty ways to say "sorry". When studying a new language, it is the first word they want to learn.

International readers of this book need to know that "sorry" is the most often used word in the Canadian English vocabulary. Most Canadians will try to work it into every sentence. Our Prime Minister, Justin Trudeau, decided to be the politician holding the record for giving the most apologies upon being elected. It is something that most Canadians boast about.

I hate to burst the bubble of the image Canadians hold of themselves, but the reality is, a large number of political and corporate leaders see Canada differently and choose to travel with bodyguards. At one time in my career, in the early 1980s, I worked for the most senior official in a large crown corporation, which was always in the news because of its unpopular (although necessary) decisions. The corporation is still in the news today. The senior official and I travelled with bodyguards, who were also our drivers. They had previously worked for the Ontario Provincial Police (OPP) and the Royal Canadian Mounted Police (RCMP).

Our bodyguards were always complaining that they weren't allowed to carry guns so, at one point, we did an analysis of whether or not this would be a good idea and concluded that the likelihood of them shooting themselves or other staff by mistake was high. One option that we considered was to give the bodyguards guns, but no bullets. Today, post-9/11, even corporate security people are armed.

For rare assignments, my staff and I travel with bodyguards. My preference is to hire those who are ex-military, ex-RCMP or ex-OPP. The ex-military police are probably at the top of my list as they are trained to police people who are taught to kill.

Bodyguards help facilitators in four important ways: they have access to intelligence and data bases that we don't have; they have a good ability to brief and secure support from local police; they are good at checking out venues and making them safe and secure; and they will become physical if the need arises.

We were asked to facilitate a very large public meeting regarding a large infrastructure project in the City of Toronto. The issue was getting a lot of attention in the media. Many local residents were opposed to the development, particularly those living right next to it.

A grassroots activist organization formed, with membership ranging from old, grey-haired, hippie radicals searching for a way to remain relevant, to alt-left anarchists looking for thuggery. This group was expected to attend. Previous public meetings were quite vocal and raucous, and we were warned that this one was not going to be easy. As well, another consulting firm had turned down this facilitation assignment. I insisted that security be provided, but my client refused, saying that they did not want anyone in uniform or police presence at the meeting. They just wanted me to facilitate the meeting.

After further discussions, during which I threatened to walk away, I was allowed to bring my own security. I hired four retired municipal and military police officers who had worked with me in the past as bodyguards. Not only were these men very clear thinkers who performed well in problematic situations, but they were also very large and fit, which added to their ability should I have needed that type of support.

That being said, my bodyguards did not have the power of arrest. Nor could they touch anyone unless a person took the first punch. We anticipated a crowd of approximately five hundred, but only three hundred and twenty-five attended. To make my bodyguards part of the team, they wore golf shirts and sweaters. Their role was to work at the registration table and, once the meeting began, to wrangle microphones and be friendly faces in the crowd.

Prior to the meeting, my security team connected with the local division of Toronto Police, giving them a heads-up that a very angry meeting was going to take place, and that we expected there might be a few people acting disorderly and possibly causing a disturbance. We warned the police that there might be one or two individuals who would need to be removed from the meeting, knowing this from intelligence gathered by my bodyguards before the meeting through police files, conventional and social media.

As the meeting unfolded, the speaker from an engineering firm was interrupted in the middle of his presentation, with three men shouting "Stop the presentation and get on with the question/answer period. We are sick and tired of hearing this stuff!" As the facilitator, I intervened, saying, "Look, I have some ground rules that say we'll be respectful to each other, we'll allow people to speak, and we'll allow them to finish their presentations, so that we don't disrupt them. You're going to want the same when you have an opportunity to speak, and I'll let you speak first."

This worked until the presentation ended about ten minutes later, and I let these people speak first, as promised. At that point in the meeting, there was no reason to have anybody thrown out. People were just being a little bit more emotional. Then, about half an hour later, another man unrelated to the first vocal group stood up exclaiming, "Everything that I've heard is just bullshit!" and called the engineers "liars".

Slander, swearing, libel and racist remarks are unacceptable so, jumping in with an emphatic voice, I yelled, "That's enough of that! I don't want to hear that language. I want you to rephrase that please without using that language!" The person apologized and rephrased the question but, as if on queue, the original group began shouting at the top of their lungs," Bullshit! Bullshit!"

In response, I went over to the group and threatened to throw all of them out of the meeting if they continued. With the worst offender, I put my hands behind my back[176], leaned over so as to be close enough to his face for him to smell my breath, and told him that I'd had enough. From that point on, I used a lot of strategic body language and closed in on their personal space. Because I was wired with a microphone, I was able to facilitate the meeting while standing beside them. If they were going to say something that was out of line, I was right there.

As it turned out, I actually thought about asking one of the men in the group, who was heckling speakers, to leave near the very end of the meeting. But, since the meeting was wrapping up, I used my better judgement and decided not to do so. Before the meeting ended, one of people from the grassroots organization opposed to the development, went over to this person and said, "Look, this really looks bad on us because we're coming across, you know, as intolerant and bad mannered. You are abusing others. You're even heckling people who agree with you. It's so bad."

The people in the crowd were actually starting to control themselves – a good development in an angry meeting. If I had decided to expel the person, my security had a speed dial connection to the local police, who would have escorted him out. I have never had to ask police to lay a charge of causing a disturbance in a meeting, but I am sure that this person would have been charged.

In addition to the roles specified earlier, I expect that my security staff or bodyguards will:

- Plan the security approach.
- Scout out the venue and identify emergency escape routes.
- Find and secure safe rooms.
- Find muster points if we have to leave.

---

176 When getting close to someone I will always lock my fingers with hands behind my back so as to not have anyone have a reason to think that I might have initiated an assault.

- Liaise with local police.
- Provide intelligence that I wouldn't have access to.
- Be able to de-escalate if required.
- Provide an additional layer of support if needed

Fire Safety and Emergency Response

Fire safety and emergency response are important considerations when planning a public meeting. I have had more than one occasion where more people were trying to get into a venue than the fire code for the maximum occupants for the room. For one meeting, I worked with the Fire Captain on site to limit the number of people who got in the door.

Fire safety also means that fire and emergency response vehicles can get access to the meeting venue. This is important because people have tripped and fallen down stairs and found other ways to injure themselves. On one occasion, a person died of a heart attack shortly after a meeting. Exceptionally vocal, red-faced and sweating profusely, this man was jumbling his words because his emotions pushed the logical part of his brain aside. I though he was going to have the heart attack during the meeting.

On several occasions, there were so many people attending the meeting that they couldn't get to the parking lot. Other parking lots in the area were filled, all the streets in the area were packed with cars, and there were massive traffic jams. When this happens, I can expect that the police hired for the meeting will get hauled off to do traffic duty or deal with issues outside of the meeting itself. In these cases, we hire paid off-duty officers. I work with police to make sure that an emergency vehicle can get into a meeting if somebody faints, or worse.

Always checking to see if there is a fire drill planned for the time of the meeting, my staff and I are aware of the procedure if a fire alarm is pulled. Depending on the venue, a fire alarm usually has two types and tones. The first tone is a notice indicating that a fire alarm has been pulled. The second is the escape alarm.

As soon as I hear a fire alarm, I stop the meeting and send out two staff to investigate. They will contact the security people that we're working with, and one staff member will return immediately to provide information, which

Who are these people and why are they yelling at me? | 209

I will immediately share with the meeting participants. If my staff don't return immediately, I will evacuate the room, asking people to leave calmly through emergency escape doors. Usually, this ends the meeting. In some meetings, where it is a false alarm, I will see if anyone standing outside wants to continue.

Security Checklist

I am a big fan of checklists, which I use religiously when planning for large, angry meetings. My safety and security checklist are as follows:

Check venue

- Where are all the doors?
- Are crash doors open and unlocked? (A door locked with a chain is a big problem.)
- Are any escape routes are blocked?
- Where are the emergency escape routes?
- What muster points does the venue use?
- Where are the accessibility ramps and other aids?
- Is there a room to be used as a safe room?
- Where is the automated external defibrillator (AED)?
- Does the rental permit allow us to control who is legally able to be on the premises?

Confirm Security and Support Personnel

- Call the hotel or meeting venue. Ask how they handle security and which security guards are working that night.
- Who are the first aid people?
- Who is situated where?
- Who is in contact with police?
- Who decides whether or not the police should be called?

Check the Site and Deal with Security in Advance

- Inform the police: who I am as a facilitator; who the client is; what the meeting is about; what is expected; the date and location of the meeting.
- Ask about any planned fire alarm drills during the same time period.
- Park our cars "'nose out".
- Explain to local police the reasons why I might need assistance.
- Advise police when the meeting is expected to begin and end.
- Do I have any intelligence that I need to share with the police?

Room Layout and Logistics for Safety

- Chairs are laid out with wide rows.
- Tripping hazards are identified and rectified.
- Outside and inside hazards are identified.
- Parking and emergency vehicle access is clear.
- We have a copy of the rental permit.
- Fire doors are unlocked and accessible.
- Am I aware of whether a fire alarm drill is scheduled?
- First aid personnel are empowered.

In summary, I try to transmit as much information as possible in a large meeting, so that people attending and the client will learn. When dealing with large crowds where people have emotions ranging from curious to vicious, boundaries need to be established. More importantly, people need to be safe.

Chapter 9:
Meeting Day

Facilitating large meetings has, and continues to be, a great job. Although it can be stressful, I'm always aware that it's going to be more so for my client. We both have a stake in how the meeting goes, but I don't have a stake in the client's decision. Ultimately, the meeting is part of a process that will result in a decision that is in the best interest of the public.

The goal of facilitating these meetings is best defined by my facilitator colleague Suzanne Ghais as follows: "The true challenge of the facilitator is to help draw out the best in individuals and in groups, and to help balance the needs of one against the other when they conflict."[177] I've met tens of thousands of people and engaged in conversations with hundreds of interesting and passionate ones. Their input has influenced major decisions.

The first thing on my mind at a meeting is who's going to show up. Facilitating smaller groups of people in other forms of public consultation is different than facilitating large, angry public meetings. As a facilitator working with a client, you can generally decide who to invite to participate in small Advisory Committees. For larger meetings, you typically want to hear from the general public, but the question of who represents them arises. Is it community leaders across a few sectors, public interest groups, governments, elected representatives or their staff?

Ghais presents this dilemma nicely: "Related to representation of the general public is the dilemma of intensity versus breadth of opinion. In other words, there can be a minority with very strong feelings and a much larger majority who hold the opposite opinion but don't feel strongly about it."[178] The challenge

---

177 Ghais, S. op cit, p. 279
178 Ghais, S. op cit, p. 86

with large meetings is the inability to select who to consult. It all depends on who comes in the door. Also, it is not possible to have the sort of sharing of information with members of the public over weeks and months that would normally occur through public participation on community advisory committees or through other public engagement techniques.

On this topic, Ghais observes, "Public meetings (ones open to the general public rather than only invited stakeholders or members of intact groups) are the most volatile forums for facilitators. Participants in public meetings have no investment in the group's success; they haven't had the validating experience of being identified as stakeholders; and they are in an ideal setting for grandstanding."[179]

Before facilitating the meeting, I begin with the assumption that I'm managing a conversation where about a third of the people will be supportive of the client, a third will be opposed, and a third will be seeking more information. Sometimes the majority of people are there to listen, with only a few people acting out.

Over the years, there has been a trend where most people attending meetings are older adults, living in families, well-educated and active voters. Younger adults with families are typically "no shows" at evening meetings because they are either taking children to activities or exhausted after a long commute home. Many attendees are baby boomers with time on their hands. They are used to speaking up and being heard.

The facilitation of large, angry public meetings involves opening the meeting, sharing information and fostering understanding, hearing all voices on the choices available, and closing. However, there are three specific areas that I feel are important to the process: facilitating the journey through an agenda; dealing with people and situation complications; and drawing the meeting to a close. I discuss each of these as follows.

Introductory Remarks

Opening and introductory remarks are presented by the facilitator in the forming stage of the meeting. Most of my work in this stage, before and after introducing myself, involves setting a tone.

---

179 Ghais, S. op cit, p. 277

Who are these people and why are they yelling at me? | 213

When I'm in front of a group, everyone is watching me and judging. "Who is this person?" they may ask. "Is he sincere? Can I trust him? Can I be confident that he will lead us over the course of the evening? Ingrid Bens[180] provides thoughtful advice on what the facilitator is trying to achieve through their introductory remarks, saying that much of their ability to facilitate during the meeting depends on how they are perceived by the public from the earliest parts of the meeting.

To start the meeting, I take care to sincerely welcome people, clearly state my name, why I've been asked to lead the meeting and where I stand in terms of being neutral and working with the group, adding that I make my living as a professional facilitator. I also make sure that people know what the meeting is about, and let them know the questions the project team wants to ask them.

During the opening moments, I occasionally make observations about the people I see, would like to see, or hope are attending, saying "I've had a chance to spend time in the community this afternoon and this looks like a very nice place to live in. I've enjoyed talking to several of you I've already met, and I'm looking forward to getting to know the rest of you."

Through these remarks, I'm affirming that the participants are good, reasonable and decent people who are contributing to their community by simply attending the meeting. I give them a heads up about who I think they are from the perspective of a visitor to their community. And, in terms of self interest, I'm effectively and informally commenting on who I'd like them to be.

What I'm hoping for is that the participants will see their better selves as I see them before the meeting starts, then act accordingly. Sometimes this will be the tenure of the meeting: nice folks providing thoughtful comments in a respectful way. It's the first effort at establishing norms.

My remarks are sincere. The bottom line is that I genuinely care about people who have decided to attend, and I respect their comments. To this, Suzanne Ghais observes, "Even if we find some people unlikable, we still need to look for the underlying nugget of gold, or at least their positive potential. We must try to see the world from their point of view, if only for a moment."[181]

---

180 Bens, I. Advanced .... P. 13
181 Ghais, S. op cit, p. 24

Because my opening remarks take up to ten minutes of the agenda, I will tell people how long I will be speaking. When there's a lot of tension and people want to get to the question and comment part of the meeting, I refer to a mini-agenda within the larger agenda. (Sometimes, for clarity, this will go up on a screen as a PowerPoint.)

During my introduction, I state that I will be introducing who's here tonight, talk about fire exits and safety, go through the formal agenda and present ground rules. Clarifying the purpose, process and expected outcomes of the meeting, this part of the introduction serves as a second effort to influence group norms. Ingrid Bens shares an observation that this, the norming stage, "…sets the climate, creates safety, negotiates additional power, or enrolls members to manage their own behaviour."[182]

Schwarz expands on this observation saying that, as we move to the Norming Stage from the Forming Stage, the facilitator's remarks also help to define group structure. My comments confirm to the group: what are we here to do? why we have come together? And, what are the boundaries of the discussion, presenting myself as the leader, at least until other leaders may emerge. Facilitators lead the group in the process, structure and organizational context.[183] As leaders at this stage, we are building trust and engaging in a sort of psychological contract with participants, leading them because we have the expertise.

The Ground Rules

Most facilitators expend great effort in establishing ground rules, and much has been written on the subject. Schwarz states, "Ground rules serve several functions. First, they are a diagnostic tool. By understanding the ground rules, you can quickly identify dysfunctional behaviour, which is inconsistent with the ground rules, so that you can intervene on it. Second, the ground rules are a teaching tool for developing effective group norms. If a group understands the ground rules and commits to using them, the members set new expectations for how to interact with each other. This enables the group to share responsibility for improving

---

182 Bens, I. p. 38

183 Schwarz, R., 2nd edition, p. 25 - 30

Who are these people and why are they yelling at me?

process, often a goal of facilitation. Finally, the ground rules guide your behaviour as facilitator."[184] Doyle and Straus add: "If you are the facilitator and make the social contract between you and your group clear from the start, many of the natural fears of a new process and of potential manipulation are put to rest."[185]

Three issues need to be addressed when crafting and communicating ground rules for large, angry public meetings: how strong or how weak to make them? getting meeting participants to agree on them in advance; and coming back to them if they are not being adhered to, and enforcing them. Coming back to the ground rules if there is group dysfunction allows me to place a check on group norms. Ground rules imply "…enforceable authority for the facilitator [however]…there are dangers to enforcing ground rules overtly".[186]

Usually, the majority of people attending an angry public meeting are from a defined community. They have a common purpose and common views, and are working from shared information about a project, program, policy or plan. They are usually either seeking information from the proponent or critical of them, as their minds are already made up based on information they've been able to glean from other sources.

Sometimes, when participants have read the reports and done their homework, this information is accurate. In other instances, only a few people have thought the issues through and are seeking a solution that serves the broader public interest. A small number want to speak and share innovative and constructive ideas.

As a facilitator, the problem I'm always wrestling with is that members of the public will intimidate or even shout down someone with a neutral or positive comment.

Recognizing that ground rules are important for this reason, I will try to create a space for dissenting views in my opening remarks. Normally, I will say that I want to hear all perspectives. If someone does share a unique perspective, I will thank them. At the same time, I will show the evil eye or send a nasty look

---

184 Schwarz, R. 2nd edition, p. 10
185 Doyle and Straus, op cit; p. 47
186 Ghais, S. p. 183

to anyone trying to shout them down. (The recipient of my evil eye gets my expression because they will respond non-verbally.)

As a rule, I always have the client allow me to present the first set of PowerPoint slides. These slides are usually basic, not necessarily branded with client logos, tag lines, graphics or colours. My first Ground Rule slide sets out the facilitator agenda for the meeting. Another slide introduces the project team, because people want to know who is in the room beside the client, their staff and the consultant. If there is a public official in a suit taking notes as members of the public are talking, I will introduce them as well. It's hard to hide in one of my meetings.

If I expect the meeting to be calm, I introduce Ground Rules as "Meeting Courtesies." Otherwise, I simply use the title "Ground Rules". The following rules/considerations are used to tee up expected behaviours and norms in advance of what may be an angry meeting.

- **Speaking/ Speakers List**

    I will announce that we will have a presentation (always pleading with the client to keep it short) and that there will be one or more speakers. People will be told that they will have lots of time for questions and comments, but I want them to have some information about what is being discussed first.

    I will state that I'm pretty good at remembering who had their hand up first, will call on people in order, and will select people who have not had a chance to speak before coming back to those who have already spoken. A later chapter will deal with how I communicate the speakers' list during the open part of the meeting.

- **Listening/ Respect**

    The next behaviour is listening. I begin by saying that I expect everyone (including the proponent) to listen to each person speaking throughout the evening in a respectful manner. I've had clients engaged in a conversation with another team member on another matter when a member of the public is speaking. When this happens, I will interrupt the speaker and call out my client if they are not listening. Respect goes both ways. What I also don't tolerate is one member of the public cat calling or criticizing another. When this happens, I will again stop the meeting and remind everyone that we promised to be respectful to each other.

I learned a lot from work I did years ago with a group called the Eastern Ontario Model Forest, an impressive organization in terms of forestry research and practice whose management techniques have been duplicated around the world. The group was basically a collaboration between Domtar Corporation, the Ontario Ministry of Natural Resources and the Mohawks of Akwesasne. At the time, Mohawk Council Director of Environment Henry Lickers shared a story with me that I use today in my introductory remarks as a way to make space for dissenting voices.

Henry shared how difficult it had been to achieve dialogue among members of his community as they went through some rather intense politics. Then the Band Mothers came up with a ground rule of treating meetings like "pot luck" dinners, with each person attending expected to bring a dish of food for others to share. The idea was, when making their pot luck dish, each person adds love, puts in the best ingredients and cooks it in a way that they think everyone will enjoy it. They bring their part of the meal to the pot luck to share with others. According to Henry, when you are eating food at a pot luck dinner, you know that everyone has brought their best meal and are happy when the food is on people's plates. Everyone at the dinner knows this. Although each person could decide to pass on a dish, they would never criticize the person who brought it.

The food dish at the pot luck meal is like an idea presented at a public meeting. People formulate their ideas based on the knowledge they have and their point of view, offering them to the group with the hope that others might accept their ideas. Knowing that they've done their best to help others with their ideas, we should never criticize.

- **Note-Taking**

Because any issue that gathers large numbers of angry people is important, someone should be taking notes on what the public says, and the public needs to know what will be done with the notes.

In order to ensure that all public comments are captured, I usually assign one of my staff members the role of independent note-taker. I will also make sure that the public knows who is taking notes and what will happen to the notes. Typically, we complete the notes, make sure the information is factual and post them on a web page. Sometimes I will also write comments on a flip chart (discussed later) in order to put an exclamation mark on individual comments. This allows people to see what I'm hearing.

For very large meetings, I will consider "live notes", which involves a staff member typing what they are hearing live on their laptop, with their computer screen projected onto a large screen for everyone to see.

The best and worst example of live note-taking happened when one of my staff was asked to take live notes at a convention-sized meeting. She is a well-educated environmental planner with an excellent understanding of the subject matter. There were few comments she couldn't record accurately and present on the screen.

It started well. The initial comments were presented to the audience almost in real time. It's interesting to be facilitating a live note meeting because you see and hear someone commenting and, several seconds later, six hundred faces turn toward the screen to see what the note-taker had typed. This went on for the whole meeting.

I think my note taker sensed this audience behaviour herself. Initially positioning herself on a stage facing the audience, about half way through the meeting, she turned her desk and laptop toward a wall (so that the audience couldn't see her face and she couldn't see theirs) as the comments became particularly snarly and loud. As the anger grew and the comments intensified, she turned completely around so that the public could not see her face. All I could see was her hunched up back. It was an intimidating process for her. But her notes were well done and not questioned.

Other issues that may come up related to note taking include whether or not the public can see the notes in draft stage. (They can, but only after they've been checked for facts with the client.); individual members of the public can correct what they feel to be inaccuracies. (No. They need to send in an alternative minute or note submission to the regulator.); the minutes should include enforceable actions that the audience demanded from the client. (No. It is up to the proponent to decide actions, but the recommended actions are usually listed for consideration).

Doyle and Straus observe that note taking instils group memory. "As the meeting unfolds, the recorder creates the group memory from what participants are saying; it becomes a powerful visual tool, a ready made instant replay, that helps members concentrate and see what is going on. Like the facilitator, the recorder is a neutral servant of the group. The recorder does not edit or paraphrase, records an idea without the name of the contributor, which depersonalizes it and transfers "ownership" to the group."[187] The recorders roles is so important that, I insure that if my recorders are lost or falling behind, that they let me know and stop the meeting and let them catch up.

- **Jargon**

Early in my career, it seemed that all of my clients were using jargon as a defense mechanism to protect themselves from an informed resident asking tough questions. Over the years, all of the technical professions have worked hard to improve how they communicate with the public. Frankly it's still not the level of communications I would like to see, but the public now has a much better chance of understanding what is being said. Schwarz[188] stresses the need to manage jargon, succinctly stating that the public wants to know what the important words mean.

As an example, I worked on a waste water project in rural Ontario where the professional team divided the presentation into the following headings: Population Estimates; Class Environmental Assessment Evaluation Criteria; Collection System Alternatives; Forcemain Alignment Routes; Wastewater Treatment Technology Alternatives; Biosolid Disposal Alternatives; Treated Effluent Outfall Alternatives; and Assimilative Capacity Study. The two hundred plus people in the audience came to the quick conclusion that they were in for an evening of techno-talk. To

---

187 Doyle and Straus, op cit; ppgs 125 to 129

188 Schwarz, R., 2nd edition, p. 112

allay their apprehensions, I used the "simple language/jargon" ground rule and said the following,

"The folks you are going to hear from tonight have a good idea how many more people might live in this town. That means we are going to have to deal with more poop. They did a study and made choices following the Provincial Environmental Assessment Act. They are going to present how they are getting the poop from your home to a sewage treatment plant. They've made a choice on how the poop will be treated. The solid material will be disposed of safely in one way; the liquids will be disposed of in another. They've concluded that the fish in the local stream will have no problem living near the waste outfall."

Ah, we get it now.

Normally it's the technical team that communicates using jargon, so I will tell them in advance that if I hear jargon or acronyms during their presentation, I will stop them and ask them to explain. The same applies to a member of the public if required.

- **Parliamentary/ Respectful Language**

This is a particularly important ground rule. Usually I'll get a chuckle out of the public when I state this rule because their view of Parliament is one of a raucous bunch of politicians whose treatment of each other is often less than respectful. That said, the House Speaker has rules that do not tolerate swearing, slander, defamation, libel, character assassination, slurs or racial bigotry. As an extreme facilitator, these are the issues that get the strongest reaction from me. I will ask a member of the public for an apology or ask them to leave.

- **Sharing Time**

I will always inform people in advance that I will be watching microphone time. In the opening part of the meeting, this goes for both the client, the professional staff and members of the public. Normally, I tell people that I'm very happy to hear their comments, and even happier if they can be brief and to the point. I'm happier still if they can provide one or two comments in order to allow other people in attendance to speak. When I see twenty-five hands in the air at the beginning of a meeting, I hope that everyone will be brief.

Sharing time goes both ways. Because it often takes the client five minutes to answer a question and there may be more than one expert who wants to respond, I also have to be conscious of how much time my client is taking. I will listen carefully to the question being asked by the member of the public. Is it a comment that doesn't need a response? If so, I will suggest to my client that it sounds like this comment should be noted, but point out that it doesn't need a response. If it looks like my client and the experts are going to take ten minutes to respond, I will intervene, suggesting that it sounds like the member of the public has received a thorough response and it is time to hear from the public again.

- **Written Material**

A handful of people will come to a public meeting with prepared notes or articles they want to read. While I'm pleased that they have done some research and prepared their thoughts in advance, they usually have no idea about the time it takes to read several pages. If you've been to a morning church service on a lovely summer day, you will have a good idea of how agonizingly long it takes for the minister or priest to read the important parts of the service. My ground rule is to ask people to summarize the material they have prepared in several sentences and bring the rest to the note-taker for inclusion in the minutes.

Dealing with people who ignore this ground rule is fairly easy. Normally, I see well in advance who has the material, so I will look for a better time to take their questions or comments. When I ask them to sum up, I will occasionally have a member of the crowd yell at me and demand that I let them read. To this, I respond that I see another fifteen people with their hands up and, as time is limited, I want to hear from them too. Then, I will stand, fold my arms and listen.

It doesn't take too long for a crowd to turn on the person who is dominating the meeting by reading written remarks. They will either ask me to interrupt the person or tell them to sit down. Either choice is fine with me.

- **Speak into the Microphone**

    Although I have discussed wrangling microphones in an earlier chapter, I need to stress the fact that the use of microphones is also a ground rule. Perhaps sometime in the twenty-third century, when we have cured cancer, traveled at light speed and found dark matter, someone will invent a microphone that responds to someone speaking from any angle or doesn't have a two-second delay before the person speaking can hear themselves.

    As part of the preparation, we will usually try to work with the audio-visual people (if such people have actually been hired by the client) to find out how the mikes work. Normally, people have to speak right into the microphone, meaning that they need to hold the bulb end somewhere near their mouth.

- **Safety and Washrooms**

    While this meeting consideration may seem trivial, I will definitely be asked about the location of the washrooms if I don't tell the public where they are. (Over the years, I've become very good at finding the washrooms and giving good instructions on how to get to them. Perhaps I've got a retirement job ahead of me.)

    Although I discussed safety and security earlier, it is important as a ground rule to point out any safety hazards, fire exits and procedures in advance of the meeting. Normally, the major safety issues have to do with cords on the floor.

- **All Views Welcome**

    I usually end my presentation of ground rules by emphasizing that I welcome all views. It takes someone with a strong constitution and an ability to run fast to say something in opposition to a dominant opinion in a room full of very angry people. Although I don't expect to get views from everyone, this is a way of conveying to certain people who I know are present that they are welcome to present their views. More than once, I've gestured to the person with an alternative view if they want to speak. With a nod of the head, they usually say "no".

The following is a good example of courtesies for friendlier meetings:

- Listen curiously and respectfully.
- Speak one at a time.
- Leave status and stereotypes at the door.
- Build upon and add nuances to help inform everyone's best thinking.
- Speak only for yourself.
- Turn off electronics.

Getting People to Agree on Ground Rules

Before the major part of the meeting begins, it is important to have people agree on the ground rules. As discussed earlier, it is an agreement about group norms. First, I ask the group, "Does everyone agree with these ground rules?", leaving a few seconds for people to respond while I scan the room for hands.

As I wait, I'm hoping that there are no comments, since I believe the ground rules have set out a fair process. On those rare occasions when someone does raise their hand because they don't agree, I probe the nature of their question or issue to determine if the comment can be incorporated into the ground rules. More often or not, the issue has to do with the notes of the meeting.

I will also ask the question in reverse, "Is there anyone who doesn't agree with my ground rules?" Usually, no one will disagree, so I will say, "It's nice to start a meeting with consensus" (knowing full well that consensus is questionable). That being said, in a particularly troublesome part of a meeting where someone is disrespectful or acting out, I go back to the beginning part of the meeting and rally some crowd support for my efforts in keeping the meeting under control because they implicitly agreed with the ground rules.

Enforcing Ground Rules

There is no sense in having ground rules if they can't be enforced. Doing so when things get hot can be tricky. I'll discuss throwing people out of meetings if they don't follow ground rules in a later chapter, but that's usually an extreme case. Normally, I will try to work with the audience to reinforce the need to stick to the rules. As an extreme facilitator, I'm at the meeting because members of the public have agreed to have me play this role on their behalf. I've established rules that instill confidence in them that there will be fairness and decorum.

The biggest issue is disrespectful language, usually coming from a particularly vocal participant. To enforce the ground rules, I remind the person about what they agreed to at the beginning, saying, "You know, at the beginning of the meeting all of these people sitting here, including you, agreed that we would talk to each other in a respectful manner. So, I'm asking everyone here tonight, 'Do you want to follow respectful ground rules or not?"

Then, to the person acting out, I will say, "All of these people said they wanted respectful behaviour, and I think it is important to respect their wishes. Please restate your comments so that we can hear them in a respectful manner".

Usually my comment grounds the behaviour, the person backs down and we can get on with the meeting. Effectively, I have used the weight of the audience and the norms established at the beginning to enforce the behaviour.

I am still surprised at how bad-mannered some people can be. It is as if they are taking their yelling at the TV and bringing it out in public. In one meeting, a person called the report from a consultant a pile of s**t, adding that the consultants were merely shills for the proponent. Upon hearing this, I stopped the meeting cold and said in a very loud voice, "Your language and your comments have no place here. Either restate, apologize or get out!" The person seemed to think that you can swear at or slander a professional without any repercussion. If I am facilitating the meeting, they are going to deal with me, and I won't take it.

Agenda Progression

Facilitation theorists focus on conducting meetings so that the goals of the group are met. The goal of a large angry meeting often involves providing people with information, clarifying information, hearing the response of the public, reflecting and responding to public comments, noting actions, and then drawing the meeting to a close. As part of their role, facilitators track the progression through the formal agenda. Since there are times when the client wants to present information and receive comments in a segmented way, each segment needs to be managed.

Moving the agenda along involves the facilitator intervening at appropriate times during the meeting. Ingrid Bens[189] describes intervention as any action a facilitator can take to improve the situation. The facilitator's training allows them to make a judgment on when to intervene. I usually watch and listen for where the public and client are in their process of exchanging information. Schwarz[190] nicely summarizes a list of considerations on the mind of the facilitator, which I paraphrase as follows:

- Do I know what's going on?
- Do I know where we are in the agenda and where we should be?
- Is a particular behaviour contributing or detracting from agenda progress?
- Should I intervene? What are the consequences if I do or don't intervene?
- Would the client/ public group expect me to make an intervention?
- What is the least I can do to intervene?

The extreme facilitator needs to have a good command of prompt questions that will move the group through the agenda. Ingrid Bens[191] cites twelve such questions in common use, with themes important to the facilitator noted below. The facilitators' prompt questions and intervention comments help them to:

- Set and maintain the context of the dialogue.
- Move the discussion from one agenda item to another.
- Probe where necessary to enrich the quality of the conversation.

---

189 Bens, I. p. 85, 84

190 Schwarz, R., 2nd edition. Ppgs. 182, 183

191 Bens, I. p. 34

- Observe and intervene to move the group from one stage to another, e.g. Storming to Reforming.
- Help to reframe conversations to achieve better results.
- Summarize at times.
- Manage the question and comment period.
- Manage emotions.
- Deal with complications.

The facilitator also needs to be conscious of the need to occasionally inform people of where they are in the agenda and meeting process.

Managing the Question and Comment Period

This is the most dynamic part of the meeting. Every time I reach this point is different. My client/ presenter may have been long-winded and the patience of the public may be running low. The PA system may not be working properly. I may have had to address outbursts or cat calls while the presentation is under way, correct poor behaviour or ask someone interrupting the speaker to hold their comment.

For most meetings, the transition to the question and comment period rolls out smoothly. My staff, who are trained to keep their eyes on me as I direct them to which person in the audience needs to speak next, are ready to bring microphones to people who want to speak. They know that I'm the one watching the audience and managing the process as I monitor group dynamics and listen carefully to each question and comment.

By watching body language during the presentation portion and listening to people during the open house period, I have a reasonable idea of who will have their hand up first. Before opening the question and comment portion of the meeting, I will thank the presenters and announce that it's the open part of the meeting. My comments at this point allow a final opportunity for me to touch base with my client and the experts, who are usually under stress. It also allows me to reinforce the tone for the public, saying, "I'm sensing you have a lot of comments and questions. I'm guessing that a few of you feel very strongly about what you've heard, and I want to make sure our presenters hear your views."

I remind people about how much time is available for the question and answer session, as they may be worried that there won't be time for them to speak. For very large meetings, there is no way that I will get to everyone, so I will make a commitment to do my best and ask everyone to work with me. We typically plan at least an hour to an hour and a half for the question and comment period. I will assure the public that I'm going to try to hear from as many people as possible.

I also assure participants that I'm pretty good at remembering whose hand went up when, and that I will call on them in this order, adding that I'm going to hear from as many people in that order before returning to follow-up questions from earlier speakers. So, thirty hands are in the air, each person believing that they have the most important question and comment, and expecting to be called upon first. I know that I won't have time to get to everyone.

The technique that I use for calling on people is finger signaling - much like a stock trader in the pit does to communicate with a broker a floor above, except that I'm using interpersonal and audience communication skills to maintain a fair process in a dynamic and stressful environment.

Managing this portion of a meeting involves more than calling on individuals to ask their questions in a particular order. People need to know that they are being listened to. I also need to give the presenters time to sort out who is going to respond to a question or comment, signalling to them when a public comment does or doesn't appear to need a response (although it is ultimately up to the presenter to make that call).

Before the question and comment period, I will mentally divide how the audience is seated in terms of front and back, left and right side of the room. For larger meetings, there may be a middle portion. To remember the order, I will simply pick the first five people and use finger signals to indicate to them whether they are first, second or fifth in line, always taking care to signal showing the palm of my hand.

During the question and comment period, I will check back with people on the list after the third speaker to assure them that I am indeed keeping the order of commenters as promised. Once the fourth person has had a chance to speak, I will ask for the next people who want to comment. In many cases, the first five people have already asked questions that were on the minds of some of the thirty people who had their hands up initially. And so, I will continue to call on people in each part of the room. This is a simple way of keeping track and honouring your commitment to maintaining a fair process.

In order to allow as many people as possible to comment, I need to be conscious of how time is being consumed. Because it takes a few seconds to bring a microphone to the next person asking a question, my microphone wranglers are trained to get to where that person is seated long before the person before them receives a response from the presenter. I quietly direct my wranglers from the front in a manner that doesn't disrupt the flow.

I also need to listen to how my presenters are responding to a question or comment. While they have been coached to be brief, sometimes a question is complicated and will require two or three people to respond. What could end up as a five to ten-minute response will cause the emotional temperature to go up in the room, as people who have already been waiting an hour to speak will have to wait that much longer.

As an independent third-party facilitator, I am in the position of managing a process without having any responsibility for the decisions being made. I am, however, usually very well versed on the issues and the community. People taking the time to ask questions or provide comments need to be understood and respected. In order to make sure that presenters are providing clear responses that allow members of the public to learn, I need to understand what every individual is saying.

The Listener in Chief

Being 'Listener-in-Chief' is another role I play during the question and comment portion of the meeting. It is a satisfying role because I'm always interested in hearing the views of the public on an issue that's also so important to them and my clients. During a meeting concerning the location in the river of the discharge for a sewage treatment plant, residents informed the client that this was also the location of a spring where people take water. That was helpful to hear. In another meeting, where a highway expansion involving the future of a local bridge was being discussed, residents pointed out there was an encampment of homeless people living under the bridge. This was something that my clients would never have known.

In order to be a good Listener in Chief, I must accomplish four things. Firstly, I need to assure the person asking the question that they are being listened to while showing an audience of over one hundred people that I'm also listening to them. To do this, I will use specific body language: a pensive, contemplative and reflecting look, rubbing my chin or raising my eyebrows.

Secondly, working with my staff as note-takers, I stop for a moment and ask my staff if they've written down what the person is saying. They know that I know they have. They are all professionals. And they understand that this pause and check procedure assures members of the public that I am not the only one listening.

I also need to listen to what the client and consultants are saying as a response to the public question and ask, "Was there a response to the actual question? Did the expert pick up on the details and nuances of the question? For a multi-part question, were all parts answered? Was the response conveyed in a manner that was respectful to the person asking the question?"

Lastly, I will often use a flip chart to jot down what people are saying. More often than not, people come up to me when the meeting is over to either elaborate on their point or provide additional comments pointing to the flip chart. I take this as a compliment because they trust this part of the listening process. Doyle and Straus discuss 'flip-charting' and recording in depth and I'm happy to direct you to their work.[192]

Several challenges almost always occur at large angry meetings that require a careful response.

---

192 Doyle and Straus, p. 125

Hogging Air Time

Every meeting will include one or more members of the public who are well-researched or have a deep emotional need to speak at length. It is not uncommon to have someone who, when it comes to their time to speak, says "I have five questions" or, when they get the microphone, start to read several pages of text that they have prepared in advance.

How do you deal with people hogging air time? To begin with, my staff and I train for this. I will never facilitate a meeting where a microphone is placed in the middle of the floor, with people standing in line waiting for their turn to speak. In a situation like this, communication breaks down because you often only hear from those people who have an axe to grind or want to grandstand, resulting in my presenters becoming no more than targets waiting for the next verbal grenade to be thrown at them.

My microphone wranglers are coached on what to do when this occurs. If a person has a lot of questions or comments, I don't hesitate to be rude and interrupt them. I will thank them for being so well researched and remind them that there are many other people who also want to speak. Furthermore, I will make a commitment to come back to them if they want to start with the first few questions and deal with the rest later. If a person has a brief to read which could take them five to ten minutes, I will ask them to summarize and bring the brief to me so that we can document their submission as part of the minutes of the meeting.

There are always people who have their hands up during the whole meeting. If there are fewer other hands, I will return to them, but I need to be careful not to allow them to dominate as the other one hundred and ninety-nine people may have a different point of view and may be simply listening or holding back their comments. If there are many hands in the air, I announce that I will go to people who haven't asked a question or provided a comment before. Then I will return to them for a second or third set of questions.

Managing the Response

A public meeting is, in part, a transaction of information. Staff and professionals have an opportunity to hear what the public has to say, while the public obtains information from them.

Who are these people and why are they yelling at me? | 231

When the transaction occurs in a dynamic group setting, people can hear what other members of the public are thinking through the comments and questions being asked. Conversely, staff and professionals are learning from the public and hearing each other respond to comments and questions they might not have thought about.

As a facilitator, it is very important to have staff and professionals respond fully to questions and comments. Doing so in front of several hundred people is usually intimidating, particularly when the media may be present and some members of the public may be recording what you are saying.

With very few exceptions, I've had the pleasure of working with seasoned and well-respected professionals including transportation engineers, water and waste water engineers, biologists, environmental planners, telecommunication specialists and others. They are highly regarded by their employers, other staff, other professionals and colleagues.

Those who are regulated professionals have a responsibility for making and defending recommendations they feel are in the public interest. Most are experienced in defending their opinions before legislative bodies and, under oath, in cross-examinations before administrative tribunals or courts. They wouldn't be given the responsibility of standing in front of several hundred members of the public answering questions if they didn't carry this level of experience and respect.

That being said, the "answering" segment in the public meeting needs to be managed. My first responsibility as a facilitator is to make sure that the team has a moment to figure out who is going to answer which question or respond to which comment. Questions may be complex, requiring more than one person to respond.

Almost universally, someone among the client team has been appointed as gatekeeper - usually the project or program manager. I will be watching for body language and listening to communication among the team (usually happening away from the microphone). In some cases, time is required to allow the team to organize a response. In order to buy time, I will repeat the question or ask the audience to allow a few seconds for the team to identify who the best person is to answer.

My second responsibility is to ensure that the person answering can do so completely and without interruption. Even though we've had the chalk talk discussed earlier, there is a big difference between preparing before the meeting how you might answer a question and actually doing so when you are on the hot seat. The professional will know that if there's a full answer to be given, I've done my homework to understand what they need to say. Once they are ready to respond, I will work with the audience to allow enough time for the answer to be given. I will also be actively intervening if a member of the public is interrupting.

My technique for allowing a full response to the question in the event of an interruption involves: breaking into the response of the professional and reminding the member of the public that they had agreed to show respect according to the ground rules; asking them to hold their comment until it's their turn to speak, or standing beside them as a way of minimizing distance.

For members of the public who are persistent I will turn off my microphone, go to where they are seated and remind them that I will make sure that ground rules are followed. The person may still be unruly, but several hundred other people in the audience got the message because they don't want to be the next person to have me standing beside them.

In advance of the meeting, we talk about the importance of getting responses out with clarity and integrity. While it would be nice, a facilitator's job is not to find a consensus point of view. Indeed, too often angry public meetings result because professionals and politicians cannot say "no". At this point, their responsibility is to state a professional opinion, whether or not the public agrees with it. There is a right and wrong, and my clients are expected to say so.

Before each meeting, I remind the team that their role as professionals is to answer honestly and completely based on the studies and research they have completed. While there is a natural tendency to be respectful and empathetic of someone else's point of view, staff and professionals are not there to build consensus. There are different types of meetings that are perfect for building consensus – a large angry public meeting is not likely to have this goal. The client has done the research and concluded their studies, and they have drawn conclusions based on their professional experience. The right and wrong answers need to be communicated, but the major challenge is that the public may not want to hear or accept the answers being given.

Although each response takes time, long-winded client rambling results in fewer people getting to ask questions or provide comments. For this reason, I watch to see if a response from the professional is raising the emotional temperature. If I see this, I use a circular finger gesture (with one hand blocking what I'm doing from the view of the public) to ask the professional to wind it up. They will have other opportunities to elaborate later in the meeting.

If a response from a professional is not clear to me, it won't be clear to the public. Observing facial expressions in the crowd, it's not hard to see when people don't understand. If I notice this, I will intervene and ask the staff person to clarify certain points. Usually, they are happy to do so but, if it's still not clear, I will ask the member of the public to come up after the meeting for a face to face conversation.

Managing Storming

During large, angry public meetings, the extreme facilitator needs to be on their game in terms of managing emotions and diffusing hostility. When a meeting is underway, I'm constantly watching the audience and my client, asking myself, "Where are they in terms of emotions and hostility? What's making the public and individuals angry?"

There are several ways to manage emotions during a large, angry meeting. One involves setting and maintaining a tone through actions and words of the facilitator and the client. Being positive, attentive, respectful, curious, patient and calm are some of the most important responses that a facilitator can share to ensure that the right tone is being maintained.

A second way involves being a very active listener. Members of the public are at the meeting because they have something to say. They may not think that the client is listening, but they absolutely need to know that the facilitator is. Conversely, Ghais[193] presents several responses a facilitator should *not* do: deal with strong emotions by claiming to be someone with authority and pointing

---

193 Ghais, S., 181, 182

to the ground rules; tell the public to focus on the facts; tell them to calm down; and try to explain one person's view to another person.

Another way of managing emotions involves taking actions to help adjust the emotional volume, such as being aware of and avoiding trigger words. I have facilitated several meetings where a trigger word uttered by a client set off an emotional response that never stopped. Trigger words often open up a window to what the client is thinking on matters of risk, health, safety and the quality of life of meeting participants.

During a particularly troublesome meeting, my client did a calculation of how many members of the public might die if their preferred project option was chosen over another. Attempting to present the life and death calculation as a once in a million-year probability, the comment actually came out as, 'If we choose this option, only three members of this community would die over this time period, and that's acceptable to us".

I am rather glad that people don't carry sidearms in Canada, because that night, we would have had blood on the floor. Not surprisingly, the people responded to my client's comment with outrage, saying, "What right do you have to make decisions about who will die? The nerve of you for even thinking of that! You don't live here! What if your children were the ones to die?" Those were some of the more civil responses.

Emotional volume can be disruptive to a meeting, but it can be adjusted in the following ways: 1) allowing people to vent; 2) refocusing the discussion on interests versus positions; or, 3) accommodating or compromising. Accommodating means the client says something like, "You know, you're right. We will make the change you are suggesting."

People and Situational Complications

While the general characteristics of people attending large, angry public meetings were discussed in an earlier chapter, as an extreme facilitator, I also need to prepare for and manage certain people and complications that can pose a challenge to the meeting process.

I refer to these as complications rather than problems because they are not always negative. For example, someone may want to hog air time as a local expert or Internet expert. This person may have thought through the issues and may have something important to add to the conversation, but they are not allowing other people to speak. They may also be intimidating because they make people who haven't done their homework feel stupid, so that they clam up. In addition, the Internet expert creates confusion because people don't know who to believe: a well-researched member of the public or an expert with a PhD and thirty-five years of experience.

People complications include: the indignant and the outraged; children; local and internet experts; politicians; anarchists.

Situational complications arise from: intoxication; people demanding to hold a vote; grandstanders; prolonged applause; chanting; dealing with citizen journalists and social media; throwing people out. I discuss each of these situations in the following chapters.

Indignant and Outraged

There will always be people at the meeting who bring this attitude and behave accordingly. These people have a very strong sense of what's "right" behaviour. They are passionate about sharing their views of moral outrage with others, which is along the lines of, "Our sense of morality has been violated by what the proponents or experts are advocating", and may say things like, "I'm outraged! How dare you?"

Occasionally, there will be outbursts with tears and comments on what kind of world we are creating for our children and grandchildren. The outraged person will often point to perceived health and safety risks and effects on the environment. These are the social justice issues.

Because there will usually be some silence following the outburst, as well as empathy for the person showing the strong emotion, I will generally allow a few seconds' pause at this point to allow the person to regain their composure. We are all human beings and we feel bad when someone is that upset. We all have our moral view of the world. The person expressing the outburst may be articulating how other people feel as well.

As a way of sharing my empathy, I will say, "I can tell you are upset. You appear to be very passionate about this issue. Thank you for sharing for views." While

I may appear a bit hard-assed after that because I keep the question and answer session going, we don't make public policy and public interest decisions on the basis of who's upset. For a society to function properly, we gather facts, weigh evidence and make rational choices.

On a shelf behind my desk is an essay[194] by Dr. George Pickering who, at the time of writing was a professor of Religious Studies at the University of Detroit[195]. Possessing a wonderful sense of humour, George was at one time a co-host of the NPR Radio Show "Ask the Professor". (He often boasted that the show was a big hit in Alaska.) On the matter of the violation of moral differences, George advocated breaking through endless discussions about conflicting moral claims by making explicit key assumptions and focusing the discussion on the principal questions. I discuss this, in part, earlier in the chapter on the causes of large angry meetings.

Essentially, a person who is indignant and outraged is referring to the issue of what is wise and right behaviour and what is wise and right policy. These are important questions. The deeper and totally fair questions that the indignant and outraged person is appealing to are almost never brought up in public discourse. To this point, George Pickering observed, "There is no strictly technical nor any strictly ethical answer to the question of what is the wisest policy for this or any other country to follow?[196]"

For some policy decisions, it is not clear where political, ethical and scientific/technical judgements take up or leave off. Moral questions underpin policy questions, and they run deep. In my humble opinion, the act of reframing some of the most pressing questions that cause conflict in society is long overdue.

---

194 George W. Pickering, 'Integrating Ethical and Technical Considerations in the Energy Debate' March 12, 1980 in "Moral and Ethical Issues relating to Nuclear Energy Generation: Proceedings of a Seminar, March 1908.

195 George W. Pickering was a professor of Religious Studies at the University of Detroit and died in 2002. http://www.ugapress.org/index.php/books/confronting_color_line

196 George referred to energy policy in his remarks.

Children

Speaking of children, it irritates me to no end seeing children brought into large, angry public meetings as props. These events are usually quite intense, and children will likely be terrified if they see their parents and others behaving badly. There are better ways for parents to teach their children about politics. I don't know if parents realize what they are doing when, on the worst occasions, they hold their two and three-year old children up at me, crying, screaming and claiming that their kids are going to get cancer. The thought going through my mind is, "What kind of parent are you?"

When there are children in the audience, I alter my style and my introductory remarks so as to explain to them what is going to happen. I want to play my role in making the children feel welcome and safe. As an example, I was asked by a cellular telephone company to facilitate a meeting in Caledon, Ontario. I obtained some intelligence that there would be children at the meeting.

The issue of concern to the parents was the proposed site of the cellular phone tower. Despite the fact that most of them had cell phones, TVs and radios, the local residents heard that the radio waves from these towers cause cancer. I suppose that no one had informed them about the radio waves beaming into their homes to make their radios and TVs operate. Several people from a local public school who had organized the concerned parents had already found the name of the farmer who owned the land where the cell tower was to be located, and were picketing his driveway.

When I walked out to the lobby of the meeting hall to greet people, I concluded that the teachers at the local public school were either also involved or had succumbed to parental pressure to have protest signs created in art class. (The art teacher obviously had talent. Compared to most protest signs I normally see, these were well done.)

The parents waited for the right occasion to tell their kids to hold up their signs. (I suspected that the grade three and four students had also been taught to shout out protest slogans.) As I was getting the meeting underway, I realized that I had an opportunity to talk directly to the parents and children.

During my opening remarks, I acknowledged the signs that the children were carrying, adding how important it was for children so young to be taking civics classes and learning about our democracy. Coming across as a kind of wise, old grandfather, I said, "Tonight, you will have an opportunity to see how your parents and other adults talk to each other when we have different views. Talking to each other nicely is the way we solve our differences in Canada. You should be proud of your parents and your teachers for taking an interest."

At this time, I also explained the importance of democracy and how it involves respecting each other and showing good behaviour in public. I said, "I hope everyone can learn from this evening. I would be proud if one of you became a politician some day - someone we could all look up to with respect." I could start to see the signs being hidden. Eventually the parents shoved them all under the chairs, and the meeting ended up well.

From: Waterkeepers Newsletter, July 28 2009

Local and Internet Experts

Formulating solutions based on the information they have on hand; local and Internet experts will challenge specialists at most meetings. The local expert will have local knowledge to share with the intent of trumping the views of specialists, saying, "You don't know the community like I do, so your facts have to be wrong". The Internet expert may have no schooling in the field of

Who are these people and why are they yelling at me? | 239

study related to the project. But they have taken the time to research a position online. Seeking to be an authority at the meeting, they might say, "I've done the research and found a study that disproves everything you are saying".

The typical meeting I facilitate starts with several specialists, scientists and consulting professionals retained by the client making a small presentation on the project. After they have finished, I field questions from the public, fully expecting to hear from the antagonists, starting with the local community experts.

In addition to presenting information, the specialists also include an argument and point of view on the conclusions they have drawn. The client expects their consultants to confirm through their studies why a particular project or policy has technical merit and should be approved. The consulting professionals are typically well-educated, well-researched and highly credible.

There is a significant difference in the way that professionals and local experts answer to the public. Professionals, bound by their respective licensing and regulating bodies, have boundaries around what they can say. The local experts are free from any restrictions, and basically say what they want.

For example, I am both a facilitator and a professional planner. As a Registered Professional Planner (RPP), I am allowed to use this professional designation under the Ontario Professional Planners Institute Act.[197] Governing my professional actions, the Institute can dish out discipline if required. When I appear as an expert witness, the judge or hearing officer expects this discipline, as it characterizes the quality of my opinion. This also applies to occasions when I express a professional opinion in public. If I'm not qualified to comment on a certain matter, I don't comment. I can be disciplined if I do.

My judgement as a planner is governed by what I believe to be in the public interest. Consistent with the objectives of the Institute, I am expected to; promote, maintain and regulate high standards of professional planning practice and ethical behaviour; further the recognition of the planning profession in Ontario; promote the value, use and methods of planning; improve the quality

---

197 Ontario Professional Planners Institute Act came into force December 9, 1994

http://digitalcommons.osgoode.yorku.ca/cgi/viewcontent.cgi?article=2265&context=ontario_statutes

of Ontario environments and communities by the application of planning principles; encourage participation and co-operation among those persons, associations and groups concerned with improving the quality of Ontario environments and communities; and stimulate the generation, development, dissemination and discussion of ideas on planning. I am governed under a Code of Practice[198] and must adhere to a Standard of Practice.[199]

In contrast, the public interest objective of some community groups while admirable, is narrowly defined as protecting the quality of life of their families and the local community. Neither local experts nor Internet experts are bound by any such requirement.

Like other professionals, I value public input and listen carefully for matters to be raised that will help me to define the public interest. What other professionals and I determine to be the public interest, however, will not necessarily change for the purpose of assuaging the views of local experts or in the face of strong public opposition. For this reason, well-informed and technically credible professionals pose a problem for communities and other individuals who either want to stop a project or advocate alternative policies and approaches.

With the exception of their doctors, lawyers, accountants or dentists, members of the public typically do not interact with technical professionals and scientists. Few of them understand what a health physicist is. They may have never met a hydrologist, radio frequency engineer or epidemiologist, and normally don't understand what they do.

With the rise of "citizen science", I've seen greater numbers of local citizen Internet experts at large, angry meetings. These "experts" with scientific opinions will typically come forward and present opposing points of view. Ironically, we have the rise of citizen science when scientific and mathematical public literacy appears to be declining in many societies. As long as the person espousing an alternative point of view appears to be researched and credible, many members of the public will accept their opinion over that of the seasoned and credentialed professional.

---

198 http://ontarioplanners.ca/Knowledge-Centre/Professional-Code-of-Practice

199 http://ontarioplanners.ca/getmedia/294feead-e2df-4271-a892-d8cfcdb4a6e3/OPPI-Standards-of-Practice.aspx

Research presented by a member of the public posing as an expert does not need to pass any peer review. Nor does it need come from published sources. Although it is also unlikely that the community expert will be subjected to cross-examination, professionals can expect it.

A variant of the local and Internet expert is the "hired gun" brought in by the community to take on the consulting professionals. This person is typically a professional with all the credentials who doesn't share the majority professional view of what constitutes sound science. Hired guns are typically under-funded and as a result may be poorly prepared. They may be asked by the public to comment on matters outside of their core field of expertise. Dr. David Suzuki sometimes accepts requests from the public to travel to a community and comment on matters of science in public meetings. While he is perceived by the public to have a huge amount of credibility, those with professional and academic knowledge of the subject matter outside of Suzuki's area of expertise may disagree with his opinions.

The challenge in preparing for and facilitating large, angry public meetings is that the "outlying" scientific research is seen by the public to be credible. Witness the global movement to stop inoculations for childhood diseases due to the public's belief in alternative, shoddy science. Or the two studies released about the health effects of exposure to electromagnetic radiation from radio waves that caused widespread public concern. Meanwhile, one hundred and fifty thousand other studies concluded that there were no effects or a slight association, but no causality. While this majority of studies was largely ignored, the two studies of concern legitimized the public opinion of health risk.

In the middle of a large, angry meeting, the public will be further enraged if the proponent or I ask for credentials or challenge the research of the local community or Internet expert. In one meeting, I had to deal with a certified day care worker presenting herself as pediatrician specializing in childhood diseases related to exposure to electromagnetic effects. In another meeting I needed to address a truck assembly line worker claiming to be transportation expert qualified to speak about the community effects of aggregate truck traffic. I typically don't aggressively challenge citizens, claiming to be scientifically-informed experts, who are well informed, yet have only read the academic literature that supports their point of view.

Although I do acknowledge that people standing up have a right to question experts. Their ability to challenge experts is a fundamental part of our democracy. Yet, this type of exchange creates a lot of confusion among the public. As a facilitator, I try to nudge the meeting process somewhat to test the scientific evidence in front of the public and allow a respectful challenge of the claims of local experts, if their opinions are inaccurate. I will do this in a manner that allows the member of the public to save face while allowing the audience to come to their own conclusion about what information is sound.

During my opening remarks, I introduce the scientific professionals in a manner that announces their credentials. If a person has a PhD in the field and thirty years' experience, I will introduce them that way. I also try to shed some light on the scientific or technical credentials claimed by the local expert. Sometimes the local expert is indeed well qualified or the client's professional needs to be held to account. There are boundaries, however. In the middle of a large, angry meeting, the local expert is trusted by the public and seen to be on their side.

My exchange with the daycare worker claiming to be a pediatrician with expertise in electromagnetic radiation causing cancer in children related to cellular telephone tower radio frequencies was very light and cordial. The conversation went as follows:

"You obviously have some expertise in this area?"

"Yes."

"It's important to hear how you got your training. Are you trained as a medical doctor?"

"No, but I do have medical training on working with children."

"I'm glad you are sharing your opinion with everyone in the room. I assume your training is also about the effects of radiation on children?"

"No. My training is in how to take care of children."

"Perfect, I can't think of an occupation more important in today's society. I'm glad that you are here and that you have certification."

"Well thank you. Yes, I have a Certificate in Early Childhood Education."

Who are these people and why are they yelling at me? | 243

The local expert felt good about what she was contributing to the conversation and about being recognized for her certificate. I was satisfied because members of the audience knew exactly how much weight to give to her comments on electromagnetic effects.

I encourage my client to ask local experts gentle but probing questions on where their data and referenced studies came from in order to allow the team members to review the material. I also make sure that the scientific point being raised by the resident is recorded in the notes of the meeting. The specialists I work with are highly trained, and I have yet to receive any information from the public that wasn't already well known to the project team. Because the meeting is about process, I will say, "I'm sure that the team will want to take a look at your research. Can you share your information and discuss your research with them after the meeting?"

The challenge in preparing for large, angry public meetings is that the "outlying" scientific research is seen by the public to be credible enough to direct the political decision. Indeed, junk science endorsed by TV personalities is seen to be credible by many members of the public.

Internet experts pose a more unique challenge in terms of group process. They may have no scientific or technical training, but take the time to do the research through the internet or Wikipedia. Typically, Internet experts are "pseudo-experts", well armed with facts and studies. They may have talked to an actual expert or specialist before the meeting. Sometimes they are very well-qualified.

We were once asked to peer-review a proposed Advanced Conversion Technology Low Temperature 'gasification' waste to energy plant in Central Ontario. My role here was as an expert and not a facilitator. A group of well-qualified local residents including a professor emeritus specializing in the biological effects of contaminants pointed to the potential emissions of nitrogen oxides, dioxides and mercury. Claiming that fine and ultra-fine particles would be emitted, the professor drew the conclusion that the emissions would result in cardiovascular disease, pulmonary disease and cancer.

The group also claimed other potential risks associated with the project, including the plant may not operating properly, unproven technology at this location, a plant somewhere else in the world that had a problem, regulations in other parts of the world which, if applied in Canada, would not allow the technology to be approved, and other risks that would make emissions unacceptable. Their scientific citations included Greenpeace and Environmental Defence studies.

That said, the professor emeritus was obviously far more qualified than a Internet expert. However, the professor was unable to acknowledge in public that the emissions were at a micro scale in the order of parts per billion and trillion. In truth, the everyday act of breathing would result in more gasses being exhaled than would be emitted by the plant. The logical conclusion was that, if we wanted to implement such a high standard of emissions, we should all stop breathing.

In light of the stature of the professor emeritus, however, none of the professionals could rebut the comment in the meeting. Not rebutting the point tacitly means that you've accepted it. This allowed the public to conclude that the plant should not proceed because the opinion on negative effects was unanimous.

Internet experts will usually not talk to a scientist or technical expert retained by the proponent. To do so would be a violation of group norms. Nor will they take a course on the topic. The reality is that we are living in a world where, once people make up their minds, it's very hard to convince them to change their point of view. Indeed, I steer my clients away from the notion that, if they merely provide accurate scientific information or proven facts, members of the audience will change their minds. They often do provide this information anyway, but it usually it doesn't work.

Project teams need to understand that the public obtains data to inform their opinion from family members and neighbours, the internet, newspapers and technical and scientific references on Wikipedia. This information is often biased or inaccurate. Sometimes it is deliberately so, and sometimes it's not. Yet, to the public, the internet and newspapers are seen to be an authoritative source where media personalities like Leonardo De Caprio are seen to be more credible than Nobel Prize winners.

Internet experts are convinced that, because they have done the research, their opinions are correct. Other members of the public at the meeting, often friends and neighbours who have not done the research, are faced with deciding who to believe: a scientist who is an expert with a PhD or their neighbourhood Internet expert who is adamant that their research is sound, and that their opinion is the right one.

Over the years I've kept a list of the ways in which local and Internet experts position their views positively and cast doubts on the views of a client or trained professional.

Using a utility pipeline as an example, they will:

- **Deny the problem**: "We don't need pipelines to transport oil. Instead, we need to move toward a low carbon economy."
- **Magnify the risk**: "A pipeline once broke and polluted a local stream. That's the risk I'm concerned about – that it will break here and be catastrophic."
- **Shift the blame**: "It's big oil and the one percenter's will benefit and local residents will pay."
- **Cherry-pick the data**: "We're not against bulk oil pipeline shipments. It's just that the pipeline will also transport lighter polluting gas that is very hard to clean up."
- **Call for more evidence**: "We know the National Energy Board reviewed the evidence before giving approval, but they did not hear from or properly weigh the opinions of local communities."
- **Ask for a delay until a better solution can be found**: "A new hearing involving information about the feasibility of a low carbon economy will result in a better solution."
- **Shoot the messenger**: "The professionals behind the studies are hired by the proponent. They are biased and they shouldn't be listened to."
- **Attack alternatives**: "The alternative pipeline alignments didn't properly consider environmental effects. And, no future alternative will have considered environmental effects adequately."
- **Find quasi-scientists to support a position**: "Professors and academics hired by an environmental think tank came up with a different conclusion than the regulator. They should be believed."

Based on the research and strategy they chose for undermining the arguments of the proponent, it is then job of the Internet expert in a public meeting to present the "Got-Ya's". This is when a member of the public thinks that they have uncovered a fact that will undermine the basic premise of the position presented by the proponent.

Alternatively, a "Got-Ya" can occur because they have found a flaw in the proponent's reasoning regarding the need for a project.

"Getting" the other person during a public meeting is the goal of the "Got-Ya". The intent is to fatally trip up the proponent with the expectation that the specialists will agree and then go away. In some instances, the member of the public will imply there is a political back door, where a powerful person has had an influence on the decision so as to strengthen the impact of the 'Got-Ya' statement.

With apologies for seeming overly critical of people who do their own research, I do want to stress that local and Internet experts do show up at many public meetings. They also help to elevate the discussion and focus the conversation of facts. And, this is desirable. My advice to clients is this: either be prepared to respond to the information and the method chosen to deliver the information, or be open- minded, accept that the person might be right and be prepared to make changes.

Politicians

I have great respect for politicians. Most of them throw their hat in the ring for the right reason. This noble attribute, however, adds a layer of difficulty when they choose to play a prominent role (or any role) at a large, angry public meeting. The issues I have observed with politicians are as follows: it is hard to get them on script; they will have opinions that may not be completely aligned with the facts, and I'm never quite sure if there are other agendas at play; and there's a large likelihood that they will be put on the spot and be forced by the public to say things that are not true or are unwise.

When issues have festered, and a large, angry meeting is inevitable, politicians joining the meeting, points to the larger question of where we are in the democratic process. Instead of residents asking their politician to make a decision in a particular way or presenting their point of view at a municipal council meeting, they bypass the regular process, declaring, "Democracy is us. It's not about the politicians. We are going to turn out en masse."

I usually ask to meet with political representatives in advance of a meeting to explain my role and to try to ascertain theirs. They usually take some comfort in knowing that I've got quite a lot of experience and that I can generally keep meetings on track. That said, I will inform the politicians that, if they show up at the meeting, they will have to respond to strong questions from the public. There's little that I can do.

I share with politicians typical questions they may be asked to address, including, "Why is the decision going this way when we don't approve? Why don't you make the decision the way we want you to? We are in control, and if you don't make the right decision, we won't vote you back into office!"

The most uncertain part of the meeting occurs when politicians are called on to speak. First, I run a little flak control. I inform the public that meeting agendas rarely include a political comment, to which I can count on cat calls and demands to let the politician speak. At this point, I will engage in strong eye contact with the politician to determine whether or not this is what they want to do.

More experienced politicians will stand up and share their views, realizing that they need to straddle the evidence and science presented by the project team as well as the demands on the public based on what they say. For the less experienced politicians, the project team and science are expendable. And as an elected politician, they are not.

Anarchists

This is most challenging group to deal with at large public meetings. Almost universally, they represent the "alt left". In the few meetings where anarchists have been an issue (and there have been very few in my experience) I try to interact with them before the meeting begins. A group of anarchists attended a meeting that I was facilitating involving a highway extension. The same group show up a few weeks later at a meeting concerning an electrical transmission line. They had little in the way of a substantive interest in either topic and instead were interested in disruption.

During the former meeting, people from the group grabbed the microphone and grandstanded. When I spotted them at the second meeting, we had the following exchange beforehand, while they were seated. "How will we be presenting your comments tonight?" I asked. "We've got something we want to say," they replied. "I have security here tonight and I need to decide whether to throw you out now before the meeting begins or later. Help me out," I said. "We'll be brief. We'd like to talk first and then we'll leave," was their response.

My strategy worked. They kept to their word and left after having the first chance at the microphone. My approach to anarchists now, if I know they are coming, is to change the format of the meeting. For example, I was facilitating an evening meeting at a community centre in a part of Toronto known for strong citizen activism. The meeting was topic innocuous. The City of Toronto wanted to hear from residents about inviting businesses to invest in the community by offering them incentives and, if so, what incentives would be best.

About thirty residents showed up and registered before the meeting. Since I expected that there would also be anarchists and local activists attending, I decided to adjust the meeting format by inviting people to sit at round tables. They were asked to discuss several predetermined questions and share their views at the end of the meeting.

About twelve late-comers entered the room. The activists had arrived. They asked when the public portion of the meeting would start, as they were clearly intent on grandstanding to present their views on all sorts of issues. When they were told that there would not be a public portion and were invited to participate in a roundtable discussion with the others, they left because the opportunity to grandstand was not available. A constructive list of priority incentives was developed by the end of the evening.

Intoxication

My clients are usually reluctant to hold Friday or Saturday meetings because they fear that no one will show up. But sometimes, in vacation or cottage country, these are the only times that you can hear from city dwellers who have weekend properties in the area. As a result, these weekend meetings are usually a combination of city types and locals.

Who are these people and why are they yelling at me? | 249

If you are like me, Friday night is your wind-down time. Should you somehow end up having more than a few beers, you can sleep in on Saturday morning. In cottage country on summer weekends, Friday night often starts mid-afternoon, so typically, Friday evening is not the best time hold a public meeting.

In a lakefront community in central Ontario, however, the local Mayor decided that Friday night was the best time to announce that the municipality will be adding $20,000 to $30,000 to every homeowner's tax bill to pay for a new water distribution system. Normally, when financial and construction impacts are involved, my clients try to mange expectations by not soft-selling what the residents are going to experience, adding something like, "We'll be tearing up your street for a few weeks, making you park your cars in an alternative area, forcing you to walk to your home."

"What could go wrong?" my client thought. "We've hired a professional facilitator to run the meeting."

When I anticipate large crowds at a Friday night or Saturday afternoon meeting my biggest fear is not that people won't show up, but that they will show up drunk and angry.

As we were registering people arriving, it was obvious that many had been to the happy store early, and had consumed a starter course of liquor, wine and beer. I sensed that several residents had also consumed a selection of herbs and pharmaceuticals. We limited the length of the PowerPoint presentation to get to the question and answer period early. This would take the professional engineers out of the firing line and put me out in front, flagging questions and dealing with insults and outrage. The idea was that we could present more information during the question and answer period when the meeting is more interactive.

To my delight, the meeting was going a lot better than I thought, with some of the comments as follows: "Tear up your street? Fine with us. They're full of potholes anyway." (Scattered laughter.) "Park elsewhere and make us walk to our homes during construction? No problem, we've got legs." (Heads nodding.) "Thirty thousand on our tax bill? Sure, why not? We're good for it."

Most of the one hundred and twenty-five people attending the meeting were quite happy, and I started to get the sense that they would rather be on their decks getting back to the festive part of their evening. When I suggested that we might be able to end the meeting on time or perhaps early, there was no objection. The mayor came up to me after the meeting, saying that I had done a superior job of facilitating; music to my ears, as ending the meeting early gave me enough time to drive home and start my weekend.

I am happy to say that, in almost thirty years of facilitating meetings, I've never had staff or professionals show up to a meeting intoxicated. However, numerous politicians and senior government officials have attended in this condition. This presents a multiple set of challenges, not the least being that they are expected to speak.

In managing every meeting, my antennae are always tuning to what is going on outside of the meeting. My staff at the registration desk are trained to look for a number of situations, including public intoxication. If a potential speaker shows up in this condition, they will inform me, and we will work out what we are going to do about it when time allows before the meeting.

My first concerns are obvious: How did they get here? Did they drive? Did someone drive them? If so, I look for someone to get them home safely. It is a conversation with both the intoxicated person and the sober person accompanying them that needs to be both delicate and firm. As it is my expectation that the inebriated person will not be driving, I will assure myself that someone has been placed in control to make sure that this happens.

My next concern is that the intoxicated person still wants to speak in front of several hundred people and the media. Two examples come to mind. The first involved a senior official, scheduled to be a spokesperson at a meeting, who turned up inebriated. Apparently, he had been at a retirement party that afternoon. (It must have been a good party.)

When he arrived, my pants must have caught fire because I decided to misspeak about his situation. Before the meeting began, I joined the official and told him that, because the agenda had been changed, he wouldn't be able to speak after all, so he had an opportunity to leave early. I said that I will tell the audience that he has to leave due to another urgent appointment.

The official minder was on board, appreciating the need to get him out of the meeting - always a good decision because, during loud and emotional meetings, it's not unusual for members of the public to want to hold a senior official accountable and demand that they speak. Who knows what he would have said.

While it didn't take place in an angry meeting, my most memorable example occurred when a senior elected Minister (M.P.P.) was given the job of formally welcoming several hundred conference participants on behalf of the Province of Ontario. When he entered the room, the minister was so inebriated that he could barely stand. His assistant was quite red-faced. Since the Minister was his boss, he was limited as to what he could do. The Minister was senior enough to have a driver. But it all became my problem.

The Minister got passed on to me because I was chairing the meeting. Asking him to take a seat beside me, I told him that his assistant had just informed me that the Minister was expected to return to the Legislature for a pressing meeting. Frankly, I don't think he knew what day it was. I also instructed the Minister to provide brief remarks then join his assistant outside of the room.

From the Minister's response, I also concluded that he didn't really know where he was, and that all he really wanted to do was go back to the bar. I said, "Minister, I'm going to welcome participants and introduce you. Your assistant didn't give me your remarks, so I will whisper them to you, and you just repeat after me."

After presenting my introductory remarks, I got the Minister to stand up, holding on to his chair for support. Standing up as well, I turned my back to the audience as if to search for something in my jacket pocket. Repeating my whispered prompts, the Minister said, "Thank you for inviting me here today and welcome to this meeting. You are doing important work and I wish you the best on behalf of the Province of Ontario. Apparently, I've been called back to the Legislature and will leave you. Thank you." Then, off he went with his assistant. As it turned out, the Minister made a positive impression, with members of the audience who were thrilled that he had taken the time to welcome them.

People Demanding to Hold a Vote

It is not unusual for me to facilitate meetings where people demand to know where consensus lies or hold a vote. Normal public meetings are usually topical sessions where people want to develop a vision or goals or prioritize tasks. There are many facilitation techniques that aid in group decision-making and group voting. The tone is usually friendly and cooperative.

Unfortunately, large, angry public meetings are not like that. It is not usual during the storming stage to have someone stand up and demand that I hold a vote "Right here, right now!" This is a sign of frustration. If a vote was held in this situation, the client or specialists would clearly be on one side, and the vocal residents on the other.

I strongly resist having a vote, for very good reasons. Firstly, there is not a "vote question" that the three hundred people attending the meeting will be aware of. Nor is there a process for deciding the question to vote on. Secondly, the more vocal members of the audience will have intimidated the quieter members of the audience who may not agree, and may not want a vote.

Thirdly, every community has thousands of residents who have a right to vote. Even though one hundred and fifty out of three hundred people may vote for an option, their vote carries no weight because it is not indicative of the will of the thousands of voters who didn't attend, and who may not agree. I'm very happy when strong politicians in the audience join me on these occasions, stating, "Your vote comes every four years through the ballot box. If you don't like the decisions that other politicians and I make, you can turf us out of office."

Among alternative decision-making methods the range of outcomes is: lose/lose, win/lose or win/win. Voting produces losers. Doyle and Straus comment on 'voting' as part of the meeting process saying that voting sets up a win lose scenario. Up to 49 percent of the voters will be losers. They state, "There are no longer only two sides to many issues – matters that can be submitted easily to the win/lose mechanisms of arbitration or the courts. As a growing result of demands for involvement and an increasing complexity and interconnectedness of issues, the need for win/win solutions is obvious."[200] There are great public consultation processes that build consensus and lead to win/win outcomes.

My response to the request for a vote in an angry public meeting is a firm "no". As this will likely be followed by protest from the person demanding the vote, I will repeat the reasons why a vote should not occur, saying, "No. Let's move

---

200 Doyle and Straus, op cit, p. 63

on". I'm used to having people completely ignore me, particularly my wife. Sometimes vocal people at angry meetings will hold a straw vote, regardless of what I say. Acknowledging that this is inconsequential, I will return to the presentations or the question and answer period.

Grandstanders

Grandstanding involves someone capturing the anger at a public meeting and giving it a voice. Most of these people are good public speakers. In contrast to what I am trying to accomplish, they will try to work up the crowd to bring home the point that the audience is in opposition to. Grandstanders typically have a fair amount of skill in group process. They will wait for a moment of emotional intensity to articulate the sentiment of the larger group. The public sees a leader, and the grandstander receives an emotional reward. But, in terms of group process, the chance of having a calm and reasonable exchange of views diminishes.

I design large, angry public meetings to minimize the potential for grandstanding. People wait their turn for the microphone, and those who have talked earlier will have to wait to talk again. In my experience, you can recognize certain individuals who are likely to grandstand. It helps to talk to these people before the meeting, informing them that I know they have strong views they want to state in public, and that the meeting ground rules also apply to them. However, once the meeting begins and the grandstander grabs the microphone, there's not much that I can do. When they run out of steam, I will get the microphone back. I will note their emotion, acknowledge their comments, and we get on with the meeting.

Grandstanding effectively involves someone with a strong opinion, some facts and a desire to take centre stage advantage with a microphone in hand. It is about getting on stage and having everyone else hearing what you have to say, with the hope that you will get a round of applause from the audience when you finish.

I can expect a grandstander or two at every large angry meeting. Sometimes, they will sense that the meeting is entering the storming stage, and their role will be to drag the meeting in that direction. The grandstander tends to be so loud and dramatic that the public will often miss their facts but support them anyway because they've given voice to the emotion in the room.

After facilitating about 1,500 meetings, I worry that I have developed a cynical personality that causes me to judge the performances of grandstanders.

Best Performance: intense diatribes; passionate; sharing special knowledge that undermines a proponent's position; comments peppered with a few humorous remarks.

Worst Performance: rambling; long-winded; hogging the microphone; reading many pages of prepared remarks.

Simon Cowell of "America's Got Talent" has perfected the stone face and I've also learned to be careful about allowing my personal views expressed through body language to spill onto the floor during a grandstand presentation. For example, during a large evening meeting in a small town in south-western Ontario, a member of the public caught some of my body language and called me out. It occurred after someone had grabbed a microphone and gave the performance of their life.

The gentleman was in his mid-sixties and rather large. He began with quiet and reasoned remarks. First, there was the bonding comment: "Like you, I love this community." Next, he found a way to bring the audience into his view legitimizing the public interest, saying, "None of us wants to pay more taxes." Then, raising his voice masterfully, the gentleman posed his challenge questions: "Do you want these people to control your lives? Do we trust government?" With his face glowing red, in his loudest voice he called out his final query, "When has government ever brought a project in on time and on budget?'

The grandstander's "storm the ramparts and hoist the flag of victory" finale was a passionate statement urging the people to push for a different project alternative or turf the government out of office. It was a brilliant performance. Full marks from me! There was a long period of applause, and I smiled. When I did so, a member of the public with a serious look on his face quietly pointed out my facial expression to me and remarked, "As the facilitator, are you laughing at the serious comment that was just made?"

I knew that the grandstander was going to take advantage of the opportunity to strongly state his support for a project alternative that was in total opposition to the one recommended by the scientists and engineers. I was trying to avoid him, but it was his turn on the speakers' list.

I smiled, partially because he had gotten me. Standing in the front row right in front of me, he had grabbed my microphone, turned his back to me and taken centre stage. As it turned out, the grandstander had a major conflict of interest, being that he was the owner of a competing project technology company which would benefit financially if the alternative he advocated was chosen. The public was not aware of this. I was. His characterization of himself as a champion of the community was pure hypocrisy.

Prolonged Applause

The most common behaviour in the storming stage is loud, continuous applause in response to what someone, usually the person grandstanding, is saying. It is a method used by the audience to expresses its agreement with what has been said, disrupt and threaten speakers, and object to what the professionals are saying. Prolonged applause usually stops the remaining members of the public from sharing an alternative point of view. Since there are usually many viewpoints in a meeting, the belief that support for someone grandstanding constitutes consensus is wrong.

In a few instances, I have actually been asked by clients during a briefing before a meeting to put a halt to any applause. As discussed earlier, there is no such rule. While I can be super sensitive in setting a ground rule and trying to achieve it by coaxing members of the audience to show respect, there's not a lot I can do about applause, short of cutting off people's hands when they register. We do, after all, live in a democracy. As a very mild form of civil disobedience, clapping should be viewed as a normal part of a meeting.

During a particularly large public meeting discussed earlier, there was a point when the applause went on for several minutes. While this is a bit intimidating, my role as a facilitator is to acknowledge the emotion behind the applause, saying, "I'm hearing that everyone of you has a strong viewpoint on the matter," and pick up the meeting where we left off after the clapping subsides.

Chanting

The response to chanting is similar to that of prolonged applause, the difference being that it is usually a declaration such as, "Stop the pipeline", "Shame", "Shut them down" or "Tell the truth." Chanting usually indicates that there are people with some sophistication in the audience who have some experience with street theatre. (Been there, done that.) The professionals are not going to go home because of chanting, but it puts them in a stressful situation as they have many people ready to pounce on the next words that come out of their mouths.

After the chanting dies down, the focus is once again on you as the facilitator. The best thing I can do is maintain my cool. I will acknowledge the emotion and the direction of the opinion being articulated, saying something like, "I hear what you are saying. You have made your views known loud and clear."

At this point, I need to find a way of bridging back to the discussion at hand. In some cases, I will have discussed with the client in advance alternative methods of directing the opposition if the meeting becomes hostile. These may include setting up a citizens' committee or conducting a small workshop to discuss the issues in depth. If I can remind residents that there are other ways to address the issues causing their anger, their frustration level decreases because, through the promise of action, they are being listened to.

When I don't have that release, I get ready to take a hit from the public. "So, Mr. Facilitator, are you going to change the agenda?" they may ask. "No," I reply. "Are you going to get the professionals to agree with us?" Again, I reply that I won't. "You said you wanted to hear our views and now you are not listening," they insist, to which I reply, "I'm listening and the team is listening, but neither of us agree with you on changing the process. You are welcome to hear what else they have to say and provide comments during the rest of the meeting, but the agenda is not changing."

In our democracy, it would appear that a meeting involving several hundred people all demanding the same thing is a clear indicator of the democratic will of the people. Yet, we need to be careful.

Citizen action in Canada's Capital, the City of Ottawa several years ago resulted in transportation engineers being shouted down for their efforts to build a bridge over an intersection with a rail track due to safety concerns. Residents would have nothing to do with it, and the bridge was never built. Years later, there was a deadly crash between a bus and a train at that same intersection.[201] While driver error was listed as a cause, the final inquiry report listed speed of the bus, the curve of the road ahead of the crossing, company practices and bus crashworthiness as contributing factors. Resident opposition to the rail separation was not listed.

Unfortunately, I have been involved in many meetings where people are totally misinformed about the facts, or insist that local will should prevail over the public good. In my opinion, decisions shouldn't be made this way in a democracy.

Citizen Journalists and the Media

I have witnessed many changes in journalism and media over the course of my facilitating career. These days, my project team and I are always on camera or being recorded. Its not unusual for me to be the subject of Tweets and Instagram posts from the time I open up the meeting. It didn't used to be that way. Then came the ubiquitous presence of social media and camera phones. Armed with a camera, everyone can now be a citizen journalist, and the "Got-Ya" types will want to film clients' presentations.

There are no laws prohibiting someone from taking a photo or filming in a public setting. However, there are two actions that can be taken to address unwanted citizen journalists. You can ask them to put down their phone/camera's and leave (if the meeting is on private property). Or, you and the clients can stop the meeting and leave.

One instance of when I've had to consider ending a meeting prematurely comes to mind.

We were working for Rogers Communications, a media and communications company that was trying to locate a cellular telephone tower in a suburban community lacking adequate cellular coverage. As usual, the issue drawing the crowds was fear of electromagnetic radiation, or radio waves. In addition to filling the meeting room and having questions posed by the local audience, the

---

201 https://www.cbc.ca/news/canada/ottawa/oc-transpo-bus-crash-report-released-1.3343729

leaders of the residents' group also decided that they wanted to film the presentations and create their own TV program documenting their battle.

Obviously, Rogers did not want a film crew at their meeting. Nor did they want a TV show that would present the company in a negative way, which would also open up the possibility that competitors could use the film for negative advertisements and other uses.

My client at Rogers Communications, was Jack Hills. Jack was one of the best people I've ever had the opportunity to work for - very bright, competent, an excellent manager, empathetic and reeking of integrity. He understood facilitation and allowed me to do some of my best work. He wasn't afraid to tell it like it is. But he did so in a way that people trusted his word.

Before the meeting started, Jack requested that I ask the residents to remove their film crew and camera. I told the residents that, as the meeting facilitator, this is what I want to happen. To this, the residents promptly replied that they had a right to film because this was a public meeting.

On checking the room permit for the meeting, I noticed that we had rented a private space, so the rules of trespass applied. Thus, I had the power to ask the film crew to leave and enforce the decision. Jack and I agreed that having residents and the film crew thrown out of a meeting, or worse, being filmed as they were thrown out, would not be desirable. Instead, Jack decided that he and his staff would exit the meeting, leaving the residents to film their own meeting, which would be a less sensational scenario. The residents couldn't believe that the client had decided to leave. Jack and his crew started packing up, at which point the residents knew that they couldn't call his bluff, and asked their film crew to leave.

The media can be expected to attend every large, angry public meeting (the angrier, the better), presenting the challenge I face of keeping reporters and camera people on track and out of the way. It is up to the facilitator is to ensure that the media do not pour gas on the fire. They want the shot of the angry, indignant mother holding up her child and crying. The more responsible media will try to get both points of view, interviewing the client when they are finished answering questions from the public.

The less responsible media, who prefer to set up the story with an angry meeting as the backdrop, may at times be effectively manipulating the meeting agenda. Their ideal TV shot is one of people lined up at a microphone screaming in anger, while other residents are pumping their fists in the air and screaming at a table of clients and consultants in suits.

In my experience, residents at a meeting today are somewhat media savvy. They know that, when the media gets this shot, the intensity of the issue is doubled because thousands more TV viewers will perceive that the thirty-second clip fully represents the totality of the meeting. Sadly, a scenario of calmer opinions and all parties agreeing to work together by the end of the meeting will not make the eleven o'clock news.

The one person that the media doesn't expect to be at an angry meeting is the facilitator, who can speak with authority and be frank about how events are going to unfold. I don't have a personal agenda, and I'm not worried about what people say tomorrow. I don't have to be re-elected next fall, and I don't have to be worried about being fired.

Without a facilitator, the media will often barge into a meeting and set up their TV cameras at the best angles, often blocking the view of participants. They will turn on bright lights while clients or speakers are trying to convey a sensitive point to members of the public. And, they will sometimes put people on stage, giving them a platform to play their parts.

To deal with the media, I coach my clients to work out the logistics and do the following: 1) accept that the media want their film shot and help to accommodate them; 2) establish a media approach well in advance and stick to it; 3) assign a media spokesperson in advance, rather than have the media only interview a person chosen to represent residents. It is important to allow the media to cover the story. It's part of the democratic process. But when the media help to create the story or interfere with clients sharing important information with members of the public, they are stepping over the line.

When a large meeting is going to happen, I will also work with the client's media spokespeople and public relations staff. We all understand who the prime media spokesperson will be in advance. If this person is busy addressing emotional questions from the floor, we will also have a back-up or temporary spokesperson. Spaces outside the meeting hall are designated for the media to set up cameras and interview people. If media personnel attempt to distract my clients and members of the public by crowding speakers, disrupting the transmission of information or conducting interviews during the meeting, it is my role to say "no".

That being said, meetings have changed with the advent of social media. Ten years ago, as I noted earlier, I would normally ask people to turn off their cell phones so that they could focus on uninterrupted communication. I don't do that anymore, because some people will be tweeting comments (positive and negative), or use Instagram, Tumbler, Periscope or Facebook to communicate with each other during the meeting.

When planning a meeting, I tell the project team that we need to assume that everything they do, both audio and visual, will be recorded, and that everything I say and do as a facilitator is commented upon immediately in terms of how I'm running the meeting.

During one meeting where my staff monitored Twitter, I was getting creamed for sticking to the agenda. People were berating me. In terms of social media, the facilitator needs to understand that both traditional and social media will look for the most extreme individuals and commenters. The cameras will roll during emotional outbursts and be turned off during moments of dialogue. The story will often be written before the facts are available.

If an issue is particularly heated, I usually suggest to my clients that they retain professional communications staff and have a media and communications plan that includes a parallel social media presence. The challenge that facilitators face today is a significant reduction in substantive news in relation to the health of our democracy. Reporters don't cover the calm meetings. Myths and misinformation spill into angry public meetings.

Communications staff and facilitators need to understand the flood of public opinion that now competes against traditional news gathering and news stories. My good friend, professional communicator Brian Smith pointed out that, in our society, we believe that freedom of speech leads to truth. So, we don't muzzle Jenny McCarthy when she says that vaccination is a cause of autism in children. Indeed, I have spent much of my career listening to angry people who have taken up a cause based on few facts.

Thankfully, for the health of our democracy, we allow people to express their views. Yet having five hundred internet bloggers providing opinions with little or no research bumps into the historical views that we've developed in North America about what constitutes responsible journalism.

The underlying premise of responsible journalism is the reporting of substantive news produced by professional journalists, who are expected to check facts and print or tweet corrections if the facts are wrong. This supports the health of our democracy.

We expect journalists to disseminate quality information.

I was pleased to read a thoughtful article by Warren Kinsella[202] on the demise of the Canadian news outlet Sun Media and loss of many traditional media jobs. Kinsella said, "… bloggers and tweeters don't generate actual news – they just comment on it. They offer opinions on someone else's work - someone else's journalism."

It is not the job of bloggers and tweeters to correct falsehoods. Meanwhile, there is an uncomfortable amount of evidence showing that professional journalists are accepting facts and Tweets without verification. Perhaps, with cuts to media budgets, this will increase.

Another supporting premise of responsible journalism is that it separates the front page and the editorial page. With the rise of social media, opinion often gets through as front-page journalism whereas, in the past, opinion was filtered because it came through the funnel of traditional news organizations.

A third premise is the role of traditional media, according to Mark Little[203], Founder and Director of Innovation at Storyful, "to separate the news from the noise". Before the rise of social media, members of the public could check the integrity of news stories because they were following several journalists.

---

202 Warren Kinsella, Dear Sun News Network folks 13 02 2015

203 Mark Little, Founder and Director of Innovation and Storyful, "The Journalism of Terror: How Do We Bear Witness When Everybody is a Witness"

Little states that the job of traditional journalists is to "filter the flood of competing narratives and connect the most authentic voices to the widest possible audience." Society today needs to scrutinize stories and facts produced by thousands of assorted bloggers, tweeters and journalists. Author Nate Silver[204], states, "We face danger [in our democracy] whenever information growth outpaces our understanding of how to process it."

A fourth premise is that, when matters are unclear, we expect traditional journalists to report that there are facts that need to be sorted out and to provide a nuanced tempered opinion on what characterizes the truth. By contrast, bloggers don't need to report this. Nor do they need to consider the importance of reasoned debate in identifying decisions that best represent the public interest.

Today, we have journalists, citizen journalists and activists communicating the news. Thousands of people possess the same tools as traditional media, but they are not bound by the tenets of journalistic responsibility. They don't need to buy into the principles of objectivity and fact-checking.

On the other hand, perhaps there is some merit in saying that social media as a whole may also contribute to the health of our democracy. We need to ask what social media does well. In the past, there was less transparency and decision makers didn't necessarily have to take the broad public interest into account. Why would they? Who's watching?

The point is that, for some issues, we need more voices at these angry public meetings, not fewer, to keep the political class accountable. With social media, decision-makers are conscious that someone is talking about their actions and decisions. Using (or misusing) a quote from Margaret Thatcher, social media provides the "oxygen of publicity".

In terms of Kinsella's comment about bloggers simply commenting on someone else's news reporting, bloggers and tweeters do in fact often get the story and photos first, and share them with the public - raw. What about Jenny McCarthy and the need for factual communication about science, the economy and complex public policy issues in a democracy?

---

204 Nate Silver, The Signal and the Noise a referred to by Little, op cit

In support of non-traditional media, the volume of scientific and health information available has increased incredibly, with more access to everyone than ever before. Yet the public is not well equipped to sort out conflicting scientific information.

The problem faced by people is, who do you trust? The growth of info-tainment (news as entertainment) and traditional media pandering for ratings, combined with decreasing social literacy about science, technology, engineering and math, social literacy about science, has made dialogue on public policy issues and science increasingly difficult.

Democratic decisions are made every day. If we see the demise of substantive news as a threat to democracy, it raises the question of who some of the other actors are influencing these decisions. Who is holding decision-makers to account? In my experience, few politicians base their decisions on what the chattering classes say. Pipelines, Official Plans, public transit expenditures and power plants are not approved based on the direction of internet gossip. Thus, when one of my meetings have gone well, the reasoned comments from the public will be an important influence on these decisions.

Throwing People Out

I rarely throw people out of meetings. When I do, I will usually have discussed with my client before the meeting starts whether or not this would be acceptable. There are times, however, when this is exactly what needs to happen.

People attending meetings that I have facilitated know and understood my ground rules, so there should be no doubt about what behaviour is expected. When I am expecting hot tempers, I will try to establish firmer rules, such as keeping to a set amount of time to present their views and having respect for the professional credentials of the client.

The strongest ground rules which I rarely state, warn people that they may be thrown out if they show disrespectful behaviour, such as physical threats, intimidating others or acting out through rude behaviour, or use disrespectful language including libel, slander, defamation of character, profanities or racial slurs.

Threats of physical violence that involve someone getting up and charging the front of the room, toward the client or another member of the public yield an immediate response from me. Moving toward the person, I shout in a loud voice, "Out right now!" If this doesn't work, I remind the person about the presence of police and security, pointing to the door. Failing this, I signal to my staff or my security to call the police. This usually works.

In 2010, I facilitated a public meeting in Nobleton, Ontario, a small suburban community in King Township (nestled in horse country) that is part of York Region just north of Toronto. The community had made a decision to have population growth, which meant that it needed to replace aging wells and septic tanks with a modern water and waste water distribution system.

Planning these systems and getting approvals can be tricky. While these services will benefit residents, it costs them a lot of money – from $20,000 to $40,000 per household. In addition, there are usually property developers in the wings who can't build homes until the servicing is installed. Although these developers pay for their share of the servicing, local residents often conclude that it is they who will be paying for the services of the developers' new homes.

The community centre held two hundred and fifty people and the meeting room was packed. About fifty residents couldn't get in. As a result, just about everyone was upset about the proposed project cost as well as not being able to allow some people to enter the meeting room.

I spotted one elderly gentlemen at the back of the room who appeared very upset before the meeting started. As the presentations were underway, he shouted out a few comments and declared that he wouldn't wait for the presentation to end before asking questions. It was clear that he was upsetting the audience. Several times, I told the gentleman that he would have to hold his comments. Once the question and answer period started, I allowed him to ask the first question. It was rambling and unclear, but the team did their best to give him an answer.

Several other people asked questions and the process was going well. People were learning that: the costs could be amortized over twenty years; the municipality could give them a low-cost loan; and the services would result in their property values going up by more than the cost of their investment. The initial negative sting was beginning to subside and the servicing proposition was beginning to be accepted as something more positive.

The gentleman, however, didn't seem to be listening and demanded to ask the next question. I explained to him that he was on the list and that I would get to him, but that wasn't enough. He marched to the front of the room, grabbed the microphone from another resident and began a series of expletives and defamatory comments.

I refused to tolerate this behaviour. Stepping between him and the other resident, I demanded that he give me the microphone in the loudest voice I could muster. The audience went silent, and I got the mike. "And, now you are going to leave," I said. He was somewhat shocked, but started to make his way to the door. Before he got there, he stopped so as to test my resolve. "Out, now!" I exclaimed, pointing to the door, and out he went.

There are times when a subtler approach can work, such as quietly asking a person to leave. Subtle approaches should always be the first to be used. A better approach is to stage comments leading to the act of throwing someone out.

Stage 1: I point out that the behaviour is not in keeping with the rules. In a respectful and conciliatory tone, I begin with a friendly reminder that I would like the rules respected.

Stage 2: I give progressively stronger warnings, pointing out that the behaviour is unacceptable and that I would like the person to change their approach. This is my quiet appeal to the sensibilities and good behaviour of other members of the audience. At this point, it is important to keep the rest of the meeting participants on my side, as I don't want the crowd to turn on me if need to throw someone out. I remind all participants that we all had agreed to certain ground rules, and that I don't see the disruptive person engaged in the behaviours that we all agreed to at the beginning of the meeting.

Stage 3: At this point, I take action by stopping the meeting. Usually, I do this by finding a time to interrupt one of the team members rather than interrupting someone from the audience. Alternatively, I will ask the disruptive member of the public to hold their question until we get acceptable behaviour, giving them a stern, disapproving high school Vice-Principal look[205], pointing out that their behaviour is not what we agreed to, and asking them to leave. The person may resist initially, but they will realize that the crowd has gone silent, and that they are now on stage. If necessary, I will ask them to leave again. To help the person save face, I will tell them that they've made their point, and it's time to go.

I do my best to allow people to leave with dignity. Under no circumstances touching them, I often put my hands behind my back to appear less threatening. If the person is threatening, I will sometimes stand in the way between them and a client or other resident.

To be clear, I don't get paid enough to be the recipient of physical violence and, in reality, I'm holding my breath hoping that the person I'm evicting is not going to throw a punch. I know what that feels like. Fortunately, most people realize that, with the pressure of over a hundred faces focusing on them and the possibility of police action, the smart thing to do is leave.

---

205 During my high school years having been sent to the Principal's Office on many occasions, that's the typical look that Vice-Principals gave me.

Chapter 10:
Final Thoughts

While I am ending the last chapter on how to deal with some of the thornier aspects of public behaviour at angry public meetings, I don't want to give the impression that this is always what to expect. In reality, over the course of my career I've met tens of thousands of wonderful people who are taking the time out of their lives to show that they care for their families and communities.

I am often asked, "What is your goal when you are facilitating an angry public meeting?" My answer is a bit complex, as I have to draw on the objectives of an assortment of skills. Certainly, it's more than being a meeting chairperson or the neutral person pointing to people who want to speak.

I'm standing between a group that needs to make a decision and hundreds of people who have something to say about that decision. Both parties are effectively part of one group. Extreme facilitation is not about conflict resolution on a large scale. The conflict is normally well under way by the time I'm hired, and it is played out on the field of a community centre meeting room, conference hall, high school gym or auditorium. Sometimes conflict is exactly what is needed. It gives energy to political change and gets the attention of policy makers.

As an extreme facilitator, it is my hope that I can create a listening process (and ideally a process of dialogue) where all parties can listen to each other and come to a common agreement. In this way I serve the group. Am I there to help my client get across their message to the audience? The answer is a firm "no". It is the job of my client to get their message across, not me. My job is to ensure that there is a mutual listening process because, when everyone is listening, there's a better chance to get the message across. The client and the consulting team are listening to the public at the same time as the public is listening to them.

I am often asked if my goal is to be a coach. While part of my job description includes coaching, it is centred on communications rather than helping clients to advocate a position. That is their responsibility; my concern is about process. While most of my clients are governments, agencies or corporations, I've also been hired by members of the public hosting a meeting. Equally in this case, my job is not to help them to advocate their point of view, but to make sure that they can get their view across during the meeting while listening to other points of view.

Is my role to be a diplomat or negotiator? While it is true that I need to have diplomatic skills and be tactful as much as possible, dealing with people in as sensitive a way as I can, I'm not there as a diplomat to represent any person or interest. Tactful language and saving face are important. When I am speaking to a particular individual while they are "on stage", I'm aware that my words can build great self esteem or inflict long-term damage. And, there are times when I need to be firm and rude. But I don't want the person to carry home emotional baggage that would be created if I had chosen to be less diplomatic or tactful.

Would the skills of a Priest, Imam, Rabbi or Minister be helpful for someone facilitating one of these meetings? Certainly, I am the first one to admit that it never hurts to have a prayer memorized and recited in silence before grabbing a microphone for the first time. But extreme facilitation is not about calming the waters (although that is certainly expected and if calming the waters leads to dialogue, that's my goal). Nor is it about helping people to reflect or find their better selves. When tempers are hot, it is not the time to do so.

As a professional facilitator, my efforts are focused on bringing people together in a manner that will foster dialogue and build consensus. The core of my facilitation training is about bringing diverse groups together, have them identify desirable joint actions and then work as teams to accomplish their goals.

In some of the more productive meetings I've facilitated, the client and the public have realized that there may be a common cause which meets both of their needs that they can work towards. At the end of the meeting, everyone wins and positive new relationships are developed. These are the better outcomes. They've usually started with a broader acceptance among most of the audience that there is a common problem that needs to be solved or a benefit for all. My role then is to help everyone move toward seeing the commonality and having them agree to take the next steps after the meeting.

Facilitation goals are a bit different from the perspective of a trained facilitator who is also a professional environmental and land use planner. The meeting is sometimes a prescribed event required by a Provincial or Federal Act. It may occur early when the agency and its consultants need confirmation of a problem statement, study process or proposed consultation process. Here, the role of the facilitator is to make sure that important questions are asked in support of the regulatory approval process and the important part that the public plays in that process.

Mid-way through the planning or environmental assessment process, the consultants have identified alternative ways of solving a problem or taking advantage of an opportunity that needs confirmation. At this point, my role is to make sure that members of the public deliberately comment on each alternative.

At the end of the process, there will be a preferred solution, and public comments will be needed once again to confirm a choice. Whether or not the tone of the meeting is calm or raucous, specific questions need to be asked and answered, and the transaction needs to be well documented.

Over a career of facilitating these large angry meetings I can't help but be a bit philosophical. After a few beers, my staff and I once reflected on what the world would be like if extreme facilitation was known as the world's third oldest profession. (You know the first two.) What if there was a facilitator at Calvary or before the trial of Galileo? Perhaps too many beers.

Between elections, modern democracies have methods of resolving public policy issues in a way that either finds common ground or selects winners and losers. Large, angry public meetings are important events within and outside the democratic process, with crowds nudging decisions in a certain direction. In this context, extreme facilitators may have a small role to play in maintaining democracy.

The world is full of peacekeepers and peace makers. Most of these wonderful people are international development workers who put themselves on the line to bring about peace, often at the most local level, in some of the deepest, darkest places in the world. While I don't do work at this level, I have great respect for those who bring these extreme facilitation skills into much tougher situations. One might wonder whether emerging democracies would be more successful if there were more professional facilitators helping large groups learn how to identify and resolve differences, without having to pick up a gun. Emerging democracies need to learn how to use public consultation, communication, facilitation and other peaceful decision-making techniques. These are the core elements of civil society, with extreme facilitators playing a role.

References

Alinsky, Saul, "Rules for Radicals: A Pragmatic Primer for Realistic Radicals", Vintage Books, Random House, New York, March 1972

Bens, Ingrid, "Advanced Facilitation Strategies: Tools and Techniques to Master Difficult Situations", Jossey-Bass, San Francisco, 2005

Bens, Ingrid, "Conflict at a Glance! Tools and Techniques for Resolving Disputes" GOAL/QPC Memory Jogger, Salem, New Hampshire, 2013

Carpenter, Susan and W. J. D. Kennedy, 'Managing Public Disputes', Jossey-Bass, San Francisco, 2001

Doyle, Michael and David Strauss, "How to Make Meetings Work", Berkley Books, New York, 1976

Ghais, Suzanne, "Extreme Facilitation: Guiding Groups Through Controversy and Complexity", Jossey-Bass, San Francisco, CA, 2005

Goleman, D "Emotional Intelligence", Bantam Books, New York, 2005

Hackett, Dr. Donald and Dr. Charles Martin, "Facilitation Skills for Team Leaders: Leading Teams to Greater Productivity", CRISP PUBLICATIONS, Inc, Menlo Park, California, Library of Congress Catalog Card Number 92-082933, 1993

Holman, Peggy and Tom Devane, "The Change Handbook: Group Methods for Shaping the Future, Berrett-Koehler Publishers, Inc, San Francisco, 1999

Kaner Sam, Lenny Lind, Catherine Toldi, Sarah Fisk and Duane Berger, "Facilitator's Guide to Participatory Decision Making", Third Edition, Jossey-Bass, San Francisco, 2014

Keating, Don, "The Power to Make it Happen: Mass Based-Community Organizing, What it is and How it Works" 1975

Killermann, Sam and Meg Bolger, "Unlocking the Magic of Facilitation" Impetus Books, Austin Texas, January, 2016

Max Cohen de Lara and David Mulder van der Vegt, "These 5 architectural designs influence every legislature in the world and tell you how each governs ", The Washington Post, March 4, 2017

Luft, Joseph "Group Process, An Introduction to Group Dynamics". Palo Alto, California, National Press, 1963

Pickering, Dr. George "Moral and Ethical Issues relating to Nuclear Energy Generation: Proceedings of a Seminar", Canadian Nuclear Association, Toronto, Ontario, ISBN 0-919307-15-9, "Integrating Ethical and Technical Considerations in the Energy Debate, 1981,

Senge, Peter, Art Kleiner, Richard Ross, Charlotte Roberts, Bryan Smith, "The Fifth Discipline Fieldbook: Strategies and Tools for Building a Learning Organization, Doubleday, New York, 1994

Schwarz, Roger, "The Skilled Facilitator: A Comprehensive Resource for Consultants, Facilitators, Coaches and Trainers", Jossey-Bass, San Francisco, 2nd Edition, 2002 and 3rd Edition, 2017

Susskind, Lawrence and Patrick Field, "Dealing With An Angry Public: The mutual gains approach to resolving disputes", The Free Press, Simon and Schuster Inc, New York, 1996

Thompson, Michael, "Political Culture: An Introduction", "An Outline of the Cultural Theory of Risk", "The Social Landscape of Poverty", "Beyond Self-Interest, A Cultural Analysis of the Risk Debate", International Institute for Applied Systems Analysis A-2361, Laxenburg, Austria, 1980, 1981

Ury, William "The Third Side: Why We Fight and How We Can Stop", Penguin Books, New York, 1999

Index

2

2010 Vancouver Winter Olympic and Paralympic Games 146

A

active assailant 198
agent provocateur 78
Alinsky, Saul xxv, 3
anarchists 247
Anglican Church of Canada 44
architecture of democracy 169
Atikokan 111
Atomic Energy of Canada 122
audio-visual equipment 179, 180

B

backstage 178
bank balance 90, 91
bar of consensus 104
Bens, Ingrid 27, 29, 46, 213, 214, 225
biosolids 13
Blind River 90
bodyguards 205
body language 53, 54, 55, 61, 62, 63, 64, 65, 66, 67, 68, 69, 70, 71, 127, 171, 173, 182, 190, 191, 207, 226, 229, 231, 254
Brampton 158
Brudy, Norm 4

C

Caledon 126
Cameco Corporation 90
Canadian Broadcasting Corporation 13
Canadian Chemical Producers Association 90
Canadian Environmental Assessment Act 124

Canadian Nuclear Laboratories 122
Canadian Nuclear Safety Commission 88
Cane, Don 102
Caring Canadian Award 90
Carpenter and Kennedy 25
centre stage 178
chalk talk 185
chanting 256
Chicago 3
children 237
choreography xx
citizen jury 97
Citizen Liaison Committee 184
Citizen's Advisory Group 28
citizen science 240
civil disobedience xvii, xxv, xxvi, 3, 5, 77, 137, 177, 197, 200, 203, 255
classroom and auditorium style 170
Clear Scents 79, 81, 82, 160
coach 8, 29, 71, 185, 189, 259, 267
Code of Practice 240
Cohen de Lara, Max 170
Comment and Disposition Table 123
Common sense 100, 102
Community Engagement and Communication Plans 33
Community Impact Assessment 94
consensus 32
Consensus 56, 103, 104
content versus process 38
core dimensions of building trust and confidence 85
Cowell, Simon 254
Cuddy, Amy 63

D
DeCraemer, Anne 159
Domtar Corporation 217

Doyle and Straus 11, 25, 42, 50, 52, 74, 169, 183, 187, 215, 219, 229, 252
dry run\" rehearsal 184
Durham Region 203
Durham Regional Police 203

E

Eastern Ontario Model Forest 217
Edelson, Abbie xxiii
emotions xvii, xxvi, 24, 27, 39, 44, 45, 46, 50, 56, 57, 77, 78, 79, 137, 150, 151, 190, 197, 208, 210, 226, 233, 234
endocrine disruptors 13
Engagement Framework 113
Environmental Assessment Study 49
Environmental Defence 244
ethics 95, 96, 97

F

Facilitator's Agenda 162, 163, 164, 165, 166, 167
Faculty of Environmental Studies 6, 96
Federation of Metro Tenants 4, 8
finger signaling 227
fire safety and emergency response 208
Fischoff, B. 14
Fleeton, Bob 159
Frequently Asked Questions 167
front of the house 176

G

G. E. Booth Wastewater Treatment Facility 79
GE Hitachi 88, 90
George Pickering 17, 18
getting the script right 162
Getting to Yes 25
Ghais, Suzanne 23, 24, 27, 28, 41, 43, 54, 56, 57, 58, 76, 156, 161, 163, 164, 211, 212, 213, 233

Gillespie, Bruce 146
Giordano, Matt 62
grandstanders 253
Green Energy Act xxiv
Greenpeace 244
ground rules 214
group facilitator 24
group leader 29, 75
group norms 137, 138, 214, 215, 223, 244
group process design 35
group psychology 52
group think 74
Guildwood 86

H

Hackett and Martin 26
Hamilton 201
Hatch Engineering 102
Hayward, Roger 87
Henry Company Canada Inc 87
He, Shu 102
Hills, Jack 258
hold a vote 251
Horgan, Ralph 104
horizontal and vertical consultation 106

I

IAP2's Spectrum of Public Participation 116
identity politics 104
independence 28
independent 21, 54, 62, 123, 136, 138, 139, 166, 193, 217, 228
Indigenous 51, 127
Interfaith Panel on Public Awareness of Nuclear Issues 97
Interim Waste Authority 203
International Association for Public Participation 120

International Institute of Applied Systems Analysis 15
internet experts 93, 122, 235
Intoxication 248
Irvine, Janise L 74
issues triage 105

J

Jackson, Jessie 3
jargon 219

K

Kaner, Sam 25
Keating, Don 4
Killermann and Bolger 24, 30, 31, 37, 58, 66, 189, 190
King Township 264
Kinsella, Warren 261
kitchen table meeting xx
KMK Consultants Limited 158

L

Lakeview Wastewater Treatment Facility 79
Layton, Jack 8
LeFaucheur, Sandi 159
Lichtenstein, S. 14
Lickers, Henry 217
listener-in-chief 228
listening xx, xxi, 9, 21, 31, 45, 46, 49, 55, 56, 58, 59, 60, 62, 63, 64, 65, 66, 68, 74, 94, 104, 105, 123, 129, 140, 144, 157, 187, 190, 203, 216, 226, 229, 230, 231, 233, 256, 261, 265, 267, 268
Little, Mark 261
Lockhart-Grace, Joan 159
LOGOs Institute 44
Luft 272
Luft, Joseph 25, 33, 34, 58

M

Mahoney, Curtis 110
Markham 125
McDonald, Bob 13
mediation 155
meeting dynamics 39, 54, 55
mental walk 136
microphone 182
Ministry of Transportation xxii
mirroring 65, 71, 185
Mississauga 158
Mohawks of Akwesasne 217
Moore, Christopher 82
moral claims 95, 97, 98, 236
moral outrage 235
Mulder van der Vegt, David 170
Muskoka 10

N

National Energy Board 96, 245
natural justice 127
Navarro, Joe 63
neutral xx, 21, 22, 24, 28, 29, 30, 32, 35, 60, 62, 95, 106, 134, 138, 145, 164, 213, 215, 219, 267
Niagara Regional Police 202
Niamh Scallan 89
Nobleton 264
norming 62, 214
Nuclear Waste Management Organization 15

O

Oak Ridges Moraine 8, 102
Ontario Hydro 96
Ontario Institute for Studies in Education 4
Ontario Municipal Board 96

Ontario Power Generation 110
Ontario Professional Planners Institute 239
Ontario Provincial Police 203
opening and introductory remarks 212
Ottawa Valley 19

P

parking lots 61
Parliamentary/ Respectful Language 220
parts of a stage 176
Peel Region 79
people and situational complications 234
People United to Save Humanity 3
perceived risk 14
personifying projects 109
Pickering 197
Pickering, George 17, 236
police xix, 5, 42, 59, 194, 196, 197, 199, 200, 201, 202, 203, 204, 205, 206, 207, 208, 209, 210, 264, 266
politicians xx, 6, 7, 19, 22, 76, 106, 107, 110, 121, 126, 159, 163, 166, 177, 180, 185, 220, 232, 235, 246, 247, 250, 252, 263
Port Hope 90
Portlands Energy Centre 109
power balance 130
probabilistic risk 14, 16
prolonged applause 255
prompt questions xxiii, 36, 37, 225
Province of Ontario xxiv, 6, 13, 124, 158, 251
public consultation xvii, xxii, xxiv, xxv, 9, 24, 73, 77, 78, 85, 89, 101, 103, 118, 119, 120, 121, 134, 140, 211, 252, 270
Public Information Centre 69

Q

Quirks and Quarks 13

R

reading written remarks 221
read the group 55
Region of Peel 84, 86, 158, 160
Region of Waterloo 13
Registered Professional Planner (RPP) 239
REWERX 146
Richmond Hill 196
Riddell, Chris 89
Riverdale 4
Riverside Church 4
Rogers Mobility 11
Rohm and Haas Canada LP 86
Ross, Deborah 159
Rotary 5
roundtables 153
Ruiter, Zack 89

S

safety and security 193
Sandman, P. 14
Save the Rouge 7
Schiller, Mark 159
Schwarz, Roger 24, 26, 28, 29, 33, 39, 43, 46, 49, 61, 155, 156, 214, 219, 225
security personnel 186, 196, 199, 200
Seger, Adrian 169
semi-circle 172
Senge, Peter 44
setting the stage 168
Shaw, James Jr 200
Silver, Nate 262
Slovic, Paul 14
Social Impact Analyses 34
social license 103, 106
social media 260

Spaulding, Jon 146
speakers' list 216
Spider Facilitation 146
Stakeholder Advisory Committee 28
Stakeholder Sensitivity Analysis 34, 94, 101, 128
Stevenson, Mark 45
St. Jamestown 4
storming 67, 135, 137, 138, 141, 144, 252, 253, 255
Storming Stage 139
Storyful 261
Sun Media 261
Sunrise Propane Explosion 87
Susskind and Field 21, 30, 44, 71, 76, 81, 82, 91, 95, 100, 113, 186
Suzuki, Dr. David 241

T

taking notes 218
Theatre in the Round 173
Thompson, Micheal 15
throwing people out 263
Toronto East CAER 87
Torontoist 89
Toronto Star 89
TransCanada Pipelines 110
Trans Mountain Pipeline 103
Trent University 89
Trespass Act 194
Trudeau, Justin 103
Trust and confidence 81

U

understanding the community 93
understanding the subject matter 53
Ury, William 25, 82, 272
U.S. Department of Homeland Security 198

U.S.E. Hickson Products 86
US Environmental Protection Act 124
U-Shaped 174

V

values 11, 12, 15, 16, 17, 18, 19, 20, 41, 43, 58, 81, 82, 83, 84, 90, 94, 108, 111, 137, 184, 264

W

Waffle House 200
Warburton, Kim 89
West Hill 86
West Hill Community Association 87
Withers, Dawn 89
Wolf, Charlie 124
words to use and avoid 61
World Café 151
wrangling mikes 191

Y

yes/and rule 65
York, Don 87
York Region 19, 61, 66, 78, 102, 264
York University 6, 96

Z

Zamojc, Mitch 159
Zimpro 158

Figures

Figure 1 Sample Facilitator Challenges 47
Figure 2 Eight Signs of Group Think 75
Figure 3 Emotional Awareness Continuum. 80
Figure 4 Measuring Public Response 80
Figure 5 HSAL Engagement Framework 114
Figure 6 IAP2's Spectrum of Public Participation 117
Figure 7 Evaluation of a Community Engagement Process 119
Figure 8 Tracking Public Comments Template. 124
Figure 9 Pairs Interviews 147
Figure 10 Round Table Comparison of Like Questions. 148
Figure 11 Reporting out in the Plenary Session 150
Figure 12 Roundtables 153
Figure 13 Mediation vs Facilitation Comparison 155
Figure 14 Classroom Style Set-up 171
Figure 15 Auditorium Meeting 172
Figure 16 Semi-Circle or Three-Sided Stage 173
Figure 17 Four-sided Stage and Theatre-in-the-Round. 174
Figure 18 U-shaped. 175

Appendices

APPENDIX 1.
Social Impact Analysis and Stakeholder Sensitivity Analysis

Sample Stakeholder Sensitivity Analysis

The roles and responsibilities for both the Consultant and the Region are outlined as follows[206]:

- Engage a Public Facilitator for the project
- Manage the responsibilities of the Public Facilitator throughout the Public Consultation process
- Provide input to the Public Facilitator
- Work collaboratively with the Public
- Facilitator to effectively deliver Public Consultation for the project

1. Complete a Stakeholder Sensitivity Analysis

The Class EA document lists the main potential "stakeholders" of a project as the public, "Review" agencies, and other municipalities. A list of the designated "Review" agencies (provincial and federal) is provided in Section A.3.6 of the Class EA document. In addition to the Review Agencies, the Region recognizes that the project stakeholders may include, but are not limited to, the following:

a) Property owners / tenants

b) Special / Local Interest Groups and Ratepayers Associations

c) York Region officials / offices, such as the Chair of Council, Chief Administrative Officer,

---

[206] Source: York Region Environmental Services, Capital Planning and Delivery, Consultant Requirements Manual Phase 4: Environmental Assessment Version 2

d) Clerk, members of Transportation and Works Committee, Corporate Communications

e) Officer, Regional Area Planner and York Region Police/Emergency Services Departments

f) Local Municipality officials / offices, such as Local / Regional Councillors, Clerk,

g) Engineering Departments, Planning Departments and the Local Architectural

h) Conservation Advisory Committees

i) York Region District and Separate School Boards

j) Canadian National and GO Transit railways, CP Rail or railway owners/operators

k) Ontario Realty Corporation - General Manager, Environment & Cultural Heritage

l) Local Conservation Authorities

m) Utility companies

n) Indigenous Peoples

The Consultant shall develop and execute a Stakeholder Sensitivity Analysis (SSA) to identify those individuals or groups whose cooperation, expertise, or influence would be beneficial to the success of the project and to develop a strategy to involve them. In addition, those stakeholders who strongly oppose the project and whose negative opinions could be "show stoppers" for the project should be identified and consulted early on. The roles and responsibilities for both the Consultant and the Region are outlined as follows:

- Engage the Public Facilitator in the planning and/or documentation of the SSA, as required
- Identify project stakeholders
- Determine which of the Review Agencies are likely to have an interest in the project

- Develop a **draft SSA** using the **SSA Outline** in Section 2.
- Submit the draft SSA no later than 14 calendar days following the **EA Initiation Kick-off Meeting**
- Incorporate feedback into the **final SSA** and submit to the Region
- Review the SSA on a monthly basis to ensure that the stakeholder relationships are being managed in accordance with the procedures detailed therein
- Provide input to the Consultant for the identification of project stakeholders
- Provide input to the Consultant to determine which of the Review Agencies are likely to have an interest in the project
- If requested by the Consultant, provide Environics Reports to support development of the SSA
- Review and provide comments on the **draft SSA**
- Ensure that feedback is incorporated into the **final SSA**
- Enter the **Stakeholder Sensitivity Analysis Completion Date** in Project Server
- Support management of the stakeholder relationships in accordance with the SSA as required

2. SSA Outline

A. BACKGROUND

- What is the history of public consultation in the area? What the expected level of consultation complexity in relation to previous projects?
- What is the level of environmental sensitivity in the study area and how will this affect the public's reaction to the project?
- What are the linguistics, cultural composition, geographic distribution and lifestyles of those to be consulted? Create a profile of the community to reflect this.

B. IDENTIFICATION OF STAKEHOLDER GROUPS

- Affected Stakeholders - Who are the stakeholders (individuals, interest groups, agencies) who may be directly affected?
- Influencing Stakeholders - Who are the stakeholders who may be able to influence the study outcome because they have knowledge to improve recommendations or regulatory / political / legal authority on the project which needs to be considered?
- Supportive Stakeholders - Whose cooperation / expertise / influence will be helpful to the success of the project?
- Opposing Stakeholders – Who will oppose the project and/or have negative opinions with respect to the project?
- Other Stakeholders – Identify anyone else who may have an interest in the project.

C. STUDY PERSPECTIVES

- Region's Expectation - What does the Region expect are the positive/negative impacts perceived by the stakeholders (i.e. hopes and concerns)? How does the Region expect the stakeholders will want to be involved?
- Stakeholder Expectation - What would be the positive / negative impacts expected by the stakeholders?
- Potential "Show Stoppers" - What might be the "show stoppers" to the project, i.e. the issues which could halt the project? What is the plan for dealing with "show stoppers"?

D. STAKEHOLDER SENSITIVITY STRATEGY

- Mitigation of Concerns - Which concerns can be mitigated and which will remain?
- Involvement of Stakeholders – When/how will stakeholders be engaged? (specific details to be included in separate Public Engagement and Communications Plan) How will refusal to participate by some groups or people be managed? What is the plan for consultation with specific groups (e.g. Indigenous Peoples)?

- Response to Concerns – What is the process for obtaining/documenting/ responding to feedback? How will concerns be addressed?
- Involvement of Supportive Stakeholders – When/how will supportive stakeholders be involved in the project?

E. NEXT STEPS

- What next steps should the Region carry out to demonstrate its "good faith" in responding to stakeholder concerns?

F. APPENDICES

- Stakeholder Contact List

3. Compile the Stakeholder Contact List

It is important that one (and only one) complete and comprehensive Stakeholder Contact List is compiled for the project. The list must remain current and must be accurate (e.g. names spelled correctly, complete address, correct incumbent in position, etc.). The roles and responsibilities for both the Consultant and the Region are outlined as follows:

- Identify contact information for the project stakeholders identified in the **SSA**
- Develop a complete and comprehensive **Stakeholder Contact List**
- If available, include the type of correspondence the stakeholder will receive (i.e. e-mail, personalized letter, hand delivered general notice, etc.)
- Continually update the **Stakeholder Contact List** throughout the course of the project as other stakeholders are identified via correspondence, phone inquiries, Public Consultation Centre attendees, etc.
- Engage stakeholders throughout the project
- Provide input to the Consultant for identifying project stakeholders' contact information
- Support the engagement of stakeholders throughout the project as described in the **SSA** and the **Public Engagement and Communications Plan**

Sample Social Impact Analysis

METHODOLOGY

The social impact assessment ('SIA') methodology involves the collection of data on the proposed project and the social environment relevant to the proposed project. The data is assessed through a standard method of assessing impacts. Based on the residual social effects identified, conclusions are drawn on whether the proposed project will create social impacts and in turn, whether the impacts are acceptable or can be successfully mitigated.

Approach to Assessing Social Impacts

Assessments of social impacts examine the characteristics of the undertaking ('project') and the potential for direct or indirect effects on the community, in terms of how people live, work and recreate. The SIA analysis considers avoidance, minimization, mitigation, monitoring and compensation measures that can be implemented by the proponent and/or the community, maximizing desirable and minimizing undesirable social effects before assessing net social impacts. After these measures are considered, assessments of social impacts typically draw conclusions about the acceptability of the project.

SIA's are informed by public consultation comments. These comments are particularly helpful in identifying local social, economic and cultural conditions that characterize the social environment. However, SIA's are not the summation of public concerns. They involve the application of social sciences and data from other technical disciplines.

SIA's can also consider the larger social effects of the project (in this case an aggregate quarry): such as the social costs and benefits of aggregate supplies in meeting society's need for roads, places of employment, building homes and institutions. Here, assessments of social impacts provide non-commercial data on matters such as how changes in the availability of aggregate affects jobs, services and the quality of life for the larger society within and beyond the community. This study did not examine these broader social effects due to the proposed quarry development.

Standard Methodology

The word 'assessment' refers to a methodology to be used to assess social impacts. The assessment of social impacts examines the effects[207] of an undertaking, such as the construction and operation of a quarry on the social environment and determines whether the undertaking will have positive or negative effects on the quality of life of local residents and communities.

Assessments of social impacts follow a standard methodology[208] involving: 1) *scoping* the social environment to be studied, 2) *profiling* existing social conditions, 3) *projecting* changes that are likely to occur due to the undertaking, 4) *assessing* the effects for relative importance, 5) *evaluating* overall social impacts and 6) drawing conclusions and *recommending* how to proceed with the proposed undertaking.

1) ***Scoping*** determines the parameters of the assessment. For the proposed quarry understanding local community/social values is important to the assessment as is the balancing of other goals such as providing shale for bricks used in the construction of housing. In addition to assessing the social effects to people in the vicinity of the proposed quarry, an assessment of the social impacts of the haul route is also performed.

2) ***Profiling*** refers to the need to develop a profile of existing social conditions of people in the area likely to be affected and establishing baseline information which can be used to determine what difference the proposed undertaking will make to the well-being of those affected. At a minimum, this involves primary data collection through meetings with local residents and other people relevant to the proposed application, making observations and drawing conclusions about their characteristics. In addition to reviewing documents and reports, as well as meeting with local residents, 'profiling' also considered cumulative effects from

---

207 Impacts are effects that have been evaluated as being significant (either positive or negative). They may be caused by desirable or undesirable external effects to people from projects, plans, programs and policies. The extent to which social effects are significant can be influenced through avoidance, mitigation, or monitoring and compensation measures.

208 As noted in the Steetley – South Quarry Landfill Site Decision and Reasons for Decision, The Joint Board, Consolidated Hearings Act, CH-91-08.

other developments and projects. Techniques typically include surveys of residents, interviews and structured observations.

3) **Projecting** refers to the need to identify the kinds of social changes that are likely to occur should the proposed undertaking proceed, who will be affected, in what way and for how long.

4) **Assessing** refers to the predicted social impacts to determine their relative importance, taking into account such criteria as magnitude and duration of potential effects, current conditions, future conditions, community goals and impact mitigation measures.

5) **Evaluating** refers to the overall social impact of the proposed undertaking on the basis of the above information. Impact minimization, avoidance and mitigation measures are applied in order to understand the net effects. The proponent is expected to evaluate whether the proposal would have any unacceptable impacts, presently and in the future.

6) **Recommending** whether and/or how to proceed with the proposed undertaking, taking into account the potential effectiveness and public acceptability of possible impact management measures.

Many quarry applications[209] in Ontario have completed an assessment of social impacts using this standard methodology.

---

[209] Such studies have provided useful information supporting the evaluation of aggregate applications, including quarries e.g. Walker Brothers, Niagara (O.M.B File O910030); Graham Brothers, Brampton; Lafarge, Camden East, (LaFarge, 1997 O.M.B. File PL 912122); Five W Farms, Bexley Township (O.M.B. File PL 970862); Rockfort (O.M.B. Flies, PL000643, PL060448).

Evaluation Criteria

SIA studies use criteria to focus data gathering and to frame the measurement and evaluation of social impacts. The criteria are often informed by comments received through public consultation on what is important to the quality of life of residents and what is important to the management of local businesses and institutions. Sample criteria for evaluating the social impacts of a quarry include:

- Displacement of residents/households
- Disruption of residents/households
- Disruption of community and recreational features
- Disruption of businesses/home businesses/institutions
- Changes to community character/image
- Changes to community cohesion
- Changes to economic structure
- Effects on the wider community

APPENDIX 2.
Sample Comment & Disposition Table

C and D sheet used to track comments on the clean-up of low-level and marginally contaminated soils in Port Hope, Ontario.

AECL EACL
Low-Level Radioactive Waste Management Office

Comment & Disposition Sheet
LLRWMO-C&D-531.4.1
Page 2 of 32
Ref. Procedure LLRWMO-531.4.1

Comment #	Page No.	Section No.	Paragraph No.	
1.	E-iv	Executive summary	2	☐ Comment Accepted & Incorporated; or ☐ Resolved as:
The Peer Review Team has				☐ Resolution Accepted by Reviewer.
Comment #	Page No.	Section No.	Paragraph No.	
2.	E-iv	Executive summary	5	☐ Comment Accepted & Incorporated; or ☐ Resolved as:

APPENDIX 3.
Sample Facilitator's Agenda

Summit of Community Associations
Building A Shared Vision / A Vision of the Community's Future
Facilitator's Draft Agenda
28 April 2018,
DRAFT AGENDA, v7, 22 April 2018

Objective

To bring together ratepayers, community associations and taxpayer associations to:

- Get to know each other and feel comfortable working together
- Share knowledge
- Begin the process of developing a vision
- Speak with one voice to advocate for action
- Foster youth leadership
- Identify next steps for working together
- Learn about upcoming activities

Parameters

- There will be an economic development-oriented conference/ meeting of all stakeholders in the fall of 2018 that will include: cultural groups, agencies, arts, sports and recreation groups, institutions, service clubs, faith groups, NGO's, and any citizen wishing to attend. The 28 April 2018 Summit is specific to community associations.
- No politicians will be in attendance – invitation will have to be specific.
- Media will be invited.
- Expected attendance 125 people.

- Students will be invited to assist with the logistics and note taking.

Preparation

- Each community association to bring a photo that best depicts their community. (and be ready to talk to the photo in the opening session).
- Bring community map
- Buy sticky dots, bring scissors

Logistics Requirements

- Outline of Friday April 27th workshop completed.
  Their requirements:
    - Take notes
    - Help to prepare kits
    - Help to count sticky dots
    - Will need to bring their laptops/ smartphone/ tablets
- Everyone needs to bring a working cell phone or ipad.
- Each community to provide photos and can scroll via power point. Photo's are received and PPT created before April 28th.
- Master list of what photos' go with what community is created for marking purposes
- Nametags
    - Each tag to have a preassigned table number arranged so as to split people up in the first part of the morning.
    - Each table to have a number (ideally a tent card)
- Information kits
    - See information kit handout
- Someone from sponsor organization assigned as media spokesperson
    - Where do the media sit?

- Permission from participants to be reported on – sometimes this keeps people quiet.
- Purchase and prepare sticky dots, folder for kit

Support

- Notes should be taken, and a report drafted and put on the sponsor web page.
- Students to be trained as note takers
    - **Create a framework to insure each student is creating consistent notes**
        - Issues arising? Comments on priorities?
        - Would be nice if one student could pull together a report.

			Program	
TIME	PPT SLIDE	ACTIVITY	SPEAKER/ STAFFING	DETAILS
9:00-9:30		Registration	WHO?? (Students)	Registration kits distributed. The 'map' will be put up and, at registration, each group will be asked to 'map – sticky note paper' the general area where they and their community is located.
9:30-9:40	Chair's slides	Opening remarks (10 min)	(Summit Chair) Why have we asked you here? Support Chair	Need to state: • We are all volunteers. • Stress that while each community organization may be addressing local and community-wide issues such as rooming houses, seniors housing or the character of infill-ing – this day is primarily about discussing larger community-wide issues and opportunities. • Community associations are often good at opposing undesirable change – but this is different, its about renewing a community • Thank Committee for organizing Summit • We have media here, please keep that in mind. • **Thank sponsors.**

				What is sponsor? What are the objectives for the day?	Objectives for the day and background • *Getting to know each other.* • *Identify ways resident's associations can work together.* • *To learn about community-wide issues needing to be addressed.* • *Identify a third initiative for sponsor to advocate for.* • *Develop the desire and mechanics for working together.* • *Thank our partners and sponsors.*
					This will be a plenary session with people seated at Tables of 6. (100 people = 15 tables). There will also be space for catering and food. And, space for displays and exhibits. Podium area to be set up.
9:40-9:45			**Agenda and Facilitator's Charge**	Dave Hardy	

	Transition slide	Dave will go through the agenda for the day. Dave will explain the first activity – "Getting to know each other"		This is how we have split you up. **Meeting courtesies.** **Breaks and lunch arrangements.** **Student notetakers, sponsor Member, Community Assn rep, speakers, volunteers, sponsors.** The groups will be split up in advance and each person is assigned a table. There will be a table # on their nametag to have representatives of different community associations siting at different tables. Staff one will photograph the map and then put the photo on a power point slide for broader viewing. Will need a good PPT Projector and large screen. Mikes will also be needed (4 wireless). Hardy Stevenson to bring their PPT projectors, screen and lap tops. **Notetaker at each table?**

9:45-10:30		Getting to know each other (50 min) – introduction piece	Dave Hardy	2-part exercise (**Handout 1**) (See Exercise in Kit) Individuals will be asked to find their survey sheet in their kits and find 7 people they don't know and ask them: Their name and affiliation (Community Association/ sponsor / Other) The one thing that makes their community great/ unique. Something that makes them unique/ interesting. The photos of each community will be presented as a Power Point slide All participants will guess which community each photo is. Participants seated back at their tables will share what they found from the interviews about what makes each community great/ unique. *Serve coffee during this time and people can fill up as they like*
				Discussion: **What do you see?** **Were there unique ideas that were keepers?** **Do you agree these are the ideas we should be forwarded to the Mayor?**
End of day			Dave closes off meeting	Thank the organizing team.

APPENDIX 4.
Chalk Talk Outline

Open House and Meeting 'Chalk Talk Outline'

Table of Contents

- ▶ Engagement goals, objectives and considerations
- ▶ Meaning of a successful open house for the client and participants
- ▶ Key messages
- ▶ How the open house will unfold:
    - Welcoming participants
    - Tour of the information panels
    - Documentation –note taking on comment forms
    - Anticipated questions and responses developed by the team
- ▶ Reviewing what you already know: general open house etiquette
- ▶ How the meeting will be facilitated

Engagement Goals

1. To provide participants with relevant information so they are comfortable commenting.
2. To answer public questions accurately and consistently.
3. To document public comments, particularly about the specific questions.
4. To solicit other comments and provide information on the go-forward engagement process.
5. To make the Open House a pleasurable experience for visitors.
6. Accurately answer meeting questions, notes and follow-up.

How the Open House Will Unfold

- ▶ Process of welcoming participants.
- ▶ Thank them for taking the time to come.
- ▶ Tour the display panels and receive background information.
- ▶ We communicate 'technical information' and 'values'.
- ▶ 'Values'
    - "The specialist is listening to me and has an interest in what I have to say."
    - "I would trust the person I'm talking to, to make the decision I would make if I had the same information and expertise."
- ▶ Active communication with clip boards.
- ▶ Direct them to the meeting at 7:00.

How to Welcome Participants

- ▶ The person greeting members of the public should:
- ▶ State the purpose of the Open House for the participants:
    - We have completed the first part of the study.
    - We want to hear your comments.
- ▶ Explain the setup of information panels, where to get information and from whom.
- ▶ Explain how to provide comments after the Open House if they wish.
- ▶ Give out comment forms and refer them to the web page for information.

Be an Active Listener: Understanding the Participant

- ▶ Ask people why they are interested.
- ▶ Try to determine if they are a resident, journalist, interested group member, elected official or government agency representative.

Be an Active Listener: Identifying Issues

- ▶ What is the person really saying or asking?
- ▶ Indicate that you want to understand their comment better.
- ▶ Ask probing questions (separate from mapping exercise):
  - Why do you feel this way?
  - What do you value about the study?
  - What are your expectations for the project?

Be an Active Listener: Dealing with Emotion

- ▶ Maintain eye contact.
- ▶ Relax.
- ▶ If the point is personal, stay with the personal response.
- ▶ Don't respond immediately with facts.
- ▶ Acknowledge feelings:
  - "you sound upset…"
  - "you obviously feel strongly about…"
  - "tell me what you are feeling…"

Be an Active Listener: Paraphrase and Summarize

- ▶ Repeat what you hear in your own words:
  - "it sounds like what you are saying is…."
  - "this is what I'm hearing you say…."
  - "let me see if I understand you…"

Inform Strategically: Be Prepared for Tough Questions

- ▶ Anticipate what questions may be asked.

- ▶ Review the list of 'tough' questions and answers in advance.
- ▶ Example: "Will you guarantee…"

Inform Strategically: Manage the Exchange

- ▶ Look at questions as opportunities to explain.
- ▶ Focus the discussion to the scope of the project.
- ▶ Introduce facts – "Let me tell you what I know right now".

Inform Strategically: Give Headlines

- ▶ Give the 'bottom-line' up front.
- ▶ Give 'messages' in descending order of importance.
- ▶ Use positive words in the headline.

Think Before you Talk

- ▶ Consider the public as 'reporters' talking to neighbours.
- ▶ If you cannot answer something, direct people to someone who can or provide a follow-up response.

Use Simple Language

- ▶ Use simple language and everyday examples whenever possible.
- ▶ Avoid jargon and other technical terms.
- ▶ Don't worry about saying "I don't know".

Be Credible

- ▶ Communicate rather than advocate.
- ▶ Be straightforward, honest, firm.

Preparing for the Meeting

- ▶ Safety and escape areas
- ▶ Managing microphones
- ▶ Watch timing of presentations and responses to questions
- ▶ Who's fielding questions to the right person to answer
- ▶ One person up to the mike at any time
- ▶ Closure
  - Timing
  - Thank guests for coming
- ▶ Other issues?

In Conclusion:

- ▶ Be friendly.
- ▶ Ask to learn more.
- ▶ Acknowledge feelings.
- ▶ Respond with facts.
- ▶ Summarize to show you are listening.
- ▶ Use simple language.

Printed in Canada